# POXED AND SCURVIED

# POXED AND SCURVIED

*The Story of Sickness and Health at Sea*

KEVIN BROWN

Naval Institute Press
ANNAPOLIS, MARYLAND

First published in Great Britain in 2011 by
Seaforth Publishing,
Pen & Sword Books Ltd,
47 Church Street,
Barnsley S70 2AS

Published and distributed in the
United States of America and Canada by the
Naval Institute Press,
291 Wood Road, Annapolis,
Maryland 21402-5034

www.nip.org

Library of Congress Control Number: 2011922552

ISBN 9781591148098

This edition authorized for sale only in the United States of America,
its territories and possessions, and Canada

Printed and bound in the United Kingdom

# Contents

*To the crew of the Alexander Fleming Laboratory Museum,*
*the assistant archivists, volunteers and interns*
*who have been such an invaluable and loyal*
*support for their captain over the years*

# *Preface*

FOR MANY PEOPLE their first exposure to the whole subject of medicine at sea may well once have come on a visit to HMS *Victory* in the days when fresh-faced young naval ratings gave guided tours of the ship, and dwelt with particular bloodthirsty relish on the death of Nelson and the conditions in which the surgeon amputated limbs in the cockpit, painted red to hide the blood. The details may not have been altogether accurate, but the imagination never failed to be stirred. What perhaps made such a tour even more memorable was that the guide, for all his youthful enthusiasm, visibly stood in a long but living naval tradition, and was a link in the chain from the days of Nelson that is missing now that the visitor can go around the Admiral's flagship unescorted and explore at his own pace. Yet even now standing in the place where it all happened, and seeing for oneself the conditions in which the seaman lived, worked, and died, and where his wounds and illnesses were treated, can still stir the imagination. Happily there are many historic ships all over the world that evoke our nautical heritage and where it is possible to visualise the daily environmental threats to the health of the mariner, and better understand the achievement of staying well at sea. Such vessels as the *Mary Rose,* the *Vasa,* HMS *Warrior*, HMS *Belfast*, and the *Cutty Sark*, to name only a few, cannot fail to inspire an interest in the past. The spark for this book came during a visit to the Royal Navy Submarine Museum at Gosport, when the guide, an ex-submariner, made the throwaway remark that the only medical care on board the submarine *Alliance* had been from the coxswain who had enjoyed about four hours' training in first aid. That made me think of the problems of health and medicine at sea, far away from the medical facilities we all take for granted, the diseases caused by confined living and hazardous working conditions at sea, and the way in which ships can carry infection from place to place, including sexual ones carried by sailors with girls in many ports. It also made me want to write about the subject.

As well as the death of Nelson, the other commonly known 'fact' about maritime medicine, dimly remembered by most people from schooldays, is the scourge of scurvy from which the sailor was saved by lemons and limes. Apart from there being much more to the story of the conquest of scurvy than the usual inaccurate summary of it, there is also a greater breadth and depth to the history of maritime medicine in general. Keeping well at sea has always been a problem since man first sailed across the ocean, and has been affected by changes to ship design, the introduction of new technology, new ways of waging war in naval vessels, and developments in medicine and society in the wider world. Naval hygiene and medicine were to be important in building up the British Empire and in establishing British naval ascendancy in the eighteenth and nineteenth centuries. Not only was there the problem of what to do without any access to medical facilities ashore for sick and injured sailors isolated in the middle of the ocean, but there were also health dangers arising from the very fact of being at sea. Ships are confined spaces in which disease can spread quickly among ill-nourished seamen crowded together. In such conditions doctors were often all at sea in more senses than one.

The medical and surgical journals of Royal Navy doctors serving at sea are a wonderful source of evocative first-hand accounts of the challenges faced by doctors on board ships which deserve to be more widely known about and studied. Now held at the National Archives at Kew, these journals, surviving from the late eighteenth century, record more than just the daily illnesses and wounds of a ship's company, but also include accounts of natural history and sociological studies of indigenous cultures encountered on voyages. Some surgeons even included sketches and watercolours in their journals. There are also journals written by surgeons on convict ships and government-sponsored emigrant vessels. Some of them have literary merit. All of them provide insights into medicine at sea in peace and war. Sir Henry Dale in his preface to the first volume of John Keevil's 1957 *Health of the Navy* was spot on in stating that 'the naval medical records are unique in their long continuity, and present the material for a study of by far the earliest of public attempts to organize a health service.' In the isolation of a vessel at sea, health experiments for the communal good could be conducted on a captive population subject to naval discipline.

No one working on such a subject as this can remain an island unto himself, and I wish to thank the many people who have assisted me in ways both large and small. Timothy Hall arranged for access to the site of the Royal Hospital Haslar after its closure and gave me an exhaustive tour of the buildings and grounds, informed by his experiences as a dental officer there. He also obtained access for me to the Historical

Library of the Institute of Naval Research. In Malta I am grateful to the security staff who listened to my request to walk around the site of Bighi Hospital, and allowed me to see the crumbling remains of what was once the largest British naval hospital in the Mediterranean. Sally Bell, Clinical Quality Consultant to P&O Princess Cruises and Secretary of the International Maritime Health Association, has been an invaluable source of contacts and kindly arranged for me to attend an open day for the recruitment of medical staff on board the *Queen Mary II*, organised by Maggie Blight, which gave me an insight into the role of doctors and nurses on cruise ships. I also wish to thank for their help, interest and support: Gale Lewis; Neil Handley; Marika Hedin, Director of the *Vasa* Warship Museum; Evi Kalodiki, who shared her memories of being a ship's doctor on a cruise liner; Charles Savona-Ventura in Malta; Tim Carter, Chief Medical Advisor to the Maritime and Coastguard Agency; Carter D Hill, Medical Director of the Holland-America Line; Johann Onnink, Manager of Nautical Operations and Administration of the Holland-America Line; Jane Wickenden, Historic Collections Librarian at the Institute of Naval Medicine; Lorenzo Glavici, Communications Manager, Brioni SpA; and Robert Gardiner of Seaforth Publishing. I also wish to acknowledge the work of the staff of the various archives, libraries and museums I have visited and consulted in the course of my research, whose behind the scenes work of collection, preservation and cataloguing ensures that we have access now and for the future to wonderful resources for the study of our naval and maritime heritage.

*London*
*August 2010*

# CHAPTER ONE

# *Deadly Cargoes*

WILLIAM SHAKESPEARE got it almost completely wrong. It was perhaps the greatest evocation of an 'Island Race', and of what made England so unique, so great, and so protected from all forms of contagion:

> This fortress built by nature for herself,
> Against infection and the hand of war,
> This happy breed of men, this little world,
> This precious stone in the silver sea,
> Which serves it in the office of a wall,
> Or as a moat defensive to a house.[1]

Yet the author of this magnificent, inspirational piece of verse could not have been more in error, when he gave the dying John of Gaunt a speech extolling England as a demi-paradise, secure from disease and political infection, in perhaps the most poetic of his history plays, *Richard II*. The historical John of Gaunt had lived through the ravages of the Black Death, brought to the British Isles by sea. Shakespeare himself had survived outbreaks of plague that had closed the theatres on which his trade as playwright depended, and lived in a society where his country's dependence on the sea had brought new diseases.[2] The sea was not only a defence against invasion and a barrier to the spread of disease, but sea travel was the very means of breaching those formidable defences. Britannia might have set out on the path to ruling the waves, but that very imperial might brought in new perils of infection and contagion. The opening up of the world by the voyages of discovery of the age in which Shakespeare lived also opened up new routes for disease to attack hitherto untouched populations.

The Black Death, which struck Western Europe with such ferocity in 1346, killing perhaps a third of the population in the space of only three years, gave a foretaste of what was to come in the age of exploration. It started in Mongolia and was carried by the Tartar hordes to the Crimean isthmus, where they besieged a small group of Genoan merchants at the trading post of Caffa.[3] Plague quickly broke out in the trading post. According to one account, it was deliberately introduced among the Genoan traders by a form of biological warfare, when the Tartars used giant catapults to lob their infected corpses over the walls of Caffa. The Genoese carried these rotting bodies through the town and dropped them in the sea, but even that could not save them from the infection. The siege was raised when the Tartars dispersed, spreading the plague as far afield as Russia, India and China. The Italian merchants who had survived both siege and pestilence fled by ship back to Italy, carrying with them a deadly hidden cargo. Some of them first landed on Sicily, where the plague in Italy initially struck, but soon their home state of Genoa was to be afflicted.[4] The chronicler Gabriel de Mussis recorded that there were no incidences of sickness during the voyage, but that within days of the galleys landing in Genoa plague had broken out.[5] It was widely believed that 'this plague on these accursed galleys was a punishment from God, since these same galleys had helped the Turks and Saracens to take the city of Romanais ... and the Genoese wrought much more slaughter on the Christians than even the Saracens had done'.[6]

Genoa, whatever its sins in aiding the infidel against its fellow Christians, was not to be the only victim of this supposed divine retribution, as the Black Death soon spread from this focus of infection to the areas with which it had trading links, including Constantinople, Messina, Venice, Sardinia and Marseilles. It was claimed that the Genoese had driven the infected galleys away from the port as soon as they realised that not only were they carrying a coveted cargo of spices, silks and other luxury goods from the East, but also a deadly disease: 'they were driven forth from the port by burning arrows and divers engines of war, for no man dared touch them; nor was any man able to trade with them, for if he did he was sure to die'.[7] The epidemic spread rapidly along the trade routes of the Mediterranean and northern Europe. Genoese ships brought it to Sicily from where it spread to Tunisia, the Italian mainland, and Provence. By the summer of 1348 it had reached the Iberian Peninsula, northern France, and the southern ports of England. It had penetrated the Low Countries, Norway and Germany by 1349, Sweden and the western Baltic region in 1350, and the eastern Baltic and northern Poland the following year. Its progress followed the major trade routes of the Black Sea, Mediterranean, North Sea and Baltic, travelling much faster by sea than by land. In all cases, its first appearance was at the ports, before spreading more slowly along roads and rivers to inland towns, and from there into the surrounding countryside.[8]

This devastating epidemic has been identified with bubonic plague, transmitted by the bite of the human flea, *Pullex irritans,* which had been infected from black rats carrying the bacterium identified in the nineteenth century as *Yersinia pestis.* The black rat, *Rattus rattus,* was also known as the ship rat, which infested the merchant ships and then came ashore in new ports, where it established burrows near supplies of grain or flour, and was bitten by fleas which then transmitted the infection to human beings.[9] Bakers and millers were often the first victims of an outbreak of plague.[10] In its simplest form, the plague was characterised by the formation of buboes or swellings in the groin or armpit. In the pneumonic form, which could be passed between people by coughing, it affected the lungs directly and the victim would cough up blood. Even more serious was septicaemic plague, in which the bacterium entered the bloodstream and swiftly killed the person so infected. In the fourteenth century, many of the victims of the Black Death were covered with small black pustules and had little hope of survival, whereas those who were afflicted with hard, dry boils or abscesses had greater chances of survival, a range of symptoms suggesting that there was more than one form of the disease.[11] For many victims, the illness began with them feeling cold and experiencing a tingling sensation. This was followed by the appearance of hard, solid boils, ulcers, and pustules in the groin or armpit. Fever followed and many people began to vomit blood; anyone who coughed up blood, rather than vomited it, was likely to die.[12] So extensive was the epidemic that 'no one could be found to carry the bodies of the dead to burial, but men and women carried the bodies of their own little ones to church on their shoulders and threw them into mass graves, from which rose such a stink that it was barely possible for anyone to go past a churchyard'.[13]

The plague arrived in England in the early summer of 1348, brought by sea to the Dorset port of Melcombe Regis by a merchant vessel from Gascony. At first its effects were confined to the West Country and the port of Bristol, but by November it had reached London and then spread throughout the country, with mortality peaking in the spring and early summer of 1349. Inland waterways and coastal shipping favoured its rapid spread. At a stroke, the population was reduced by about a third. Villages were depopulated, fields were left untended, and tax revenues fell. Given time, the English economy and social structure would have recovered, but recurrent outbreaks of the plague, especially in 1360–2, 1369 and 1375, had more lasting effects. As labour became scarcer, those peasants who survived were able to demand a better return for their hire, rents and food prices fell, and ultimately living standards rose. Psychologically, the effects also went deep.[14]

The frightening sudden advent of the Black Death was interpreted by the medieval mind as a punishment from God for moral transgressions and as the harbinger of the Apocalypse. The pious were encouraged to undertake acts of penance and to go on pilgrimage, like Geoffrey Chaucer and his fellow pilgrims in *The Canterbury Tales,* to seek the intercessions of those saints who 'them hath holpen whan that they were seke'.[15] Processions of flagellants travelled from town to town, whipping themselves in formal procession as they went along. The *danse macabre* became a popular theme in religious art, in which Death held out his hand to the living from all ranks of society as a reminder that mortality could strike anyone at anytime. Scapegoats were sought from groups seen as outsiders and unclean, such as Jews, foreigners who were not only alien, but had often themselves come in by the sea routes that had now brought disease, Muslims in Spain and Portugal, and even the practitioners of 'foul trades', including prostitutes, butchers, tanners and fishmongers.[16] Expulsion was the more humane response. At Strasbourg nine hundred Jews were burnt alive on St Valentine's Day 1349, in a futile attempt to avert the Black Death, an atrocity condemned by Pope Clement VI, who believed that, rather than being the result of Jews poisoning wells or allowing Jews to practise their religion in a Christian world, plague was caused by demons trapped in steel-framed mirrors.[17]

Physicians saw the plague in terms of a pestilential fever rather than a new disease and fitted it into the classical Galenic theories that disease was caused by an imbalance of the humours. Medieval and Renaissance medical practice was based on the ideas of the Greek Hippocrates, the Roman Galen, and the Arab Avicenna, especially the idea that disease was a result of an imbalance between the four humours thought to make up the human body. Just as the world was made up of the four elements of earth, air, fire and water, so was the body made up of four humours, each with its own particular qualities: blood was hot and dry; black bile or melancholy was cold and dry; red or yellow bile was hot and dry; and phlegm was wet and cold. In the healthy body these humours were all in proportion to each other, but if this balance broke down, disease would result. Plague was thought to have been caused by an increase in the hotness of the heart, exacerbated by miasma and noxious vapours produced by the 'corruption of the air' caused by rotting matter, an excess of humidity, and the foul breath of the sick.[18] The response in many Italian and Aragonese towns in 1398 was to sweep the streets clean of such refuse as human excrement, butcher's offal, and leather workers' refuse, and ensure that the putrefying bodies of Black Death victims were swiftly buried.[19]

Religion and self-help against the plague came together in the Hanseatic ports of Livonia,[20] where young, unmarried German shipowners and merchants banded together in the fourteenth century to form Brotherhoods of Blackheads, under the patronage of the black warrior and martyr St Maurice, whose turbaned head was depicted on the coat of arms of the Brotherhoods and also on the facades of the Houses of the Blackheads in Tallinn and Riga. As well as serving as a trade guild and a social club, the Brotherhoods also carried out military duties and were concerned with medical care. The Tallinn Blackheads erected a triptych altarpiece imported from Flanders, dedicated to the Virgin Mary, in the Dominican monastery of St Catherine, in which members of the fraternity are depicted praying to the Holy Trinity for protection, while St Mary is depicted enthroned and attended by St George, St Victor, St Francis of Assisi, and St Gertrude of Nivelle, saints representing chivalrous fighting for Christianity, nursing the sick, and following the word of God wisely and compassionately. St Gertrude, patron saint of the sick in hospitals, is depicted with a rat at her feet in reference to her supposed ability to drive away plague-carrying rodents. For the Blackheads of Tallinn, the plague was as great an enemy as any opposing army or navy. As shipowners and merchants far away from home, the Blackheads had to be concerned for their own health and that of their brethren. As social and welfare guilds for ethnic Baltic Germans, the Blackheads continued in existence until the Soviet occupation of the Baltic Republics in 1940. Where the plague could not vanquish the Blackheads, modern politics did.[21]

As the Black Death progressed and subsequent epidemics of plague broke out, civil magistrates in the ports, seeing the epidemic as something that had been imported, took steps to prevent disease being brought by ship to their cities. Venice appointed three guardians of the public health, with powers to inspect ships' crews for evidence of infection and impose isolation on any ships with sick crew or passengers, when the Black Death struck there in 1348. In 1377 the Republic of Ragusa introduced a thirty-day quarantine against travellers to Dubrovnik coming from plague-stricken areas; this period of quarantine was raised to forty days in 1397, following the example of Marseilles, which in 1383 had introduced what would become the standard period of isolation. Venice followed suit in 1423, Pisa in 1464, and Genoa in 1467. A clean bill of health, originally known as a *patente* or 'health pass', issued by the port of departure and certifying that the ship and its port of origin were both free from infection, was required from the late fifteenth century before a vessel could land and its crew and passengers disembark at Marseilles. Other ports soon adopted this measure, which made trade and travel so much easier if quarantine could be avoided for ships free of infection.[22]

The first recorded quarantine detention station was established at Pisa in 1464 near the church of San Lazzarro, giving the world the term 'lazaretto' for such places. Such lazarettos were not only used to isolate the sailors and passengers from ships, but plague victims from an affected city would also be sent to them when, despite all precautions, plague struck. In Edinburgh an official known as the 'Foulis Clenger' was appointed to dispatch plague victims to quarantine, destroy their contaminated chattels, and disinfect their houses. The Venetian notary, Rocco Benedetti, in 1577 described the Lazzaretto Vecchio, on an island in the Venice Lagoon to which sufferers from the plague were sent, as 'like Hell itself' with its 'stench that none could endure', the groans and sighs of the sick and the clouds of smoke from burning corpses. By contrast, the Lazzaretto Nuovo, in which contacts of plague victims and people suspected of harbouring the disease were isolated, was 'a mere purgatory, where unfortunate people in a poor state, suffered and lamented the death of relatives, their own wretched plight and the break-up of their homes'.[23] Luckier and wealthier Venetians, such as Benedetti, who was confined to his own house for forty days after losing his mother, brother and nephew to the plague, might be quarantined at home until certified as free from plague. Generally, it was the poor who were removed to pest houses, not only to prevent the spread of infection but also to contain any possibility of social unrest.[24]

The island of Malta, occupying a crossroads position for Mediterranean sea traffic, played a vital role in the adoption of quarantine measures, not only to protect its own inhabitants but also as protection of the western from the eastern Mediterranean. Ships suspected of harbouring infection were directed to Marsamxett Harbour from the late mid fifteenth century, where infected cargo would be burnt, the crew placed in isolation, and the ship sunk if disease were suspected. Even more stringent regulations were adopted after the Knights Hospitaller of the Order of St John of Jerusalem were granted the island by the Emperor Charles V in 1530. These regulations, including a quarantine period of forty days, had been developed by the Knights Hospitaller at their previous base on the island of Rhodes. Ships were forbidden to disembark passengers, crew or merchandise without the permission of the port sanitary authorities. All goods were disinfected before being brought ashore, and both passengers and crew were cleansed before being allowed ashore. When the *Assistance* put into Valletta in August 1675, the captain declared that it lacked any bill of health other than 'what was in his guns' mouths' but the crew were still allowed to land, though an outbreak of plague soon followed hard on their heels. The ship's chaplain Henry Teonge, however, visited the area set aside for passengers free from disease who were still obliged to undergo a period in quarantine, which 'lies close under their outermost wall and is extremely neatly kept and provided for'.[25] This was the *Barriera,* with its facilities for the accommodation of passengers, and warehouses for the storage of luggage and provisions, where a series of ropes linked by bollards, some of which are still visible to this day, provided a barrier between the inmates quarantined for between nine and fourteen days and their visitors from Valletta. Wealthier passengers were given more palatial accommodation in a building that still survives in a now ruinous state. Augustus Hervey was visited in 1775 by the British consul 'at the pratiqua-house as I could not be out of quarantine.'[26] However, when George Sandys arrived at Valletta in 1610 without a bill of health he was 'left alone on a naked promontory right against the City, remote from the concourse of people' until he could be admitted to quarantine.[27] Anyone showing any signs of infectious disease was immediately isolated in the Lazaretto on Manoel Island, from which the usual and only release was death.[28]

It is not surprising that ships which did not possess a clean bill of health attempted to get round the system. The surgeon James Yonge's ship landed at Genoa in 1664 without the necessary documentation: 'we had no bill of health to certify the place not having the pest whence we came'. Not wishing to undergo the full period of quarantine, Yonge forged one from the Governor of Newfoundland in order to obtain 'prattick', permission to call at a port having satisfied the quarantine officers of the health of the ship.[29] Such an action, whilst understandable, hardly conformed to any code of medical ethics and could have resulted in an outbreak of the plague despite the best efforts of the Genoese authorities. Even mail was disinfected, since paper was considered to be a potential focus of infection, and most of the major ports disinfected international post. Post carried by ships with a clean bill of health was not exempt from this process if it came from an area where infection was rife. Letters were handled with pincers and slit in two with a scalpel, or even with a chisel, so that disinfectants, known as 'perfumes', could penetrate inside them, and also to ensure that they did not contain enclosures of wool, silk or thread which were considered to be carriers of plague. They were then dipped in vinegar and fumigated with burning straw and aromatic herbs for between fifteen and thirty minutes.[30] Fumigation was the standard naval response to all infectious diseases. On the *Montagu* in 1661 'we had many men sick of the scurvy, flux and spotted fever. Our carpenter used to burn some sweet-smelling thing in a chafing dish of coals in his cabin every morning' until 'his chafer overset and set the deck on fire.'[31] Despite all of these precautions, the plague could not be averted and continued to be transported along the great maritime trading routes of Europe.

Britain was a late adopter of quarantine but followed the precedents set by the maritime states with which the country traded or attempted to rival. Specific plague threats made action essential. In 1711 an outbreak of plague prompted quarantine legislation on vessels entering British ports from infected areas. Parliament responded to an outbreak in Marseilles with further legislation which remained in force until another Act of Parliament introduced new regulations in 1753. An Order in Council could require the customs officials of a port to quarantine ships arriving from named destinations.[32] During the eighteenth century the Barbary Coast of Africa and the eastern Mediterranean were feared as sources of the plague, which went unchecked in the Ottoman Empire and North Africa until well into the nineteenth century. Ships arriving from the plague-ridden coasts were escorted to an isolated anchorage where they would be kept under watch for forty days. When the vessel was 'on station' (at the quarantine anchorage), a customs officer held up a 'Quarantine Testament' or 'Plague Bible' at the end of a long pole for the ship's master to swear an oath that there was no sickness aboard his vessel.[33] He also had to fill in a questionnaire recording the ports the ship had visited, the origin of the cargo, the number of people on board, the length of the passage, and whether there had been any sickness or deaths among the crew and passengers during the voyage.[34] No one was allowed to go onshore during the period of quarantine and any breaches of this regulation were punished with six months' imprisonment and a £200 fine. In 1750 the Customs officers at Portsmouth were directed that if the *New Phillis* arrived from Constantinople with a 'foul bill of health', as plague had broken out there, they must 'not suffer the captain or any of the crew to come on shore, but acquaint them that they must forthwith repair to the place appointed for quarantine and remain there until directions shall be given in relation to the ship and cargo.'[35] The ambassador to the Ottoman court had sent warning to London of the sailing of this ship from a plague area. Vigilance was ever necessary along the trading routes.

Until the middle of the fifteenth century sea voyages tended to be mainly coastal in nature or confined to the inland seas, with ships seldom being at sea for longer stretches than eight or ten days. All was to change with the design of new sailing ships that supplanted the oars-driven galleys of the Middle Ages. The caravel, with its slim hull, axial rudders and triangular sails, developed by the Portuguese, was better suited to sailing along uncharted coasts. Henry the Navigator considered that 'the caravels of Portogallo being the best ships that sailed the seas and being well furnished with every necessity' had the advantage that it was 'possible for them to sail everywhere'.[36] Larger, multi-decked ships propelled by wind and sail could indeed travel longer distances. Contemporary with the transition from oar to sail came improvements in the art of navigation. The development of the mariner's compass and the ability to determine a ship's position at sea made possible the long transatlantic voyages of discovery of Christopher Columbus, Vasco da Gama, Ferdinand Magellan, Jacques Cartier, and Sebastian and John Cabot, which opened up new continents to the Europeans. However, longer voyages had their effects on the health of the mariner, prone to disabling injuries and sickness in the confined, ill-ventilated decks of the sailing ships. Scurvy was to become the scourge of the seaman for the next three centuries.[37] The voyages of discovery also took diseases with them to virgin soil where they could wreak havoc.

Almost as soon as Europeans landed in the New World, Old World diseases spread rapidly among the indigenous peoples of America in a process described by Emmanuel Le Roy Ladurie as 'the unification of the globe by disease'.[38] It was inevitable that such European diseases as smallpox, measles, influenza and typhus should exact a heavy toll on the lives of people who had no inbuilt immunity to the infections. The European newcomers had long been exposed to these diseases and had built up a degree of resistance to them. Domesticated animals back in Europe had acted as reservoirs of infection and the well-developed system of trade had helped to spread and mix germs. The transport of these pathogenic diseases to the Americas in the wake of the voyages of Columbus has been dubbed the Columbian Exchange and offers an explanation for the ease with which a comparatively small number of Spanish conquistadores were able to lay low the mighty Aztec and Inca empires, beginning a pattern to be repeated when the English began to explore and settle North America in the next century.[39]

The Taino inhabitants of Hispaniola were the first recorded victims of the diseases brought by Columbus and his crew. It is estimated that in 1492 there were more than a million Taino living in what is now Haiti. They soon suffered the exactions of their Spanish invaders seeking gold, labour and tributes, and when they resisted were subject to a sustained campaign of terror in which the conquistadores 'hacked to pieces' children, old people and pregnant women, 'slicing open their bellies with their swords as if they were so many sheep herded in a pen'. The native leaders and nobles were tied to 'a kind of griddle consisting of sticks resting on pitchforks driven into the ground' and were then 'grill[ed] over a slow fire, with the result that they howled in agony and despair as they died a lingering death'.[40] In the midst of these atrocities in 1493, worse was to come when the native peoples were to be stricken by an influenza epidemic imported from south-west Spain. The final blow to their survival was when the survivors of influenza and Spanish brutality were attacked by an outbreak of smallpox in December 1518, which was to have such momentous effects on the South American mainland, having reached Mexico after devastating Puerto Rico and Cuba. By 1550 the Taino were extinct.[41]

The Aztec Empire was at its peak when Hernán Cortés and his small band of conquistadores landed in April 1519. Identified by some of the Aztecs with the black-bearded god Quetzalcóatl, whose second coming from the sea had been predicted as imminent, Cortés received a warm welcome from Moctezuma, emperor of the Aztecs, and was welcomed to the capital Tenochtitlán in November 1519 with gifts and luxurious quarters. Bernal Díaz del Castillo, a soldier serving under Cortés, later wrote that 'with such wonderful sights to gaze on we did not know what to say, or if this was real that we saw before our eyes', but, in the midst of these wonders, he was only too conscious of the warnings from the subject tribes of the Aztecs 'to beware of entering the city of Mexico, since they would kill us as soon as they had us inside', and that the Spaniards were 'scarcely four hundred strong ... What men in the world have shown such daring?'[42] Cortés, with the audacity of the born adventurer, took Moctezuma hostage in his own capital, but soon had to leave it to return to the coast to deal with a Spanish army under the command of Pánfilo de Narváez, sent by the governor of Cuba, Diego Velásquez, to curb his growing power. On his return to Tenochtitlán, having defeated Narváez and recruited some of his troops, he found the Aztec capital in revolt following the massacre of Aztec nobles during a religious festival in the Great Temple. Moctezuma met his death trying to pacify his people and the Spaniards were driven from the hostile city, not to return until their final victory over the Aztecs in August 1521. However, with them was a black slave porter infected with smallpox, who had been drawn from Narváez's forces and may have been among a cargo of young slaves recently brought across the Atlantic from Africa to work in the plantations that were now being established. The Aztec army may have been able to withstand the Spanish conquistadores militarily, but they could not fight against the even more lethal but insidious enemy that would soon sweep through Mexico.[43]

Smallpox was to devastate the Aztecs. It killed over half the population of the central zone of the Basin of Mexico in 1520. One of the survivors related the horrors of the epidemic in his native Nahuatl language to the Spanish chronicler Bernardino de Sahagún:

> And before the Spaniards had risen against us, a pestilence first came to be prevalent. It was Tepeilhuitl[44] when it began, and it spread over the people as great destruction. Some it quite covered [with pustules] on . . . their faces, their heads, their breasts. There was great havoc. Very many died of it. They could not walk; they only lay in their resting places and beds. They could not move; they could not stir; they could not change position, nor lie on one side, nor face down, nor on their backs. And if they stirred, much did they cry out. Great was its destruction.[45]

Among the victims was Moctezuma's brother Cuitlahua, who had declared himself emperor during Moctezuma's captivity and rallied opposition to the Spaniards. His death was to lower morale among his warriors, who also saw many other nobles and leaders die. Although his successor Cuauhtemoc, the son-in-law of Moctezuma, a vigorous 25-year-old who appeared to Bernal Díaz as 'very much of a gentleman for an Indian and very valiant',[46] swore to fight on until the last Aztec warrior was dead, the ravages of smallpox had weakened his forces both physically and in terms of morale, and Tenochtitlán, wasted by the epidemic, finally fell and the last Aztec emperor was captured whilst fleeing. In such a hierarchical society, the loss of its leaders led to political fragmentation and disruption. The fact that the Spaniards seemed immune to the worst effects of the epidemic had a psychological effect on their enemies and seemed to proclaim their superiority and invincibility to fatalistic Aztecs.[47] Similarly, when smallpox claimed the life of the Inca ruler Huayna Capac and his heirs in 1525, Francisco Pizarro was able to take advantage of the succession crisis to plunder the capital Cuzco.[48] Smallpox brought across the ocean had helped to lay low two great empires.

The effect of the epidemics was devastating. The Mexican Gulf, Pacific coast of Mexico, the Basin of Mexico, the coast of Peru and the fertile Rimac Valley were virtually depopulated. These consequences were to be long lasting. The Marqués de Varinas travelled from Lima to the Peruvian coast in 1685 and saw for himself the results along his route, 'mounds of skulls and bones of those miserable beings that horrify those travelling the road'; he estimated that only twenty thousand remained of the two million Indians who had once lived in the region through which he was travelling.[49] Among the descendants of the victims, the memory of the havoc wrought was even more vivid. Francisco Hernandéz Arana, the grandson of King Hunyg of Yucatán, remembered that 'great was the stench of the dead. After our fathers and grandfathers succumbed, half the people fled to the fields. The dogs and vultures devoured the bodies . . . We were born to die'.[50] The role of smallpox in establishing a Spanish Empire in South America was to set a pattern for English settlement in North America.

Smallpox was not to reach North America until later in the century, when the voyages of discovery and settlement carried it with them, but its effects were to be equally calamitous for the native peoples. Jacques Cartier reported on deaths among the natives of the St Lawrence River in the winter of 1534 shortly after his arrival; he did not identify the cause of the disease brought by him and his companions but it seems to have been smallpox.[51] The North American Indians had no inbuilt immunity. Pocahontas, the Indian princess who had helped the Virginian settlers, died of smallpox aged only twenty-one during her visit to England in 1616, unable to fight against the infection.[52] When the Pilgrim Fathers landed on Plymouth Rock in 1620, they found neatly cleared arable fields but no hostile warriors since 'the natives are near all dead of the smallpox, so the Lord hath cleared our title to what we possess'. This belief in smallpox as an agent of divine providence was shared by many of the settlers, one of the Pilgrim Fathers commenting that 'the good hand of God favoured our beginnings in sweeping away the multitude of the natives by the smallpox'. In 1634, William Bradford reported that at Plymouth Plantation 'the Indians that lived about their trading house there fell sick of the smallpox and died most miserably . . . not one of the English was so much as sick, or in the least measure tainted with this disease.'[53]

Whereas the voyages of exploration had transmitted many diseases, to which the indigenous population had no immunity, from the Old World to the New with such disastrous results, the 'great pox', syphilis, was the only serious disease to be brought in the opposite direction from the Americas to Europe. The new and repulsive disease was first observed in 1494 in the aftermath of the French siege of Naples by Charles VIII, as the French armies retreated through Italy leaving a trail of the new infection in their wake. The Venetian doctor Alessandro Benedetti described how

> Through sexual contact, an ailment which is new, or at least unknown to previous doctors, the French sickness, has worked its way in from the West to this spot as I write. The entire body is so repulsive to look at and the suffering so great, especially at night that this sickness is even more horrifying than incurable leprosy or elephantiasis, and it can be fatal.[54]

It had been noticed that some of the Spanish mercenaries defending Naples against the French had accompanied Columbus on his second voyage. They had actually withdrawn before the arrival of the French, but not before they had had the opportunity to sleep with local prostitutes, who thought nothing of sleeping with the erstwhile enemy and thereby passing on to them the repulsive new disease. Fernandez de Oviedo proposed this as the origin of the pox as early as 1525; his theory was backed in 1539 by Ruy Diaz de Isla, who had attended Columbus' pox-stricken crew in March 1493 when Columbus reported his discoveries in the New World to Ferdinand and Isabella, the Catholic Kings, at Barcelona. These unfortunate sailors had originally thought that their disease was merely the effects of the hardships of their voyage, but had then spread it among the inhabitants of Barcelona, before taking it to Naples with them. Diaz de Isla identified the disease with the Serpent in the Eden of the newly discovered demi-paradise of Hispaniola, now better known as Haiti, and named it the serpentine disease because 'as the serpent is abominable, terrifying and horrible, so is this disease'.[55] Meanwhile, in a futile attempt to avert the malady, the people of Barcelona responded to the pox with prayers and fasting.

The idea that the disease had been imported from the Americas soon became the most common explanation of the origin of the sickness, despite the attempts of many university-educated sixteenth-century physicians to deny that the disease was new to Europe, in the belief that if an illness had been unknown to the classical authorities on medicine it could not exist; they tried to link it with elephantiasis and

13

leprosy in the ancient writings of Hippocrates and Galen. The theory of an American origin depended on the co-incidence of the date of Columbus's return from his second voyage with the first great European epidemic of syphilis. Spanish sailors had undoubtedly raped Indian women, and there were frequent allusions to sickness and exhaustion of his sailors in Columbus's own accounts of his voyages, but no conclusive evidence as to the nature of that illness.[56] Despite the brutality of the behaviour of Columbus's crew, a New World origin for the pox could be depicted as evidence of a decay or weakness in the New World that might justify its conquest and colonisation by the European powers.

By contrast, the Amerindians experienced much milder cases of syphilis than the Europeans, since they had immunity to it, unlike the virgin population of Europe soon to be ravaged by the new disease.[57] Indeed the medical folklore of the indigenous cultures of Central and South America shows familiarity with syphilis-like diseases. Mayan medical texts had terms for gonorrhoea (*kazay*), syphilitic sores (*yaah*), and buboes (*zali*). The warlike Aztecs had several gods concerned with venereal diseases: Titlacahuan, Tezcatlipoca, Macullxochital (god of pleasure) and Xochiquetzal (goddess of love), all of whom punished any breach of vows or unchaste behaviour with an infliction of repugnant diseases affecting the genitals of their victims.[58] This would suggest that the disease was already familiar in these parts of the New World when the conquistadores arrived.

The New World origin of syphilis was the subject of an epic poem in Virgilian hexameters, *Syphilis sive Morbus Gallicus*, by the Veronese physician and humanist Girolamo Fracastoro, whose Latin verse has given the disease its modern name. Begun in about 1511 but not published until 1530, the work was dedicated to Cardinal Pietro Bembo, a humanist scholar and lover of the infamous Lucretia Borgia.[59] In this modern romance, the voyages of Columbus are compared to those of the Argonauts who similarly sailed through uncharted oceans. After suffering hardships at sea, the adventurers find an earthly paradise inhabited by noble, unsophisticated herbalists and gardeners whose simple, natural, sylvan lifestyle is threatened by the European newcomers. Divine retribution is visited on the Europeans when one of the sailors uses an infernal modern weapon, the gun, to shoot parrots, birds considered sacred to the sun. The punishment for this sacrilege is the prediction that the sailors will have to face many battles, monsters, dissension amongst themselves, and a strange disease for which they will find a remedy in the holy wood of the guaiacum tree.[60]

This disease is already endemic among the natives of this demi-paradise as a punishment for the sins of their ancestors, survivors of the lost legendary city of Atlantis. The shepherd Syphilis had blasphemed against the sun god Apollo and encouraged his king Alcinthous to declare himself to be a god. The punishment for this impiety was a pestilence characterised by foul sores that could only be washed away with quicksilver and which brought on sleepless nights and tortured limbs. The first victim was Syphilis himself, and the impious shepherd was offered as a scapegoat in expiation. However, Juno and Apollo took pity on him and allowed the sacrifice of a bullock in substitution for him. They had also provided the sacred guaiacum tree as a remedy for the disease unleashed by Apollo in his rage.[61] This cure, the use of guaiacum, was to offer hope to the new European victims, too, now that the disease was 'spreading in the sky of Europe and harassing cities alarmed at the lack of remedies' and 'the fleet, and a far from negligible number of its young men, were in the grip of this illness, their limbs all wasting away'.[62] Guaiacum was the wonder cure of its day, though distrusted by Protestants as a Catholic cure, because its import was a monopoly of the Fugger merchant dynasty of Augsburg, who had underwritten the indulgence of Cardinal Albrecht of Brandenburg that had triggered the German Reformation, and who had established a pox house in their native town for the relief of victims of the disease as part of an extensive almshouse complex. It was believed that the dark hardwood guaiacum had been used for the True Cross on which Jesus was crucified, which gave it its healing qualities. Portuguese mariners, believing themselves to have been cured by it, hung it in their churches in thanksgiving for a cure.[63]

There may be a symmetry, and indeed justice, to the idea of the Columbian Exchange, with both sides of the Atlantic not going un-scathed, but the notion has not gone unchallenged with regard to syphilis. Archaeological excavations have uncovered skeletons from before 1493 that show such signs of syphilitic infection as star-shaped scars on the skull and traces of inflammation in the bones.[64] Yet indications of syphilis in skeletons are difficult to distinguish from damage caused by other diseases such as leprosy, and relatively few medieval European skeletons show signs of syphilis compared with those from after 1492, though many more characteristic features are found in skeletons in the Americas from the pre-Columbian era.[65] If syphilis was already present in Europe, its apparent sudden appearance in the 1490s could only be accounted for by a great increase in the virulence of the infection by a mutation of the bacterium, *Treponema pallidum,* which causes it, spread by sexual contact rather than by touch.[66] An equally plausible explanation was that treponemal infections native to Europe had combined with others imported from overseas, such as non-venereal yaws, which the Portuguese may have brought from Africa as a result of their voyages of discovery in the half-century before Columbus set out on his voyages, and that this combination proved more potent and devastating than the two infections had ever been singly.[67] Thomas Sydenham, a seventeenth-century physician, actually blamed the slave trade, 'that barbarous custom of changing men for ware', for the introduction into Europe of what he called 'the contagion of the Blacks bought in Africa'.[68] However, the evidence still remains strongest for an American origin for syphilis.

The infection was spread throughout the world by the great voyages of discovery. It was taken to the coasts of Africa and to India in 1498 by the crews of sailors on Vasco da Gama's voyage which left Lisbon in July 1498 in search of the fabled wealth of the Indies. Portuguese explorers also took it to Japan, where it was known as 'manakabassam' or the 'Portuguese Sickness'. Nation after nation ascribed responsibility for it to an alien or enemy nationality. The Italians called it the 'Spanish' or the 'French Disease'. To the Turks, it was nothing more or less than the 'Christian Disease.'[69] In the eighteenth century the Tahitians called it 'Apna no Britannia', the British disease, to the chagrin of Captain James Cook, who thought that it was not his men who were to blame for spreading it to Tahiti, but that it was all the fault of the French.[70]

Whoever may have been to blame for the spread of syphilis, the new disease posed a major public health problem, especially in the seaports. Syphilitics would be driven from the towns in the early days of the panic about the spread of this new disease. Innkeepers were forbidden to offer hospitality to anyone showing signs of the dreaded disease. Public bathhouses were seen as breeding grounds for disease since they were associated with sexual licence, and throughout Europe were compulsorily closed, leading to a decline in the late medieval practice of communal bathing.[71] The physician Gaspar Torella suggested in 1500 that 'the Pope, the Emperor, kings and other lords should send matrons to investigate the disease, especially among prostitutes, who if they are found to be infected, should be confined to a place designated for that purpose . . . and treated by a physician or surgeon paid to do so',[72] while the religious reformer Martin Luther called for the closure of licensed brothels in 1520.[73] In Scotland the town council of Aberdeen issued an order on 21 April 1497 forbidding prostitution on pain of being branded on the cheek, and the town council of

Edinburgh passed a 'Grandgore Act' on 22 September 1497 banishing all syphilitics and anyone claiming to be able to cure the infection to the barren island of Inchkeith in the Firth of Forth.[74]

Sailors, especially, were prone to catching the disease because of the wandering nature of their calling. The apprentice naval surgeon James Yonge visited a brothel for the first and, by his own confession, only time when in Lisbon with the English fleet accompanying Catherine of Braganza to England for her marriage to Charles II, the 'Merry Monarch' not himself averse to the pleasures of the flesh:

> I one day went with some of our people to Mount Whoredom. It is a street on an hill and when you go through it, they call 'I am an Englishman' and pull up their coats and commend their privities as best and soundest. As soon as you kiss one woman, all the rest leave her to you . . . and I satisfied my curiosity and went there no more, it seeming too much like beasts.[75]

Yonge was stronger minded than many other mariners who did not share his abstinence – with the inevitable consequences.

The impetus to set up special hospitals for the treatment of syphilitics came from private charity, initially in the major ports. In Italy the initiative came from the Oratories and Confraternities of the Divine Love, a movement founded in Genoa in 1497 by the layman Ettore Vernazza, under the influence of the noble-born mystic Caterina Fieschi Adorna. The Genoa Compagnia del Divino Amore was dedicated to the twin principles of celebrating individual faith by means of the Eucharist and providing charitable aid for the sick. Vernazza and his colleagues had set up a refuge for the sick in the port of Genoa in 1497, and as the movement spread through Northern Italy similar hospitals for the *incurabili,* the chronic sick among whom pox victims formed a majority, were established.[76] In Venice they attracted the patronage of many patricians who supplied the 'very abundant alms' that financed them, and even 'with great humility washed the feet of the impoverished and ill syphilitic men, and the gentlewomen washed the feet of the women, that is, the females sick with this disease'. Such public shows had the desired effect on onlookers and 'many were moved to piety seeing the pious work performed by the prominent people of the city.'[77] Many Counter-Reformation religious orders were active in treating the *incurabili.* The constitution of the Jesuits specifically stipulated that a novice should spend a month of his training in just such a hospital, usually the Spedale di San Giacomo in Augusta in Rome, established in 1515 with an intensely moralistic regime in which patients were forbidden to swear, play cards, or display the 'dishonest parts of the body'. The founder of the Jesuits, Ignatius Loyola, had himself nursed patients suffering from the pox in 1537 in the Spedale degli Incurabili in Venice, founded in 1522 and later renowned for its buildings designed by the architect Jacopo Sansovino, and for the girls' choir of its attached orphanage. The Capuchin Order was founded in 1528 in a small house near the Spedale di San Giacomo in Rome and its monks nursed the sick in hospitals for incurables in Rome, Naples and Genoa.[78]

The opening up of the oceans had ushered in a time that seemed to be of fundamental change for mankind. In the quest for the fabled wealth of the Indies, a New World had been discovered and an era of exploration begun that was to expand the horizons of the Old World at the expense of older, previously unknown, cultures in the New. Trade was stimulated and new empires carved out. Yet there was a cost, not only in the toll taken on the health of sailors and passengers faced with long voyages, but in the exchange of disease. The sea routes had not only carried riches, they had borne disease and death for sailors and for people onshore that were to have consequences for centuries to come. England was a comparative newcomer to naval adventures and the pursuit of empire, compared with Portugal, Spain and the various Italian adventurers, but in subsequent years was to supersede them at sea and face similar maritime medical challenges to those had bedevilled the earlier naval powers of the age of discovery. Henry VIII may have declared England to be an Empire when the Reformation Parliament broke with Rome, but no island, especially not one dependent upon trade, could be safe from the mixing of disease that had been unleashed.

CHAPTER TWO

# *Surgeon's Mate*

IT WOULD HAVE been a baptism of fire for most fourteen-year-old boys, but James Yonge was already an experienced surgeon-apprentice when the *Montagu,* on which he was serving as the youngest of three surgeon's mates, saw action against the Turks off the coast of Algiers in 1661. As the battle began he quickly went into action.

> Here I began my slavery, for boiling gruel, barley water fomentations, washing rollers, and making lint, spreading plaisters and fitting the dresses, was wholly on my hands, besides often emptying the buckets they went to stool in, a nasty and mean employment, but such as usually chyrurgeon's mates formerly did in the navy.[1]

An improvised sick bay had been set up on a platform in the after part of the hold, where beds had been made up for the wounded, who had to descend to it through a shuttle with only a pile of cloths to cushion their fall. Only two of the crew were killed outright in battle but there were many minor casualties from scalds, bruises, and 'slight hurts not worth minding'. Among the other casualties there was a lieutenant with splinters in his buttocks, a volunteer officer with the upper part of his foot torn with a splinter, a seaman whose buttocks had been lacerated by a shot, and a boy with the calf of his leg torn by a splinter. Another sailor had his kneecap torn by a bullet, which the surgeon 'dressing up without amputation till the next day cost the poor man his life'.[2] In his journal, Yonge described the scene almost dispassionately. Life could be short, nasty and brutal in the seventeenth-century navy for a surgeon if he was over-sensitive. Yet his role had long been vital in maintaining the health of the ship on which he served.

There had been naval surgeons ever since classical antiquity. Homer in his *Iliad* describes the brothers Polidalirus and Machaon, sons of Asclepius, god of medicine, as 'skilled healers' and the commanders of 'forty curved black ships'.[3] When Machaon, referred to as 'a man who can cut out shafts and dress our wounds – a good healer is worth a troop of other men',[4] is summoned by Agamemnon to treat the wounded Menelaus, his role is almost that of a fleet surgeon, though nowhere in the epic is there any definite mention of naval medicine.[5] It is not until Imperial Rome that there is specific evidence of the role of the doctor at sea. The gravestone at Naples of Marcus Satarius Longinus, serving on the trireme *Cupidon,* is a memorial to a senior medical officer in the fleet of Augustus, one of the earliest known by name.[6] Other monumental inscriptions also indicate that doctors were carried on the larger ships of the Imperial fleet, although the evidence does not indicate whether all ships had surgeons, or just the flagships of the small flotillas.[7] Their role was not only to treat the wounded, but also to enforce hygiene aboard ship and tend to the sick, such as Claudius Terentianus who was laid low with food poisoning on board his ship *Neptune,* while serving in the Egyptian fleet based at Alexandria. Terentianus wrote to his father of 'so dreadful and violent an attack of fish poisoning' which had confined him to his bed, and 'for five days I was unable to drop you a line, not to speak of going up to meet you'.[8] The medical officers enjoyed a certain amount of prestige and reward for their expertise and role in maintaining the health of the fleet. Augustus exempted military and naval doctors from combatant duties and the naval doctors, for whom there was an age limit of twenty-one years at enlistment, may have received twice the rate of pay as an ordinary member of the ship's crew.[9]

There is less evidence to tell us about medieval maritime medicine, although by the thirteenth century it was considered desirable to have a barber-surgeon onboard ship. The maritime republics of the Mediterranean, the bulwarks against the infidel, led the way. There were surgeons serving aboard Venetian galleys as early as 1317 and on Genoese ships by 1337.[10] When Philippe of Valois agreed with Jean Aithon Doria for the supply of forty armed galleys from Genoa in 1337, it was stipulated that a master surgeon should be carried at a salary of forty florins a month.[11] The Knights Hospitaller, founded in Jerusalem to provide and protect hospices and hospitals for pilgrims to the Holy Land, and recognised by the Pope in 1113, were to be based successively on the Mediterranean islands of Cyprus, Rhodes and Malta following the Saracen conquest of Palestine in 1219, and re-established themselves in their successive island homes as a maritime power, still with the intention of protecting pilgrims; they had their own naval medical service both when based at Rhodes and then at Malta. Although the Order of St John did not have a purpose-built hospital ship, they would equip one of their ships as a hospital ship with beds, surgical instruments, medicine, doctors, nurses and nursing orderlies, for the care of battle casualties whenever a squadron of the Hospitaller fleet sailed into action. When Rhodes fell to the Turks in 1523, the carrack *Santa Maria* was converted into a hospital ship to transport the sick and wounded knights and their followers into exile.[12] A member of the entourage of Count George Albert of Erbach in 1617 could not praise too highly the medical attention he had once received on one of the galleys of the Knights of St John: 'they made me a bed among the knights, one of whom was always carefully tending me, and after meals two of them would come to make my bed afresh, covering it with red damask, and in the morning they did the same again.'[13] Even sick and wounded galley slaves were cared for by a Christian slave, under the supervision of a young knight, and, if in port, were transferred to a special ward set aside for slaves in the basement of the Sacra Infermeria in Valletta, considered to be one of the finest hospitals in Europe with its massive great ward, at 508 feet the longest room in Europe, food served from aseptic silver platters, and its rule of treating all comers equally regardless of their wealth, race or religion.[14]

Christopher Columbus took three surgeons with him on his first voyage of discovery, one for each of his vessels. A doctor, described only as 'Maestre Juan', was left behind at La Navidad with some of the crew when Columbus, having lost two of his three ships, set off on his return to Spain with those mariners he could fit into one ship in January 1493.[15] On his second voyage in 1493, Columbus was accompanied by two physicians, Guillermo Coma of Barcelona and the royal physician Diego Álvares Chanca, who totally underestimated the likely discomforts of the voyage, yet later waxed lyrical on the wealth of the Caribbean 'whereby, our sovereigns can certainly consider themselves henceforth the richest and most prosperous rulers on earth for nothing comparable has ever been seen or read of till now in the whole world'. The inclusion of a physician in the pay of Ferdinand of Aragon and Isabella of Castile was part of an attempt by the Catholic Kings to control Admiral Columbus. Such physicians were more than medical practitioners, but were learned and perceptive reporters of what they might witness, as well as trusted royal servants.[16]

The French explorer Jacques Cartier was also accompanied by at least one surgeon during his exploration of the St Lawrence Seaway in 1535. In the course of that expedition, many of his men were stricken with a strange sickness. In some cases they 'lost all their strength, and could not stand on their feet, then did their legs swell, their sinews shrink as black as any coal'. Other men 'had all their skin spotted with spots of blood of a purple colour: then did it ascend up their ankles, knees, thighs, shoulders, arms and neck; their mouth became stinking, their gums so rotten that all the flesh did fall off, even to the roots of the teeth which almost fell out'.[17] The surgeon was ordered to perform a post-mortem examination on a hitherto healthy 22-year-old seaman, but it threw no light on this strange disease. What Cartier did not know was that it was the vitamin-deficiency disease, scurvy. He and his men were saved by the advice of the Indians to drink 'the juice and sap of the leaves of a certain tree'.[18]

It was not until the reign of Henry VIII that there is much evidence for the regular employment of surgeons at sea in the British naval forces. Until this time, kings and noblemen had taken their own physicians on military campaign with them but a ship's doctor appointed to serve the whole ship was a new development. The basis of welfare for the ill or injured mariner in England, however, went back to the thirteenth-century Laws of Oléron, originally compiled under the authority of the English monarch to govern the Gascon trade passing through the island of Oléron, which were soon recognised as a code of maritime law and included provisions for the sick or wounded; they were to be landed and cared for at the ship's expense with either one of the ship's boys being left to tend the unfortunate seaman, or else a woman being engaged as a nurse.[19] The Laws of Oléron, initially drawn up for merchant vessels, were to be the basis of all future medical provision for English Royal Naval and merchant navy care of the sick, both at sea and on land. They can be considered the foundations of English medicine at sea.

Henry VIII is often described as the founder of the Royal Navy for the energy he displayed in expanding the size of the English fleet, building dockyards, and establishing a board of professional administrators that later became the Navy Board. Much of his interest in maritime affairs was as a means of displaying such magnificent symbols of his might as the *Harry Grâce à Dieu*, popularly known as the *Great Harry*, which when launched in 1514 was, at over a thousand tons, the largest warship in the world. In these new warships, now seen as distinct from the merchant vessels which in the Middle Ages had been pressed into royal service whenever military needs demanded, guns were placed between the decks, a development which not only altered the construction of the ships but also had effects on the life of those on board. The only and inadequate means of ventilation between decks was by means of the hatches, scuttles and gun ports. Meanwhile, there was a need for more men to man the guns as well as sail the ships, resulting in overcrowding.[20] It was in the context of the king's expansion of the navy that the ship's surgeon first became an important and permanent feature of life at sea.

Perhaps the best known ship today in Henry VIII's fleet is his favourite warship the *Mary Rose,* launched in 1511, sunk on 19 July 1545, and raised from the waters of the Solent in 1982. Among the most fascinating of the archaeological finds was a surgeon's chest, containing ceramic and wooden medicinal jars that once held various medicines and ointments, glass phials storing mercury globules and scented oils for the shaving of officers, copper alloy mortars, spoons, bandage rolls, pewter syringes for urethral irrigations in the treatment of gonorrhoea and for the irrigation of wounds, wooden needles, spatulas, a maplewood feeding vessel, a leather wallet for storing instruments, ear scoops for cleaning out the ear, combs, razors, a brass shaving bowl, and the handles of surgical instruments. These instruments, of which the blades had long since rusted away, once would have included amputation saws, probes, forceps to extract bullets and foreign bodies from the wounds, cautery irons to stop bleeding, a dilator to open wounds in order to take out bullets, arrowheads and darts, splints, and a trepan with a screw mechanism to remove pieces of bone from skull fractures. The surgical instruments show signs of being sophisticated for their time, and analysis of the traces of medicines indicates that some of them may have been imported from Europe, a sign that medicine had some importance on Tudor warships. They also show the dual role of surgeon as doctor and barber, although haircutting, trimming of beards and shaving were most probably tasks relegated to the assistant surgeon. They were found in one of the two small cabins assigned to the barber-surgeon and his assistant, one of which was probably the surgeon's own cabin and the other his surgery complete with a wooden treatment bench.[21]

In 1513 there were thirty-two surgeons serving under four master surgeons and one chief surgeon in the Henrician navy, all of them appointed for the duration of each major campaign. Robert Symson served on the *Mary Rose* at a salary of 13s 4d a month. His assistant surgeon and servant Henry Syme earned 10s a month. Not surprisingly for the times, the wages of both men went 'unpaid for five months', and a warrant had to be issued to pay them the arrears that they were owed. A wounded gunner, Andrew Fysh, was granted compensation of 13s 4d, the same as the wage of the surgeon.[22] The main role of the surgeon was to treat injuries suffered in battle, but the surgeon also had a general responsibility for health onboard ship and there are very few references to outbreaks of disease on the ship, notwithstanding the outbreak of plague and dysentery on Lord Lisles's ships in 1545. Most of the 415-strong crew were large-boned, strong, and fit young men, the majority of them under the age of thirty, according to the palaeopathological study of the remains of those recovered from the depths.[23] On a daily basis the surgeon would have treated cuts, bruises, and fractures from lifting heavy weights, extracted decayed teeth, and dealt with upset stomachs. In maintaining health, the role of the cook was as important as that of the surgeon. The standard diet was dull but reasonably nutritious, mainly consisting of bread or hard ship's biscuit, cheese, butter, bacon, dried or salted beef, peas, and beer. Food was cooked in a massive brick oven in the bowels of the ship. Two daily meals were provided for an economical 2d a head.[24]

The maintenance of health and hygiene aboard ship was the responsibility of the barber surgeon, a difficult task considering the rudimentary sanitary conditions on all sailing ships of the time. A pewter chamber pot, presumably belonging to one of the officers and for his own personal convenience and comfort, was recovered from the area where the officers would have had their cabins. Most of the crew on similar ships would instead have used the beakhead, an area forward of the bowcastle open to the sea and decked with gratings, through which the waves could break and so keep the area clean, but no physical evidence survives of the beakhead from the *Mary Rose*. This area was known as the 'heads' giving future generations of sailors a convenient term for their ablution areas. Sailors were encouraged to use the leeside depending on the weather and prevailing wind direction, so that effluent would fall cleanly into the sea.[25] Among the crew the swabber was responsible for the cleanliness of the decks and the liar for cleaning the heads; this particularly unpleasant duty was assigned for a week to the first man to be found out telling a lie on a Monday morning.[26] Despite all attempts to ensure the hygienic state of the ship, the ship was infested with fleas, latrine flies, bluebottles, and rats. It was impossible to eliminate the regular stench of the ship, and at least one of the officers was fastidious enough to have a boxwood pomander, which would have contained dried herbs, flowers or spices, suspended from his sword scabbard or belt to combat noxious smells.[27]

When the pride of the Tudor navy heeled over, flooded, and sank when caught by a gust of wind with her gun ports open as she was about to discharge a broadside at enemy French galleys on 19 July 1545, within sight of Henry VIII dining at Southsea Castle, the surgeon's cabin was unoccupied. Yet the hold, where traditionally the surgeon would have operated, was full of skeletons when the ship was excavated. It is unlikely that there would have been many casualties at this early stage in the naval battle, but it has been suggested that these men might have been suffering from the dysentery outbreak which was to result in great sickness among the fleet in August 1545. If this was indeed the case, the ship's company might not have been able to react quickly to the capsizing of the ship.[28]

Although records have not survived of the name of the barber-surgeon on board the *Mary Rose* when it sank, his cabin contained a black velvet coif, which showed that he was a liveryman of the Company of Barber-Surgeons.[29] Although regarded by university-trained physicians as little better than quacks and charlatans, the barber-surgeons were actually fully trained in the practice of surgery after an apprenticeship of seven years. The Mystery and Commonalty of Barbers and Surgeons of London had been granted a royal charter by Henry VIII on 25 July 1540, uniting earlier guilds of barbers and surgeons exercising a monopoly of surgical practice within the City of London since the late fifteenth century. The control of the guild over the trades of both the barber and surgeon in the City of London was confirmed. Barbers were forbidden to practise surgery within the bounds of the City and for a mile outside it, except for tooth drawing, and surgeons were similarly prohibited from setting up as barbers within the same limits. Surgeons were exempted from military service and were allowed to keep apprentices, who after their seven indentured years could themselves become Freemen of the Company and be eligible for elevation to the status of Liveryman when a vacancy in the Livery arose. The Company of Barber-Surgeons was granted the power to examine sea-surgeons applying for naval appointments in 1606 and retained this role until 1745, when the Company of Surgeons was formed from surgeons who had separated from the barber-surgeons and now took over the privilege.[30] Any apprentice who became a sea-surgeon would pay a fee of seven guineas on admission to freedom of the Company, coming under its jurisdiction just as much as if he lived and practised in the City of London, but the majority of sea-surgeons and surgeons' mates were pressed into service in the provinces and were exempted from serving as a journeyman. They were admitted to the guild as foreign brothers without the privileges of full membership, such as attendance at Company dinners, and were not entitled to the right to the freedom of the City of London.[31] When called upon by the monarch to supply surgeons for the navy, the Company would press men into the service. The wealthier surgeons would pay for a substitute to carry out their duties, often with unfortunate results if the substitute proved incompetent. On 6 February 1599 the Company of Barber-Surgeons heard that 'one Richard Halliday, mariner, made his complaint of Ralph Rowley for setting forth an insufficient man not approved to serve as a surgeon at sea in the ship called the *Costeley* of London by whose unskilfulness he was dis-membered of his arm and is in great danger of life.'[32] Yet, even before the Company of Barber-Surgeons was given a formal position with regard to naval surgery, many of its members played a prominent role in the development of medicine at sea.

At first many of the regulations for the maintenance of good health at sea, on the advice of surgeons, were drawn up for the use of trading vessels. In May 1553, Sebastian Cabot, governor of the Merchant Adventurers' Company, issued a set of regulations for a planned voyage to Cathay in which hygiene played a major part. A dirty ship was not to be tolerated and 'no filthiness was to be left within board; the cook room and all other places to be kept clean for the better health of the company'. For this reason there was 'no liquor to be spilt in the ballast'. The men were also to be provided with a livery, which would have put the Merchant Adventurers well ahead of the Royal Navy in providing a uniform, but this was only to be worn when the captain 'shall see cause to muster or show them in good array', rather than for any hygienic purpose. Care was also to be taken of the sick and injured: 'the sick, diseased, weak and visited person to be tended, relieved, comforted and helped in the time of his infirmity, and every manner of person, without respect, to bear another's burden'. If the sick man had the misfortune to die during the voyage, his clothes and other personal possessions were to be kept so that they could be returned to his wife and children or other heirs, together with the wages due to him up to the day he died.[33] It was not until 1596 that similar instruc-tions were issued for the use of the navy and then they were simply that 'you shall give orders that your ship may be kept clean daily and sometimes washed; what with God's favour, shall preserve from sickness and avoid many inconveniences.'[34]

Francis Drake, privateer, national hero and the veteran of five ocean voyages, was well aware of the importance of good health among his crew when he set sail on his voyage of circumnavigation of the globe on 15 December 1577, with a chief surgeon aboard the *Pelican*, soon to be renamed the *Golden Hind,* and another on the *Elizabeth* for the care of the 164 gentlemen, sailors and boys on the expedition. By the time that Drake reached the Pacific, the *Elizabeth* had turned back and the chief surgeon was dead, leaving all medical care for the expedition to the surgeon's mate, who was no more than 'a boy, whose good will was more than any skill he had', and the concern of their leader. A watering party from the *Golden Hind* was attacked on the Chilean coast on 26 December 1578. Drake, who had been grazed under the right eye by an arrow, was credited by his 'good advice and the diligent putting to of every man's help' with saving the lives of nine wounded men, by giving 'such speedy and wonderful cures, that we had all great comfort thereby and yielded God the glory whereof.'[35] Drake was not unique in having some rudimentary medical knowledge, as most of his officers understood the use of 'lotions, plasters and unguents'.[36] They took every opportunity to find fresh supplies of fish, water, fruit and vegetables; at their first anchorage in the Cape Verdes they had loaded up with grapes and bananas, and had learned how to tap the milk of coconuts which Drake found to be 'very delicate and sweet, but most comfortable and cordial.'[37] Only on their return home through the uncharted waters of the Pacific, after their discovery of 'New Albion' (California), when they had been without sight of land for sixty-eight days, were many of the seamen reported to be 'sick, weak and decayed'. Nevertheless, Drake was successfully to bring his crew back to Plymouth on 3 November 1580, restored to health after putting in at Barateve in the Moluccas, with its wealth of nutmegs, ginger, lemons, cucumbers, peppers and coconuts, 'wherein we found more comforts and better means of refreshing' than anywhere else during the long voyage.[38]

The maintenance of good health on a long voyage was not to be so easy when Drake set sail again in 1585, on a privateering expedition against the Spanish colonies in the Americas with the support of Elizabeth I. After the fleet raided Santiago in the Cape Verde Islands in November 1585, sparing only the hospital, 'there began among our people such mortality as in a few days there were dead above two or three hundred men'.[39] The sick were stricken with 'extreme hot burning and continual agues, whereof very few escaped with life, and yet those not without great alteration and decay of their wits and strength for a long time after'.[40] Many of the men who recovered were 'much decayed in their memory.' Although the men who died had small spots resembling those of the plague, it is more likely that they were suffering from malignant malaria which Drake and his men called 'Calentura', and blamed not on the bites of mosquitoes but on 'the night air . . . who so is then abroad in the open air, shall certainly be infected to death, not being of the Indian or natural race of these country people'.[41] As malaria continued to deplete his fleet, Drake was forced to abandon his plan to go overland to Panama and instead returned home.

Diseases such as malaria and scurvy were to scupper other voyages and be a disincentive to settlement in North America. In June 1586 Martin Frobisher had to rescue after ten months the survivors of an attempt by Richard Grenville to establish a settlement at Roanoke Island, Virginia, after the colonists succumbed to malaria. When Frobisher's fleet reached home waters some five weeks later, he had buried at sea two-thirds of his men, 'above three parts of them only by sickness'.[42] Against disease there was very little that the surgeon could do, which did nothing to enhance their status or decrease the lack of respect in which they were held by some of the tougher of the privateers, who confused hygiene measures and sick regimes with luxury and softness. During Thomas Cavendish's circumnavigation of the world from 1586 to 1588, one of his men was shot in the thigh with a poisoned arrow when washing his shirt whilst part of a landing party off the coast of Sierra Leone. The man, William Pickman, plucked out the arrow himself but broke it and could not remove the shaft. He would not allow the surgeons to attend his wound but had instead 'plucked out the arrow, because he would not have them lance his thigh'. As a result, 'the poison wrought so that night, that he was marvellously swollen, and all his belly and privy parts were as black as ink, and the next morning he died.'[43]

Despite the low esteem in which some of them were held, surgeons had by 1588 become a recognised and accepted part of life at sea, even though some of them may have lacked any recognised qualifications, and smaller ships lacked any medical expertise. Thomas Brown, gunner, and other members of the crew of the *Delight* of Bristol, becalmed in the Straits of Magellan, complained in February 1589 of the 'want of a skilled surgeon' on board a ship which had lost twenty-two of its crew, as well as of the actions of the captain Matthew Halls and his officers in consuming 'those sweetmeats, which were laid up in the ship only for the relief of sick persons (themselves being healthy and sound, and withholding the said meats from others in their sickness)' which were more likely 'to starve us, than to keep us strong and in health'.[44] The Barber-Surgeons' Company impressed surgeons to serve at sea during the Armada campaign, and the Privy Council ordered physicians to join the fleet of Lord Howard of Effingham: 'whereas a disease and sickness began to increase in Her Majesty's Navy, for remedy of the diseased and for stay of further contagion their Lordships thought meet that some learned and skilful physicians should presently be sent thither ... to have care of the health of the noblemen, gentlemen and others in that service ... and to carry with them a convenient quantity of all such drugs as should be fit for medicine and cure.' [45] Elizabeth I even sent her personal physicians to sea in 1596 and 1597. That noblemen were now seafarers was a sign that service at sea had become respectable and worthy of the occasional attendance of the physician on a ship rather than the artisanal surgeon.[46] At a time of anti-Catholic feeling, as England faced the prospect of a Spanish invasion and the overthrow of its excommunicated Queen, the ship's surgeon's respectability came not only from his qualifications and ability but also from his religious soundness. A surgeon serving on Lord Sheffield's ship was suspected of papacy, despite being pressed by the Company of Barber-Surgeons, having 'sailed often in Her Majesty's ships' and being 'accounted a very honest man', but he cleared himself of the charges by proving that he possessed his personal copies of the New Testament in English, the Book of Common Prayer and the Book of Psalms, 'which he daily sang with the company'.[47]

Good Roman Catholic credentials would have been more appreciated among the Spanish surgeons than the Protestantism of the psalm-singing English surgeon. The invading Spanish Armada, with its eighty-five surgeons and assistant surgeons, was better prepared for dealing with casualties than the English fleet, which was working on the assumption that the wounded would be removed to the cable tier or laid on the ballast where they would be safest and least likely to get in the way of the fighting, until they could be safely landed to receive treatment as soon as possible.[48] Yet it was physicians, not surgeons, who were most needed when an epidemic of dysentery broke out as a result of men drinking putrid water and eating decayed provisions. An outbreak of typhus followed, though their enemy were not aware of this poor state of the Spanish forces until later.[49] The English, too, suffered so severely from dysentery that Howard was to write to Francis Walsingham his fears and hopes that 'God of his mercy keep us from the sickness, for we fear that more than any hurt that the Spaniards will do . . . I would Her Majesty did know of the care and pains that is taken here of all men in her service.'[50] When the Armada was sighted off the Lizard on 30 July 1588, the English decided to force the enemy to sea before disease and hunger lessened the English powers of attack.

The surgeon William Clowes, whose writings on military and naval surgery and on the pox, based on his experience of naval service from 1564 to 1570, were to be a major influence on the next generation of naval surgeons, was appointed to serve as surgeon on the flagship the

*Ark Royal* during the Armada campaign, but did not describe his experiences in any of his books, probably because there were actually very few casualties for him to deal with. The real need in 1588 was for physicians to deal with the sickness and disease caused by poor sanitation and bad food. There was little the naval surgeon could do for such cases, as he could by law treat only external injuries and was prohibited from practising internal medicine. Clowes accordingly believed naval surgeons should have some knowledge of physic and the right to practise it as they 'cannot always have physicians at the elbows to counsel them'.[51]

It was an iconic victory over the Armada, but was followed by a major medical disaster. The loss of life from wounds among the English forces was so negligible as to be considered too 'tedious to rehearse' by Richard Hakluyt in his account of the action.[52] Much more serious was the outbreak of infection reported by Lord Howard in the moment of victory:

> Sickness and mortality begins wonderfully to grow amongst us . . .
> It would grieve any man's heart to see them that have served so valiantly to die so miserably. The *Elizabeth Jonas*, which hath done so well as ever any ship did in any service, hath had a great infection in her from the beginning, so as of the 500 men which she carried out, by the time we had been in Plymouth three weeks or a month there were dead of them 200 and above, so as I was driven to set all the rest of the men ashore, to take out her ballast and to make fires in her of wet broom three or four days together, and so hoped thereby to have cleansed her of her infection, and thereupon got new men, very tall and able as I ever saw, and put them into her. Now the infection is broken out in greater extremity than ever it did before, and [they] die and sicken faster than ever they did, so as I am driven of force to send her to Chatham . . . It is like enough that the like infection will grow throughout the most part of our fleet, for they have been so long at sea and have so little shift of apparel, and so [few] places to provide them of such wants, and no money wherewith to buy it, for some have been – yea the most part – these eight months at sea.[53]

There was a widespread belief that sour beer had been the cause of the sickness and Howard wrote that 'the mariners have a conceit (and I think it true . . .) that sour drink has been a great cause of this infection amongst us.'[54] Things were even worse in 1589 when as many as eight thousand soldiers and sailors were lost during the expedition to establish the exiled Dom Antonio on the throne of Portugal, then occupied by Philip II of Spain. The *Dreadnought* lost 114 out of a ship's company of three hundred, and only eighteen men were fit enough to work the ship into Plymouth.[55]

Outbreaks of epidemics regularly devastated the fleet throughout the sixteenth and early seventeenth centuries. The outbreak of typhus which swept through the English fleet in 1625 and 1627 was the inevitable result of large bodies of ill-clad and ill-fed men being crowded together for long periods of time in cold weather. At the time the disease was attributed to the offensive odours on the ships. Slops or seamen's clothes had first been issued in 1623 'to avoid nasty beastliness by continual wearing of one suit of clothes and thereby bodily diseases and unwholesome ill smells in every ship'.[56] Badly made, expensive, and unpopular with the seamen to whom they were issued, slops still made it easier for men to desert than if they were wearing their own rags and 'it was not intended to clothe the mariners in harbour to make them handsome to run away'.[57] Chewing garlic was one way the individual seamen could attempt to ignore 'the prodigious scents, smells and savours . . . betwixt the decks where our men lodged'.[58] For removing the offensive miasmas from the ship itself, it was standard practice to air the bedding and hammocks on shore when possible, and to wash the decks daily with water and twice weekly with vinegar. Sir Henry Mervyn on the *Vanguard* at Plymouth in December 1627 tried everything possible to rid his ship of infection but to no avail. The vessel was even 'perfumed with tar burnt and frankincense' and 'aired twixt the decks with pans of charcoal', but conditions remained so bad that he 'would rather quit my employment than go to sea in her'.[59] A fortnight later conditions had deteriorated still further and 'the men lodge on bare decks . . . their condition miserable beyond relation; many are so naked and exposed to the weather in doing their duties that their toes and feet miserably rot and fall away piecemeal, being mortified with extreme cold'.[60] It was little wonder that morale among them was so low when the sick were so grievously neglected.

Epidemic disease was to play a crucial role in the sea fight between a squadron of fifteen ships under the command of Thomas Howard and a 53-ship strong Spanish fleet off the coast of the Azores on 31 August 1591. The majority of Howard's ships, laid low with 'the one half of part of the men of every ship sick and utterly unserviceable', escaped leaving the *Revenge* under Richard Grenville to fight alone against the massed Spanish galleons for some fifteen hours, despite herself having 'fourscore and ten sick, laid in hold upon the ballast'. At midnight Sir Richard Grenville was 'shot into the body with a musket' and 'as he was dressing, was again shot into the head and withal his Chirurgion wounded to death'. In the hold the water had risen six feet and the sick and wounded, lying there without any surgical aid, were drowned. Grenville, 'very unquiet in his mind' and 'wounded in the brain', wanted to blow up the ship, but was unable to stop his crew from surrendering to the Spaniards, who were shocked at what they found on the *Revenge*, 'the ship being marvellous unsavoury, filled with blood and the bodies of dead and wounded men like a slaughterhouse.' Grenville was removed to the Spanish flagship where, despite the attentions of a Spanish surgeon, he died within three days. The few English survivors of the fight were drowned, together with the Spanish prize crew, when the *Revenge* was lost in a storm.[61]

Whilst the sea-surgeon may have been able to do little to prevent or contain disease, he was on surer ground when dealing with wounds, where his practical skills could best be used. Many captains, while happy to leave surgery to the surgeon and to seek expert medical advice when necessary, had strong views on ship healthcare based on their own experiences. Richard Hawkins on a trading voyage to the tropics in the *Daintie* in 1593 was only too conscious of the limitations of medical knowledge when his men were 'consumed' with scurvy and commented, 'then leave I the remedies thereof to those physicians and surgeons who have experience. And I wish that some learned man would write of it, for it is the plague of the sea, and the spoil of mariners; doubtless, it would be a work worthy of a worthy man, and most beneficial for our country'.[62] As a good commander with a grasp of the importance of keeping his crew healthy, Hawkins did his best to combat the effects of scurvy, which he believed was the result of stagnant water, an intemperate climate, salty water and salted food, and a dirty ship. The ship was cleansed by sprinkling water and burning tar; the men were forbidden to wash their shirts in salt water and were given clean clothes to change into when their own were wet; they were encouraged to exercise through dancing and the use of arms which he believed would 'help to banish this infirmity'; they were given beer or wine with bread every morning so 'that the pores of the body may be full when the vapours of the sea ascend up'; he installed a distillation plant on the ship so that they would have 'wholesome and nourishing' water to drink; and they were given what he observed to be the best cure of all for scurvy: 'many with the sight of oranges and lemons seemed to recover heart. This is a wonderful secret of the power and wisdom of God, that hath hidden so great and unknown a virtue in this fruit, to be a certain remedy for this infirmity'.[63]

While Hawkins had strong views on medicine and nautical hygiene, he also had great confidence in the ability of his surgeons to deal with wounds, especially during a skirmish with a Spanish squadron which led to his capture in June 1594. Many men were slain in the fighting and many were wounded. Hawkins himself received six wounds, including one in the neck and another 'through the arm perishing the bone, and cutting the sinews close by the arm pit'. The master of the *Daintie* 'had one of his eyes, his nose and half his face shot away'. Nevertheless, 'God so blessed the hands of our surgeons (besides that they were expert in their art) that of all our wounded men not one died, that was alive the day after our surrender, and many of them with eight, ten or twelve wounds', even though the surgeons had lost all their instruments and salves when 'their chests were all broken to pieces, and many of their simples and compounds thrown into sea'. Nevertheless, with what they could salvage, the surgeons were able to treat not only their own wounded but the Spanish, too, 'for the Spanish surgeons were altogether ignorant in their profession, and had little or nothing wherewith to cure. And I have noted that the Spaniards in general are nothing so good or curious in accommodating themselves with good and careful surgeons, nor fit them with that which belongeth to their profession, as other nations are, though they have greater need than any, that I do know.'[64]

Hawkins may not have been overly impressed with the standard of healthcare that he witnessed on a Spanish galleon, but generally the fleet of Philip II was well provided with surgeons. Spanish ports, too, were well provided with medical facilities and asylums, many of them provided by religious organisations such as the Orden de San Juan de Dios, founded in 1543, and others established at Coruña, Santiago and Laredo for the casualties from the Spanish Armada of 1588. Philip had personally stated that 'the people in this fleet will arrive exhausted and in want of succour and comfort, particularly the wounded and sick, and therefore it is necessary to give them our special concern ... making provision for all in the best possible way'.[65] The ordinances for the government of the Spanish fleet issued by Philip IV in 1633 gave instructions for the construction of hospitals, for seamen in all the naval bases, and for the care of sick mariners at sea and on land. All ships were to carry physicians or surgeons. If a man was invalided, his pay book was to be landed with him and he was to be visited in hospital or at home by the fleet surgeon.[66] Yet it was concern with cleanliness that really distinguished the English ships from the Spanish: an English captain would 'overlook the ship once or twice a day that she be kept sweet and clean for avoiding sickness, which comes principally by slothfulness and disorder', whereas for the Spanish 'their ships are kept foul and beastly, like hog sties and sheep cots in comparison with ours.'[67]

In Sweden, the poor conditions in which the ordinary seaman lived contrasts with the mighty magnificence of the great but top-heavy royal warship *Ny Wassan* (*Vasa*), which keeled over and sank in the harbour at Stockholm on 10 August 1628 as it set off on its maiden voyage and, like the *Mary Rose,* was raised from the depths in the twentieth century, revealing itself to be a time capsule of its age. Several of the recovered skeletons of the crew showed signs of old bone fractures, their tooth enamel indicated periods in their lives of undernourishment, and some of their remains displayed indications of having had pus-formation in their jaws. The wealth of everyday objects and contents of sea chests recovered in remarkably good condition from the *Vasa*, including slippers and a well-preserved velvet hat, indicated that the men's personal equipment was meagre, with no signs of any warm or waterproof clothing. The Swedish naval authorities in 1675 commented that 'the cause of sickness among seamen . . . has been that they had no other clothing, except what they wore daily', and ordered captains to supply their men with enough coarse cloth to make themselves a hammock and a cover.[68] They lacked that back in 1628. In the crowded, damp, unventilated warships of the day, where even the officers were living in spartan conditions, dysentery, typhus, and scurvy were common. In 1628, two-thirds of Admiral Henrik Fleming's squadron in the Baltic off Danzig succumbed to fevers. Medical care was in the hands of the barber, who could do little more than blood-let, provide enemas and emetics, and prescribe herbal medicines mixed with aquavit. Traditionally, a grater, whisk, and pestle and mortar found on the *Vasa* have been identified as medical equipment. Also among the archaeological finds was a pewter flask containing a litre of a spirit resembling rum.[69] Even more important were the four litres of beer a day allowed for each seaman, to counteract scurvy, wash down the salty diet, and keep the men from drinking sea water. Gustavus II Adolphus believed that the navy was second only to God in safeguarding the welfare of Sweden and took an interest in the welfare of his navy. In 1628 Admiral Fleming issued instructions that 'for the young men, both land and sea folk, to be even rougher and braver when they go into battle with the enemy, then one shall give them a pair of barrels of beer of the best kind to drink.'[70] Fleming also boosted morale with his pledge that should any seaman 'have received some incurable injury or has lost his life, I shall with the greatest energies (in so far as God spares me my life) help him, his wife and children for a piece of bread from His Royal Majesty and the Crown.'[71]

The welfare of the sailor was also of importance in the Dutch Republic, as befitted another great maritime power. The Dutch East India Company, founded in 1602, was aware from an early stage of the commercial importance of employing surgeons on its ships, and of supplying instruments and a well-stocked medical chest. Following the hierarchy of surgeons ashore, each East Indiaman would carry a surgeon and two mates. The Company physician of the Amsterdam Chamber was responsible for oversight of the Company's pharmacy, the examination of surgeons for their suitability for service, the examination of sick employees, and making recommendations on any disability pensions that the Company might be liable for with regard to its employees. Surgeons were recruited from the barbers' companies of Amsterdam and Middelburg. In 1622 a hospital was opened at the Company factory in Batavia. This highly organised medical department was advanced for its time, in its recognition of the importance of what amounted to occupational health services for the welfare of its employees. Observing the value of citrus fruits in maintaining health at sea and preventing scurvy, the Dutch East India Company planted orange orchards at Mauritius and St Helena to maintain access to fresh fruits on their trading routes, and even experimented with shipboard gardens.[72]

Naval surgeon James Yonge was, despite himself, impressed by the standard of Dutch naval hospitals when taken prisoner in 1665. The hospital was a 'fair house with several long rooms', in which the beds were 'enclosed like little cabins the whole length of the house, each having a window in it, and very good bedding and linen, each bed fit for two.' It was well staffed with surgeons and physicians, but Yonge was not impressed with the calibre of the surgeons who were 'the worst of the profession I have ever met with, and their operations and dressings are most clownish and indecent'.[73] Yonge had been admitted to the hospital from a prison where he had used brandy and tobacco in an attempt to save him from the diseases which he believed the stench of the prison would bring on. When he finally succumbed to gaol fever, typhus, he had been removed to the hospital where 'we were stripped of all our clothing, linen and all; and clean put on, without warming, and then put into clean, cold sheets, feather beds, enough to have killed any man'.[74]

James Yonge may have been biased by nationalism when he was not impressed by the Dutch surgeons, but the Dutch East India Company was undoubtedly in advance of the medical provision made by his own country's East India Company. The high death rate among their crews made the development of a Company medical service an economic necessity. Yet when a new factory was opened in the East Indies, it was only provided with one surgeon. However, whilst there may have been few surgeons appointed to the Company's trading posts, the salaries of £27 a year paid to them were high, which meant that talented men were attracted to such positions.[75] Even so, not all Company surgeons lived up to the standard of Francis Kelly, who when he served on the *Consent* not only preserved the good health of the ship's company but also parleyed with local headmen for supplies, and even acted as hostage when a pledge of good faith was needed in dealing with the tribesmen.[76] By contrast, another surgeon with the East India Company, Abel Price, was imprisoned by the Dutch in February 1623 for drunkenly threatening to burn down the house of a Dutch trader at Amboyna in the East Indies. He had then confessed under torture to a non-existent English plot to seize the Dutch castle, resulting in the arrest and beheading of twenty innocent English and Japanese merchants for their supposed part in the plot.[77] This incident was part of the growing friction between the English and Dutch which would eventually lead to armed conflict and, in turn, to the need for new advances in English naval medicine in the second half of the seventeenth century.

Some measure of control over the surgeons of the Company was needed and in 1613 John Woodall was appointed as the first surgeon-general to the East India Company, on the recommendation of his patron Sir Thomas Smith, Governor of the Company. He was responsible for the selection of surgeons, the supply of surgeons' chests to the East Indiamen, and for the treatment of injured workmen at the company's small dockside hospitals:

> The said Chiurgion and the Deputy shall have a place of lodging in the Yard, where one of them shall give attendance every working day from morning until night, to cure any person or persons who may be hurt in the service of this Company and the like in all their ships, riding at anchor at Deptford and Blackwell, and at Erith, where he shall also keep a Deputy with his chest furnished, to remain there continually until all the said ships have sailed and appointing fit and able surgeons and surgeon's mates for their ships and services, as also the fitting and furnishing of their Chests with medicines and other appurtenances thereto.[78]

He had served as a military surgeon in Lord Willoughby's regiment in 1591 on an expedition in support of Henry IV against the Catholic League in Normandy, accompanied Smith on a trading mission to Poland in 1604, practised in Germany, and was to be elected as surgeon to St Bartholomew's Hospital in 1616. He had invested financially in the East India, Virginia and Somers Island Companies, and so had a vested interest in the success of these overseas ventures. When the Virginia Company, of which Sir Thomas Smith was the first treasurer, received its charter in 1609, Woodall was heavily involved in shipping medical and surgical provisions and cattle to the colony's plantations, and was later involved in the import of tobacco from Virginia and Bermuda. Ever the astute businessman, even after his dismissal by the East India Company in 1635, he retained his monopoly over the supply of surgeons' chests to the Company until his death in 1643.[79]

Woodall's great contribution to maritime medicine was the publication in 1617 of *The Surgions Mate,* a textbook for 'the benefit of young sea-surgeons employed in the East India Company's affairs' in which he distilled his experience and which was to become the standard reference work for the next half century and went through a number of editions, though the fact that relatively few copies survive suggests that they were much used at sea. It also gave a model for future manuals for the ship's doctor. The first duty of the surgeon's mate, in Woodall's opinion, was to God, his second to the surgeon of his ship, 'towards whom he must be careful to behave himself wisely, lovingly and diligently . . . as the wife is to her husband', and third to his calling as a surgeon.[80] He was warned against openly disagreeing with his chief, as this might undermine the confidence of the ship's company in the medical administration of the ship. He was also exhorted to give a good example by abstaining from idling, excessive drinking and smoking, and not neglecting his duties. These included keeping a record of his medical experiences in the form of a surgeon's journal, maintaining his instruments, preparing pharmaceutical preparations, nursing the sick, being 'compassionate to the meanest creature . . . even as others should do to you in like case', and cutting the hair of the crew.[81] With an emphasis on practical information, Woodall began his book with a detailed description of the nature and uses of instruments and medicine which should be contained in the surgeon's chest, including incision knives, dismembering knives, cauterizing irons, forceps, probes, enema syringes, head saws, and even a razor that in 'one barber's case . . . ought not be wanting . . . if the Surgeon's Mate cannot trim men.'[82] The contents of such chests changed very little over the next two hundred years and would also have been familiar to the surgeon on the *Mary Rose*. This account of the chest was followed by a discussion of how to deal with the surgical and medical conditions that might be encountered at sea, and a treatise on alchemy and chemical medicines in which Woodall showed himself to have been influenced by the ideas of Paracelsus. His section on scurvy gave a clear clinical account of the disease and recommended lemon juice for its prevention and cure.[83] In 1628 he wrote a short treatise, *Viaticum, being the Pathway to the Surgeon's Chest, intended chiefly for the better curing of Wounds made by Gunshot,* for the instruction of young surgeons with the English forces attempting to relieve the Huguenots besieged at La Rochelle. Other writings on the plague and the importance of amputation in the treatment of gangrenous wounds also became standard works for the military surgeon, just as the *Surgions Mate* was for those at sea.

The emphasis in the *Surgions Mate* on the content and order of the surgeons' chest, 'which was never undertaken before by any, although very requisite',[84] was linked with the monopoly Woodall exercised over the supply of such chests to the surgeons of the East India Company, and the role of the Barber-Surgeons' Company in supplying chests for the navy, merchant marine and army. On 10 July 1626, after a petition to the Duke of Buckingham from naval surgeons pressed into service during Lord Wimbledon's expedition to Cadiz, calling for the supply of adequate sea chests and medicines, the Privy Council began to pay the Barber-Surgeons' Company fixed allowances to supply medicine chests to the army and navy, ordering that an allowance of £10 for each of the royal ships should be given to the Barber-Surgeons 'for a supply of physical drugs and medicaments to be provided for the surgeons appointed to go in this next fleet'. The chests were to contain 'all the medicines as well physical as surgical together with all other provisions belonging to a chirurgion's chest either by themselves or by their appointment' and were to be delivered locked at Tower Wharf.[85] When in 1629 Charles I granted a new charter to the Barber-Surgeons Company, it provided for the mandatory examination of sea-surgeons at Surgeons' Hall and for the inspection of their chests and instruments. Woodall, on account of his experience with the East India Company chests, was given 'the whole ordering, making and appointing of His Highness's military provisions for surgery both for his land and sea service.'[86] Thus began a lucrative venture for Woodall but also the long monopoly enjoyed by the Barber-Surgeons over the supply and inspection of ship's surgeons' chests. This ensured a standardisation and uniformity in what drugs and items of equipment were available, ensuring a degree of consistency in treatment.

Skills learned in a naval vessel could be of value to a surgeon on other ships. James Yonge served his apprenticeship on naval vessels, but was later to spend some time as a surgeon in the employ of English fishermen in Newfoundland in 1663. Ships without a surgeon would agree to pay a suitably qualified man to provide them with medical care for a fixed rate for each man aboard the ship, the fee being paid by the master of the ship at the end of the fishing season. The fishing boat owners also contributed towards the cost of the surgeon's chest, while the master paid his share of the costs of a surgeon and every man gave half a crown. The surgeon also received a hundred dried fish as part of his fee.[87] The main illnesses suffered by the Newfoundland fishermen were sores on the wrist, minor colds and coughs, and scurvy, the symptoms of which were such that 'their gums rot, thick-breathed, swollen, black, ulcerated hams and thighs, tumours of the legs, jelly to the touch'. Yonge believed that this was caused by the men eating too much herring and cod's liver. He treated it by purging them with roots of stinking gladwin steeped in water, followed by tops of spruce, wild vetches, agrimony steeped in beer, and by bathing them in similar decoctions.[88]

Health at sea was very much the province of the lowly ship's surgeon yet it was not the skills of the surgeon that were needed in an age when infectious disease, not wounds, was the greatest problem. Service at sea offered few attractions to the more lordly physician whose knowledge and skills, even given the limitations in medical knowledge of the time, might have been more useful. Apprenticeship continued to be the way of educating new generations of surgeons, who learned their skills by observing and practising surgery themselves. James Yonge was able to transform 'a lad of very loose practices, negligent, gamesome when he came to me' within two years into 'a well bred, good-natured, understanding lad of a tall stature', but unfortunately this promising surgeon's mate, William Wits, 'contracted a malignant fever by visiting a ship that was infected and for want of due care he died' aged only twenty-two in 1678.[89] Yet the position of the surgeon onboard ship was ill-defined and depended very much on the support and informed interest in hygiene of such captains as Francis Drake and Richard Hawkins. Captain John Smith, Governor of Virginia, also saw the importance of a ship having a good surgeon, especially during naval action: 'The day is spent, the night draws on. Chiurgion, look to the wounded, and wind up the slain, with each a weight or bullet at their heads and feet to make them sink'.[90] More typical was the role in tending the sick of the surgeon, his mate and the 'loblolly boy', a rating assigned to assist them and who was said to be named after the porridge he served to the bedridden. Everything depended on the individual captain and surgeon, yet what was needed was a more consistent and coherent policy and example from the centre. In England this was to come under the Commonwealth, and provide the basis for the health of the navy that was to establish a maritime empire into the eighteenth century.

CHAPTER THREE

# Sick and Hurt

IT WAS THE problem of how to deal with an overwhelming number of sick and wounded sailors during the series of wars for commercial supremacy with the Dutch, fought off the south coast of England between 1652 and 1674, which laid the foundations of the English system of naval medicine in the seventeenth and eighteenth centuries. The large numbers of wounded men in need of succour spurred the Council of State to ask the Admiralty Board on 7 September 1652 to consider 'how the sick and wounded who are sent into Dover from ships in the service of the Commonwealth may from time to time be provided for both in respect to the supplying of them with money, as also for the appointing of some able physicians and chirurgions to attend the recovery of the said men.'[1] The Admiralty Board in turn issued a series of instructions on 20 and 21 December 1652 to try to deal with the immediate problems, but which were also to map out the future way ahead. The sick and wounded were to be treated in civilian hospitals requisitioned for military use or were to be boarded out in private lodging houses under contract to the Admiralty; the contractors were to be paid at 'so much a head which is the custom of the time'.[2] Initially, this was a flat rate of one shilling a day to contractors regardless of the severity of the illness or wound. The London hospitals, St Bartholomew's and St Thomas's, to which patients were also sent, only received two shillings a week. Meanwhile, it was decreed that 'the moiety of hospitals in England be reserved for such as shall be wounded in the service of the Navy, as they become void, from and after the first of January next.'[3] A percentage of prize money was to be appropriated for the relief of the sick and the aid of the dependents of the dead. The Dutch wars, moreover, demonstrated the need for a central medical department to co-ordinate arrangements for the reception, treatment, and disposal of casualties. The following year, on 29 September 1653, a Commission was set up to oversee the care of the sick and wounded, and to 'give reasonable and timely direction to mayors and chief officers of all sea port towns to make provision for all sick and wounded men as they shall be set ashore from any of the ships in the State's service'. A wartime temporary expedient to ensure 'that the recovery and care of the distressed may not be retarded or prejudiced',[4] the Sick and Hurt Board was dissolved in 1659, only to be revived in 1664 and on a further four occasions in wartime, until its responsibilities were taken over by the Transport Board in 1806. Until 1796 it had no responsibility for surgeons and medicine at sea. A modified form of the contract system, whereby local civilian surgeons and agents were appointed throughout the country for the care of sick sailors where no naval medical facilities were available, survived up to the 1970s.

Up to this time provision for the sick and wounded had been made on an ad hoc basis, but had never been necessary on such a scale for such a long period as in the Anglo-Dutch wars of the seventeenth century. In the Middle Ages the incapacitated seaman had no choice but to rely on the charity of the hospitals and hospices established from religious motives, and often staffed by members of religious orders. The care offered to the disabled seaman was often of a temporary nature, as at St John's Hospital, Winchester, where 'sick and lame soldiers [were] to have diet and lodging thereto fit and convenient for one night or longer as their abilities to travel gave leave'.[5] At first none of these hospitals or almshouses were specifically for sailors. The first hospital for aged and indigent mariners was founded in Venice in 1318 by the sea-surgeon Gualterius, who was one of the foremost surgeons of his times; this was provided with medical stores and instruments at the expense of the Venetian Republic.[6] In the Hanseatic ports of Tallinn and Riga, the young, unmarried German shipowners and merchants who had banded together in the fourteenth century to form Brother-hoods of Blackheads were concerned with mutual self-help and medical care, showing a devotion not only to their patron saints, the Virgin Mary and St Maurice, but also to St Gertrude, patron saint of the sick in hospitals.[7] Meanwhile, in the chief Hanseatic town of Lübeck, the Brotherhood of Captains, founded in 1401, similarly organised welfare services for their members from their magnificently ornamented guildhall, the Schiffergesellschaft, with its models of ships hanging from the ceiling, and long tables and benches made from oak ship's timbers. Close by the Schiffergesellschaft was the Heiligen-Geist Hospital, where sick mariners would receive medical care.

However, it was not until the late Middle Ages that seamen's guilds in England were sufficiently well-organised to support hospitals caring for their members. At York the Merchant Adventurers became patrons of the nearby Hospital of the Trinity in 1365, to gain guaranteed beds for the sailors manning their ships. The Guild of the Blessed Trinity at Kingston-upon-Hull established an almshouse for thirteen mariners 'which by infortune of the sea shall hap to fall in poverty by loss of goods' in 1457, using charges levied on the ships using the port. In Bristol the mariners also supported a hospital for seamen through a levy of 4d on each ton of cargo passing through the port, supplemented by a contribution from the wages of the seamen, because 'the craft of mariners is so adventurous that daily being in their voyages sore vexed, troubled and diseased, the which by good means of the prayers and good works might be graciously comforted and better relieved of such troubles.' However, in Bristol they had taken over control of an existing institution, St Bartholomew's Hospital, rather than set up a new one.[8]

A mutual medical aid scheme on a national scale, known as the Chatham Chest, was established by Francis Drake and John Hawkins in 1590 for the aid of sick and disabled mariners. Each parish in England contributed a small weekly sum for the maintenance of invalid sailors born or living within that parish, and seamen were invited to make their own voluntary contributions. In 1604 a compulsory deduction of 6d a week was made from the wages of all seamen serving in the navy. Additional funds came from prize money and the fines levied at courts martial. The money raised was kept in a strong brass-bound chest in the parish church at Chatham, and the five keys to it kept by a master attendant, a shipwright, a boatswain, a purser, and a principal officer of the navy who appointed his four colleagues.[9] It was then down to the individual sailor in hardship to apply for assistance from the fund and he had to attend in person at Chatham, where the governors of the Chest met only once a month. This was not easy for men who had been landed at far-off Harwich, Portsmouth or Plymouth. Moreover, despite the high incidence of infectious disease in the Elizabethan and early Stuart navies, there were relatively few casualties from enemy action or long-term disablement, with the result that most of the applicants to the fund in its early days had suffered amputations following wounds, frostbite or exposure polyneuritis. Not surprisingly, as the funds in the Chest increased and demand on it remained limitless, there was scope for abuse and embezzlement.[10] Sir Robert Cotton, a member of a commission appointed to enquire into the state of the navy in 1608, complained that the money was 'lent by those that have no authority and borrowed by those that have no need', and that the administrators 'care not though the poor souls that have spent their youth or wasted their ability or lost their limbs consume and pine, so as *their* own turns may be served and their hunger satisfied'.[11] A seaman who had served with Drake and been disabled on the *Adventure* in 1595 was still vainly petitioning for an allowance in 1627.[12] However, by the mid–1640s the Chatham Chest was running much more efficiently in refunding the travelling expenses of applicants for relief, helping them to reach their own parishes which had responsibility for them under the 1601 Poor Law Act, reimbursing the cost of medical treatment, surgeons' fees, and charges for lodgings and diet.[13] What was missing was any use of the fund for building a permanent naval hospital, something that the experience of the 1650s showed to be sorely needed.

Traditionally, wounded mariners had long been sent to the medieval London hospitals of St Bartholomew's and St Thomas's, both of which had been refounded after the dissolution of the monasteries, and to the Savoy Hospital founded by Henry VII and housed in the former Savoy Palace. St Bartholomew's Hospital was 'in a condition to receive presently wounded and sick mariners to the number of fifty if there shall be urgent occasions' by 3 January 1653 for casualties of the First Anglo-Dutch War.[14] However, the admission of naval patients disrupted the main charitable purpose of such hospitals as St Bartholomew's, which was the care and treatment of the sick poor of London. The sailors were also disruptive in the hospital wards, and on 22 May 1654 were summoned to the Counting House to be warned that 'if they did hereafter disorder themselves by drink or did lie out of their wards or did not observe the rules of this house, that they should be presently dismissed this hospital, and put out of the state's pay'. Two 'sea soldiers' disobeyed this instruction, being 'commonly drunk and distempered', and were discharged for drunken unruliness and for fighting in the King's Ward.[15]

The Savoy Hospital and another hospital set up at Ely House, once the London residence of the Bishop of Ely and subsequently used as a prison, were wholly under military discipline, and were governed by regulations drawn up especially for naval patients by commissioners appointed by the Commonwealth. The Savoy Hospital was reserved for surgical cases and Ely House for medical. Wounded and sick seamen were escorted to the hospitals and admitted to the wards. Bed cradles were provided for men who had had an amputation, and their wounds were dressed with cotton that had been dyed red, and bandaged with a linen roller made from surplices confiscated by the Puritans from the City churches. Men who had lost their legs were supplied with crutches and then with iron or wooden legs fitted with straps. Disruptive patients, gamblers, and drinkers were threatened with expulsion, though a man could not be punished or expelled for being drunk without having first been examined by the Overseer of the Savoy Hospital or a surgeon at Ely House. Then for the first offence, he would be 'set in the stocks', for the second he forfeited a week's pay, and for the third and final transgression he would be discharged. Even so, beer was issued, as were clay pipes for men wishing to smoke.[16] The hospital at Ely House also contained a ward known as the Hothouse, staffed by two male nurses and fitted with a copper bath, in which the patients were 'sweated'. This was a standard treatment for syphilis and was intended to drive the corruption out of the body; it would be carried out as long as the patient could stand the high temperatures, for between three days and a week, during which time he would be denied food in case it allowed the noxious odours to build up.[17] Even in the godly days of the Commonwealth, vice still flourished.

Meanwhile, Daniel Whistler, a 34-year-old physician, had been appointed in March 1653 to take responsibility for the daunting number of naval casualties. An energetic and determined young man, his initial appointment had been only to look after the naval patients in Portsmouth, but his responsibilities were soon extended to cover all casualties and the sick nationwide, as a roving medical agent. On arriving in Portsmouth his first action had been to send off by cart the serious and chronic patients, accompanied by surgeons and nurses, to the London hospitals, and to return the convalescent sailors to their ships 'where salt meat will not do more hurt than strong drink would here.'[18] He had then tried to co-ordinate the work of the surgeons operating in Portsmouth. He complained of the evils of 'exposing sick and wounded men long in the open air upon the ground in expectation of quarters before they are received into any house; and then the long being in that house before notice given to the physician and chirurgions'. He also despaired of the difficulty and expense of treating patients scattered around numerous inns and lodging houses, and the temptations to which they were exposed: 'besides the difficulty and charge otherwise of ordering their diet, nursing; the thronging of weak men into poor stifling houses; the temptations to them of drinking inordinately in victualling houses who have no other but strong drinks'. Alcohol may have been readily available, but there was a 'want of linen and medicines timely which should be in readiness aforehand in store'. Whistler thought that the only sensible solution to the problem was to establish a hospital. Portchester Castle, near Portsmouth, was considered a suitable location, 'for air and water healthful', for such a hospital, though Whistler reserved judgement as to 'whether it may not cost as much to repair an old castle as to build a new house by'.[19] His hopes of establishing a hospital were in vain.

Even worse than the crisis in Portsmouth was the problem of caring for the large numbers of sick and wounded being landed in the East Anglian ports in the summer of 1653. They were lodged in farms and inns throughout Norfolk and Suffolk. The Bailiffs of Yarmouth were 'very pitiful and careful of all sick and wounded men sent to them' and 'the seamen generally give a good character of the country people with whom they have been quartered for their care and tenderness over them', but the innkeepers and farmers' wives found it difficult to provide the care when their expenses went unpaid.[20] Whistler was indefatigable in co-ordinating local efforts with the work of the surgeons sent from London. He reported at the end of August 1653 that in the previous week he had visited four hundred men in the towns and villages around Aldeburgh, and 'for the better administration of means to such sick as wanted more help than air and fresh diet for their recovery, caused such to be returned hither', 374 new arrivals at Ipswich, and five hundred men who had been sent to Ipswich from an earlier naval engagement. He also reported eighty-four wounded and eighty-seven sick at Harwich, and the death of thirty-one men from wounds at Great Yarmouth, hoping for the future 'by the blessing of God there will not men die of their wounds.'[21] Whistler, an affable man considered good company by the gregarious Samuel Pepys, but who was to die in debt in 1684, amidst accusations of dishonesty and mismanagement of the affairs of the College of Physicians of which he had become President, went straight on from his work at the East Anglian ports to act as physician to Bulstrode Whitelocke's embassy to Sweden in 1653 and while there wrote verses in Latin on the abdication of Queen Christina. He was in the 1650s not only a competent medical administrator but also took pains 'to communicate my experiences to the surgeons . . . having more than ordinary studied and observed by my employment therein the surgical part of physic.'[22]

Whistler had been helped both in Portsmouth and East Anglia by Elizabeth Alkin, a noticeably corpulent woman in her fifties, popularly known as 'Parliament Joan', and described by one Royalist pamphleteer as an 'old bitch' who could 'smell out a loyal-hearted man as soon as the best blood-hound in the army'.[23] Her husband had been hanged as a spy by the Royalists in Oxford and she herself had spied for the Commonwealth. She had provided information about George Mynnes, a Surrey ironmaster who was supplying royalist forces with iron and wire, and had also infiltrated the London printing trade in search of the printers and publishers of illicit royalist propaganda. She volunteered to nurse the wounded after the Battle of Portland in

February 1653 and had immediately set off for Portsmouth, returning to London three months later with the men whose arms and legs had been amputated. She had then gone to Harwich where she used her own money on her patients, 'to have them cleaned in their bodies and their hair cut, mending their clothes, reparations and several things else.' She had also paid for medicines and other nurses, whose work she organised and supervised, since 'it pities me to see poor people in distress. I cannot see them want if I have it'.[24] The Commonwealth was less concerned about what it owed to Elizabeth Alkin, who returned to London a sick woman, but could get payment of neither her expenses, nor a pension granted to her for her espionage activities, and was reduced to selling her bed and household goods to pay for the medicines she needed.

Concern about the possibility of further epidemics impairing the performance of the English fleet in the war with Spain led the Lord Protector Oliver Cromwell to appoint the first Physician to the Fleet in 1654. His choice, Paul de Laune, was over seventy and had no naval and very little military experience, apart from a short period of army service in 1643. He set sail for the West Indies in December 1654, stating in his will that 'I am now going upon the State's service Physician to this great Fleet of ships for land and sea service'.[25] His appointment was a reflection of the division of the medical profession into university-educated physicians and more practically-trained surgeons, as indeed of the rivalry between the College of Physicians and the Company of Barber-Surgeons. The Commonwealth was opposed to monopolies and disregarded the traditional claims of the surgeons to control of naval medicine, not only in the appointment of a Physician to the Fleet, responsible for medical supplies at sea and attendance on the commander-in-chief, but also in allowing the Society of Apothecaries to advise on and supply the contents of sea-surgeons' chests.[26] Later in the century the monopoly of the Barber-Surgeons received a further blow when in 1691 naval physicians were appointed to the four home ports of Chatham, Deal, Portsmouth and Plymouth and to the Red and Blue Squadrons of the main fleet.[27]

Many seamen remained unimpressed with the surgeons, physicians and apothecaries they came into contact with at sea. Edward Barlow, a seaman under the Commonwealth and in the Restoration Royal Navy, complained about their lack of concern for the sick sailor:

And the surgeons and doctors of physic in ships many times are very careless of a poor man in his sickness, their common phrase

47

being to come to him and take him by the hand when they hear that he hath been sick two or three days, thinking that is soon enough, and feeling his pulses when he is half dead, asking him when he was at stool, and how he feels himself, and how he has slept, and then giving him some of their medicines upon the point of a knife, which doth as much good to him as a blow upon the pate with a stick. And when he is dead then they did not think that he had been so bad as he was, nor so near his end.[28]

Barlow may have been something of a pessimist with a tendency to exaggerate the blackest picture, but there was some basis of truth in his portrait. One ship's captain complained in 1673 that 'I was informed there was a surgeon belonging to the ship but never saw him till I returned from Newcastle and then he told me he was minded to leave the ship, which I thought he had done before.'[29] An absentee surgeon might have been preferred by other captains whose surgeons were not up to the position. Richard Woodall from Bedfordshire served on five ships as surgeon, but had damaged his eyesight which rendered him unfit for further sea service and made him seem 'old and feeble' at the age of fifty-seven.[30] The surgeon of the *Baltimore* was described as being a 'pitiful fellow of a barber who knows nothing.'[31] It was made all the more difficult to obtain decent surgeons when pay rates were low, having been fixed at £2 10s a month in 1653, regardless of the size of the ship, and when there was often a long delay in their getting paid at all. Robert Moore was surgeon on the *Bonetta Sloop* for four years without being paid, and as a result was suffering from 'a deluge of misery and a labyrinth of sorrow'.[32] On occasion, surgeons aboard naval vessels were forced to get together to petition for payment of the money they had expended on medicines and transport for wounded soldiers.[33] Other surgeons were not given the assistance they needed. Even a man of some status like John Conny, surgeon to the naval dockyards at Chatham and mayor of Rochester, had to appeal for the restoration of his servant, the lack of whom was 'tending so much to your petitioner's damage'.[34] It did nothing for the reputation of naval surgeons when they were not replaced if they died or left the ship, and their duties were carried out by someone without any qualifications. James Jacob, surgeon on the *Happy Return* in 1687, died in service, leaving 'on board the same ship his chest of medicines and instruments to a considerable value'. After his death 'there was no other chirurgion ordered on board . . . but the party that did officiate on board on behalf of the chirurgion did till the payment of the said ship use and expend the medicines and instruments belonging to the said James Jacob'. The value of the contents of this chest was £2 and his heirs were determined to obtain compensation for them.[35] The use of unqualified surgeons was not a matter for comment onboard ship. In 1665 the Privy Council, faced with the difficulties of ensuring that every ship carried a surgeon and mate in wartime, had allowed surgeons to serve at sea who were not members of the company of Barber-Surgeons, and did not oblige them to become 'foreign brothers' of the livery company with restricted privileges, as had been the practice hitherto. Although this had chipped further at the monopoly of the Barber-Surgeons with regard to naval surgery, it was accepted by them because of the war emergency, and they were still supposed to examine the candidates and satisfy themselves of their ability and qualifications.[36]

Nevertheless there were many other sea-surgeons who had the respect and admiration of their men for their attention to duty and their concern for their charges. Sir John Berryman praised his surgeon Mr Howard in 1674, who 'hath served these two years in the *Resolution,* he hath behaved himself very diligently in his employment. He hath been at great charges for medicine for the sick and wounded men.' [37] The seamen themselves aboard the *James Galley* in 1680 had nothing but praise for their surgeon:

> We the mariners belonging to His Majesty's Ship *James Galley* have many of us been desperately sick of malignant fevers and fluxes, and by the scurvy, and others of the crew were wounded and bruised by accidents aboard the same ship but all of us and many more have been safely cured again by the care and skill of our chirurgion in Mr John Moyle who hath . . . sufficiently proved himself both a very able surgeon and an honest man by his behaviour, hath been so civil towards all men that he hath an extraordinary respect from the ship's company in general.[38]

Moyle was without any doubt an exceptional sea-surgeon who was to write a manual, addressed to junior surgeons at sea, which contained sound practical advice on what stores to take to sea with them, and what medical and surgical cases they might expect to treat once onboard ship. Having served in the Third Dutch War, on anti-piracy patrols off the North Africa coast and on the Newfoundland banks, Moyle understood the needs of the ordinary surgeon and wrote simple helpful tips from his own experience.[39] James Yonge, another surgeon who had begun his career as an apprentice on a naval vessel, was also to write a number of medical texts, be elected mayor of Plymouth, and be elected a fellow of the eminent Royal Society.[40] Significantly, most of these able men had to abandon an active sea career if they wished to advance in the world.

Perhaps one of the most highly placed of the distinguished sea-surgeons of the seventeenth-century was Samuel Pepys's friend James Pearse, who, having served as surgeon on the *Naseby* from 1658 to 1660 under Sir Edward Montagu, became surgeon-general of the Restoration navy and surgeon to the Duke of York and to the royal household. Pearse's appointment as surgeon-general, first made in 1664, was initially in an occasional and advisory capacity, lapsing in peacetime and renewed in wartime, but in 1675 he was officially appointed to the post of 'Chirurgion-General of His Majesty's navy', with authority over the care of all the navy's sick and wounded. His brief was to economise and retrench in peacetime, through standardising procedures and clamping down on any opportunities for peculation. The Savoy Hospital was closed and casualties were sent to St Bartholomew's and St Thomas's Hospitals, whose payment of 2d a day for each naval patient received was cheaper than the expense of boarding them out in the ports and employing local surgeons to attend them. The governors of these hospitals felt that this was an imposition on them. Where surgeons were used in the ports to attend men in their quarters, Pearse contracted with them for a standard charge of 6s 8d a man and a further 12d a day for victuals for each patient. He was also responsible for supervising the payment of pensions to disabled seamen from the Chatham Chest.[41] James Yonge wrote highly of Pearse as being 'famed for a good man', and for the way in which he 'always provides the chyrurgeons with the spices and other necessaries, which during the war he could not remit to them on this coast' of Devon, not surprisingly when he was appointed Pearse's deputy for dealing with sick men landing at Plymouth.[42] Samuel Pepys, another efficient naval administrator, also thought highly of him, most especially when he brought him gossip about the Court, and even more so of his wife, whom he dubbed 'la belle Pearse'.[43]

Pepys, who suffered badly from seasickness when he did go on a long ocean voyage to Tangier in 1683, was not directly concerned with the health of the navy, but he was with the efficient victualling of the ships and keeping their crews fed and thus well.[44] Eight men from each of the two watches on the ship formed a mess which had its own table, usually between two of the guns. Seamen were entitled to a gallon of beer a day, often ladled from a barrel. They were also given a pound of ship's biscuit each day, and two pounds of pork a week, together with fish, peas, butter, and cheese. When stationed in the Mediterranean this diet was replaced by one featuring wine, raisins, rice, stockfish, and olive oil, a diet which was not popular with the men; Edward Barlow characteristically complained that the 'sour beverage wine' laid many of his shipmates low with the flux.[45] He also criticised the mouldy bread, the 'little small beer, which is as bad as water bewitched' and the tough beef provided 'when all the best was picked out, leaving us poor seamen the sirloin next the horns'.[46] He considered that the Christmas dinner served to him and his shipmates at Cadiz on Christmas Day 1665 was 'nothing but a little bit of Irish beef for four men, which had lain in pickle for two or three years and was as rusty as the devil, with a little stinking oil or butter, which was all the colours of the rainbow, many men in England greasing their cartwheels with better.'[47] Barlow was not alone in his grumbling. Sir Robert Robinson, captain of the *Assistance,* complained that 'the provisions were so bad that several of the men chose rather to eat dry bread alone almost to the starving of themselves, than eat the other victuals.' These despised foodstuffs included fishy-tasting pork, sour oatmeal, hard peas, and wine that was so undrinkable that the men actually 'chose rather to drink water'.[48] Pepys recognised that the victuallers were cutting corners but also commented that 'Englishmen, and more especially seamen, love their bellies above everything else, and . . . to make any abatement from them in the quantity or agreeableness of the victuals, is to discourage and provoke them in the tenderest point, and will sooner render them disgusted with the king's service than any one other hardship that can be put upon them'.[49]

Sanitary arrangements were even more important than ever when the food was bad. Just as their counterparts had done earlier on Henry VIII's *Mary Rose,* the more fastidious officers, including the chaplain Henry Teonge, provided themselves with personal chamber pots.[50] Improvements were made on many of the larger ships from 1670 onwards, with the introduction of seats in the heads, a 'pissdale', or urinal, on the upper deck, and private sanitary provision for warrant officers in the stern. Many men, though, urinated wherever they were caught short, and regulations punishing 'he that pisseth between the decks' with up to twelve lashes were introduced to discourage such practices. In 1673, a consignment of thirty tons of vinegar was delivered to the fleet 'to wash their decks, to keep the men in health'.[51] There could be other hazards involved when the 'necessary seat' was so exposed right forward in the bows. James Yonge, in his early days at sea, 'narrowly escaped drowning, for going into the main chains to exonerate nature, the ship yawed to port and heeled so deep to starboard that I was dipped head and ears, the affright of which, together with the surface motion of the sea, had almost forced me from my hold.'[52]

Dealing with minor accidents took up much of the time of the surgeon in times of peace and in the lulls between engagements in wartime. Every day the surgeon would prepare a dressing box with six or eight partitions, into each of which he placed his pots of balsam, oils, and plasters ready spread. He would carry this box 'every morning to the mast between the decks where our mortar is usually rung, that such as have any sore or ailment may hear in any part of the ship, and come thither to be dressed.'[53] Men too ill to attend the surgeon would be visited where they lay and, if necessary, moved to some position where their hammocks could be slung where they would not obstruct the mess decks or guns. John Moyle dealt with cases of venereal disease by improvising a hothouse to eliminate the poison by sweating. He advised that 'if you were ashore a hot house were best', such as the one provided at Ely House during the Commonwealth when it was requisitioned as a naval hospital. However, he was ingenious enough to devise his own hothouse in the officer's cabin, which 'must be hung about with warm hangings, that no cold come in; and if there were a small pot or pan of fire in the cabin, it were so much the better.' The patient being sweated would be wrapped in 'flannel stockings, drawers, shirt and waistcoat, as likewise flannel muffler and cap', which the surgeon 'must have ready'.[54] Another of John Moyle's patients was a young sailor who had hit his head against a cross-beam when running to the steerage door. Moyle had set up an operating theatre in the cockpit, where he successfully trepanned him to relieve the pressure on his brain from the resulting haemorrhage.[55]

The cockpit became an operating theatre and dressing station when the ship saw action, while the adjoining orlop platform became a collecting centre and ward. The medical chests in the cockpit became operating tables and beds for the injured. The orlop platform would be covered with sailcloth to prevent blood staining the wood. Onto it were placed 'two vessels, one with water to wash hands in between each operation, and to wet your dismembering bladder in; and for other services; and the other to throw amputated limbs into till you have opportunity to heave them overboard.'[56] The bladder was used to slip over amputation stumps as a waterproof dressing that could collect discharges of pus and blood. The operating theatre would be lit by flickering candles in horn lanterns. Richard Wiseman, an English royalist surgeon who had served with the Spanish navy during the Commonwealth and Protectorate, wrote of men having limbs amputated that 'at sea they sit or lie; I never took much notice, nor do I remember I had ever anybody to hold them; with the help of my mates, and some one or two that belongeth to the hold, I went on with my work.'[57] During the Four Days' Battle against the Dutch in 1666, Edward Barlow was hit in the leg by a cannonball and, with his leg swollen, he 'was forced to go down amongst the wounded men, where one lay without a leg and another without an arm, one wounded to death and another groaning with pain and dying, and one wounded in one manner and another in another.'[58] The Duke of York, the future James II, witnessed for himself the carnage of a naval battle in action on the *Royal Charles* against the Dutch off Lowestoft on 3 June 1665. Pepys, who was not present but recorded in his diary the impressions of eyewitnesses, noted the deaths of the Earl of Falmouth, Lord Muskerry, and Richard Boyle, and 'their blood and brains flying in the Duke's face – and the head of Mr Boyle striking down the Duke', whose hand was wounded by a fragment of that young man's skull.[59] Many men lost limbs in that battle. In the heat of battle many surgeons amputated indiscriminately. Young Lieutenant Stephen Martin was wounded in the leg during a skirmish with the French off Bantry Bay in May 1689. The surgeon wanted to amputate because 'upon these occasions they are in too great a hurry and confusion to consider properly the circumstances of every patient, so the surgeon had determined to cut off his leg', but Martin refused to allow this to happen and the fracture was set instead. When he was landed with the rest of the wounded at Portsmouth, Martin had it reset again by a surgeon he considered more competent than the man whose only answer to a wound had been amputation, thereby saving his leg and allowing him to pursue his career in the navy.[60]

Despite the drama of wartime surgery, it was still disease which had a greater impact on the health of seamen. James White, a surgeon serving with the fleet in the Mediterranean in 1694–5, observed that, out of a ship's company of almost five hundred, 'we lost about ninety or one hundred men mostly by fevers', and that 'those who died were commonly the young, but always the strongest, lustiest, handsomest persons.'[61] James Pearse considered that such high mortality rates might have something to do with the large number of aristocratic volunteers who flocked to join the fleet, but who were unused to the diet and the methods used by seamen to keep themselves clean at sea, insinuating that such volunteers, however fastidious they may have been in their fashionable clothing, at sea were relieving themselves between the decks when suffering from diarrhoea, and that this was causing endemic sickness in the fleet. Others thought that men seized by the press gangs were less particular about hygiene than the professional mariners. Commissioner Peter Pett of the Navy Board even deplored the arrival of quantities of 'filthy and destitute' pressed men at Chatham in 1664, 'who are fit for nothing but to fill the ships full of vermin and smallpox.'[62]

Prompt action was taken to avoid the havoc which the Great Plague of 1665 might have inflicted on the fleet, which was at that time based in the Thames and manned by men from London. The plague and other epidemics did still influence naval action. An attempted blockade of the Dutch coast by the English fleet in August 1665 was abandoned as a result of sickness and lack of victuals. Meanwhile, the Dutch admiral Michael de Ruyter, lying off the Thames with ninety ships in October 1665, was forced to withdraw to Holland in November after plague broke out in his fleet.[63] Sick men were not allowed to remain on their ships, but were landed immediately and not allowed to return aboard, even if they appeared to have recovered. Many captains believed that the plague was carried in clothing and refused to allow any new supplies of slops onboard ship.[64] Any signs of plague among men rounded up by the press gangs gained them their release. When one man in a draft of 131 pressed men at Sheerness was found to have a 'rising' in his groin, 'nobody would take the rest' for fear that they too might be carrying the plague, and they were given their freedom to return to their homes from which they had been snatched.[65] Any ships suspected of carrying plague victims were quarantined. Such measures of quarantine against the advance of the plague from the East had been adopted as early as November 1663, when two small naval vessels on the Thames were anchored 'as low in the River as with assurance they may so speak with every ship that shall attempt to pass by and strictly examine from whence they come, and if they find any to come from Amsterdam, Hamburg or any other infected places, then peremptorily to command them to turn back to sea or perform their quarantine for thirty days in Hole Haven.'[66] When the *Convertine* arrived at Harwich from Gothenburg with its crew 'all the voyage very sickly and is yet . . . some of them dying from a spotted fever', it was immediately sent into quarantine at Hole Haven.[67] John Evelyn even requested the use of a pest ship for the quarantine of infectious sailors 'who were not a few'.[68] The ships were regularly cleaned as a matter of course and rarely came alongside the wharves where infected rats could get aboard, which helped to reduce the spread of plague. Moreover, the navy was at sea at the height of the summer epidemic. On land in the dockyards suspected plague victims were also isolated. At Portsmouth Dockyard, all the carpenters who had been in houses infected with the plague in August 1666 were ordered to go on board the *Little Francis,* remain there for a fortnight's quarantine, and 'wash themselves and their clothes, and burn rosin and brimstone fourteen days before admitted to the yard'.[69]

The Navy Board moved from London to the comparative safety of Greenwich to escape the plague, though Mr Secretary Pepys remained in the capital at the height of the sickness, taking such precautions as buying 'some roll tobacco to smell to and chew – which took away the apprehension' caused by seeing in Drury Lane for the first time 'two or three houses marked with a red cross upon the doors and "Lord have mercy upon us" writ there.'[70] He was alarmed when news was brought to him of a suspected plague victim among the servants of his friend George Cocke, a timber merchant and navy contractor: 'Sir William Batten ... did tell me that Captain Cocke's black was dead of the plague', and 'I did send to him that he would either forbear the office or forbear going to his own office', to avoid possibly spreading the infection. Even when he overheard the searchers employed to inspect and clean the houses of a plague victim saying that 'the fellow did not die of the plague', the ever cautious Pepys was sceptical since 'he had been ill a good while, and I am told that his boy Jack is also ill.'[71] Eventually Pepys followed the Navy Board to Greenwich in the autumn of 1665. He considered that 'I have never lived so merrily (besides that I have never got so much) as I have done this plague time', despite the great expense of moving his family to Woolwich and his office and clerks to Greenwich to avoid the sickness in the capital.[72] Content with his own prosperity and disregarding the deaths from plague of his aunt and the children of his cousin, Pepys was aware that 'the great burden we have upon us at this time at the office is the providing for prisoners and sick men that are recovered, they lying before our office doors all night and all day, poor wretches.' The problem was that 'having been on shore, the Captains won't receive them on board, and other ships we have not to put them on, nor money to pay them off or provide for them. God remove this difficulty'.[73]

What God could not do, and Pepys had tried to no avail, was to reform the maladministration of the Chatham Chest, which might have alleviated the condition of some of the sick men. Pepys had been a member from 1662 until 1664 of a commission of enquiry appointed to investigate the management of the Chest, and 'how it hath ever been abused . . . and what a meritorious act it would be to look after it'.[74] With his usual efficiency, Pepys worked late into the night on examining the accounts of the Chest, despite such distractions as when he 'this night first put on a waistcoat'.[75] Nevertheless, despite the evidence of men that 'hath abused the chest and hath now some £1000 of it', he was unable to achieve any great reform.[76] Of much more value were the proposals of his friend and fellow diarist John Evelyn, one of the Commissioners for Sick and Wounded Seamen, for a hospital; he 'entertained me with discourse of an infirmary which he hath projected for the sick and wounded seamen against the next year, which I mightily approve of – and will endeavour to promote, it being a worthy thing – and of use and will save money'.[77]

The need for a general naval hospital had become ever more pressing during the Second Dutch War of 1665–7. John Evelyn, concerned that five thousand casualties, including prisoners of war, were dying because of inferior accommodation, drew up plans for a hospital with four or five hundred beds to be built at Chatham to deal with a situation where 'His Majesty's subjects die in our sight and at our thresholds without our being able to relieve them, which, with our barbarous exposure of the prisoners to the utmost of sufferings must needs redound to His Majesty's great dishonour and to the consequence of losing the hearts of our people.'[78] Evelyn had been appalled by what he had seen during a visit to St Bartholomew's and St Thomas's Hospitals in April 1665 'with the doctor and chirurgion to attend the wounded, both enemies and others of our own', where he had 'visited my charge, several their legs and arms off, miserable objects God knows.'[79] His response to the immediate emergency facing him, with the landing of casualties in Kent and Sussex, was to set up an improvised thirty-bedded hospital in a barn at Gravesend, and to reopen a hospital at the Savoy, where he saw 'the miserably dismembered and wounded men dressed' during his visit to that hospital.[80] The Savoy Hospital seemed to him to be inadequate for naval needs and it was obvious that a longer term solution to the problem was needed. As a young man, he had been impressed on a visit to Amsterdam by the Soldatenhuis there, a hospital set up in 1587 for fifty-one invalid soldiers. Something similar was needed for English naval casualties.

With the encouragement of Charles II, Evelyn worked on plans and financial estimates for his proposed naval hospital, which also met with a sympathetic response from the Duke of York in his role as Lord High Admiral of England, the Navy Board and the Navy Commissioners, who on 20 February 1666 'having seen the project of the infirmary, encouraged the work, and were very earnest it should be set about speedily'. However, Evelyn remained sceptical about this show of enthusiasm as 'I saw no money, though a very moderate expense, would have saved thousands to His Majesty and been much more commodious for the cure and quartering of our sick and wounded, than the dispersing of them into private houses, where many more chirurgions and tenders were necessary, and the people tempted to debauchery.'[81] A navy-run hospital close to where the men were landed would have saved expense by economies of scale and eliminating the rapacity of contractors, as well as allowing greater control over the invalided sailor. However, at a time when the Sick and Hurt Board was heavily in debt and the Chatham Chest almost empty, it came as no surprise to anyone that there should be no money available for establishing and supporting a new naval hospital. Nevertheless, Evelyn went ahead with his plans and on 13 March 1666 visited Chatham to choose a suitable site. This was as much progress as he was ever to achieve with his laudable project.

It was not until 1690 that proposals for a dedicated naval hospital were again seriously considered, when the Admiralty appointed the physician Richard Lower to review the naval medical services and 'he is desired to propose in writing in what manner he thinks it will be best to have the business managed and what physicians, chyrurgions and apothecaries to employ at the several ports and the salaries to be allowed them.'[82] His immediate response was that all existing provision was grossly inadequate, especially when 'the Commissioners for Sick and Wounded Seamen put the charge of bringing the men from the waterside into the hospitals here in London, on the hospital and that some of the wounded men are suffered to lie two days on Tower Hill till there are maggots in their wounds.'[83] He found the current arrangements of the contract system to be inadequate and, keen to avoid unnecessary expenditure, advised that Carisbrooke and Dover Castles should be converted into hospitals. Lower had also suggested that houses suitable for hospital use should also be purchased in Greenwich, Liverpool, Chatham and Plymouth.[84] Just as proposals for converting Portchester Castle into a hospital had been dismissed as unsuitable four decades earlier, the approach to Carisbrooke Castle was found to be too steep for a hospital and too inaccessible from the sea. However, Lower's plans were accepted in principle but imperfectly executed, with the fitting up of temporary hospitals in the major ports,[85] and the conversion in 1692 of the King Charles Block of the unfinished royal palace at Greenwich into a temporary hospital for the sick and wounded.[86] Lower's report was resurrected in 1693 when Richard Gibson, a clerk in the Navy Office, recommended that William III should order 'a true settlement of curing seamen by Dr Lower's method, and not as now let them lie dispersed under cure in lewd ale-houses, or by the method now practised by them.'[87] Lower's recommendations were reviewed yet again in January 1703 and temporary naval hospitals were set up and run by contract. Captain Isaac Townshend complained that the hospital in Plymouth was 'very inconvenient and not fitting' for the treatment of his crew. The rooms were too small and low-ceilinged with the beds so close together that 'you cannot easily pass from one to another'. Some of the men, two to a bed, were 'lying in their excrement and the linen in general very foul and scandalously nasty'. He was adamant that 'men cannot reasonably be thought to recover so indifferently attended, pent up in such miserable lodging where they must certainly poison one another.'[88]

There was a prejudice against having military or naval hospitals in fixed places where contagion might gather, and which might not always be in the most convenient places for the receipt of casualties, when battles could take place anywhere, and were not always well-located for the landing of casualties from a particular naval engagement. Temporary and moveable hospitals were preferred as being more flexible and responsive to changing wartime conditions. A compromise was the fitting up of hospital ships, which offered more permanence than the contract system allowed, and more flexibility than a land-based hospital. The earliest English hospital ship, the *Goodwill*, had been fitted out to accompany an expedition to Algiers in 1620 and had doubled as a stores carrier. Hospital ships were commissioned primarily for the transport of the wounded in 1665 at the instigation of James Pearse.[89] The Barber-Surgeons' Company had advised on the equipping and staffing of the first hospital ships commissioned in 1665, but Pearse was more generous in his estimates of what was needed when called on for advice in 1672, even including six pounds of Castile soap in his list of essentials in addition to the mattresses, bolsters, rugs, sheets and standard medical chests recommended by the Barber-Surgeons. He recommended that each ship should be staffed by one master-surgeon, assisted by three or four able mates and two or three landsmen acting as cooks and nurses.[90] It was one thing for recommendations to be made about the equipment of hospital ships, but when Hugh Ryder took up his appointment on the Hospital Ship *John's Advice* in April 1672 he found that nothing had been done to adapt the ship to its hospital role, other than it having been hired for that purpose. He was given no storage space for his medical supplies and was refused two cabins for his four mates to share.[91] A request for gratings to be cut to allow for better ventilation between the decks when the vessel was crowded with patients was only authorised when Prince Rupert intervened.[92] The reluctance of lodging-house keepers ashore to accept sick seamen, because they often had difficulty in getting paid, made it even more important to accommodate the sick and wounded in hospital ships. The desertion rate among the sick men who were landed also made a nautical solution to hospital provision more attractive. The hospital ships were not the real answer to the problem of dealing with epidemic disease, but they did provide more specialised care than the men might have got ashore, and allowed men with infections to be isolated from ships' companies.[93]

The ad hoc hospital arrangements that ruled, although challenged, in England were not always possible on foreign naval stations, and the first permanent hospitals for the sick and wounded were established abroad. A hospital was built at Jamaica, where malaria and yellow fever were prevalent, in 1704, and one at Lisbon in 1706. A hospital was also established in 1708 at Port Mahon, Minorca, which had been captured from Spain in 1708 and ceded to the British by the treaty of Utrecht in 1713. In 1711 work began on the construction of a purpose-built hospital on a small island in the harbour at Port Mahon, convenient for the landing of the sick from ships, but offering a deterrent to drinkers and deserters. It cost £715 a year to maintain.[94] Until the completion in 1741 of a naval hospital at Gibraltar, also ceded to Britain in 1713, the hospital at Port Mahon remained the only purpose-built British naval hospital.[95]

Although plans for a naval hospital for the sick and wounded in England did not come to fruition in the seventeenth or early eighteenth centuries, the welfare of the naval pensioner was not forgotten. The Royal Hospital at Chelsea had been founded for aged and disabled soldiers in 1682 by Charles II, in direct emulation of the palatial Hôtel des Invalides founded in Paris by Louis XIV in 1670. William III and Mary II wished to found a similar institution for naval pensioners and the scheme, which had been a pet one of Queen Mary, was given a greater impetus by the death of Queen Mary from smallpox in 1694, and William's desire to build a memorial to her. William and Mary had abandoned the partly rebuilt but unfinished Greenwich Palace in favour of Kensington Palace and Hampton Court. Its conversion to a temporary naval hospital in 1692 made it seem a likely site for a hospital for old and disabled sailors which Queen Mary, realising that England 'ever made the most insignificant figure when the naval power was either sunk, neglected or broken', asked Christopher Wren to build 'with great magnificence and order' to project an image of naval might.[96] Charles II had considered that Winchester Palace might have been a suitable location for a naval hospital because of its proximity to the expanding port at Portsmouth, but though it would have been a good site, it was not one 'in the view of the world'.[97] Greenwich, close to the Thames and to the capital, was. Queen Mary's plans for Greenwich had included an infirmary for sick and wounded seamen in wartime but this was not built. Indeed, an infirmary for the pensioners living there was not erected until 1763.

The first forty-two pensioners were admitted in March 1705. Their lives were tightly regulated. They were required to attend services in the chapel daily. They were to wear at all times a coat of dark grey lined with blue,[98] a waistcoat and breeches of brown cloth, blue stockings, and a black cocked hat. Boatswains were marked out by the gold braid around their hats and sleeves. They lived in wards divided into individual cabins, but with beds instead of the hammocks they were accustomed to at sea. Their diet was basic and consisted of the beer, bread, and boiled meat that would have been familiar to them from their life aboard their ships. Dinner was eaten in the undercroft of the hall except on Founder's Day (11 April, the anniversary of the coronation of William and Mary) and the Sovereign's birthday when they dined in the magnificent splendour of the Painted Hall under William Thornhill's allegorical ceiling with its apotheosis of William and Mary. They were only allowed to smoke in the Chalk Walk, and could be punished for any misdemeanours such as drunkenness, uncleanness, perjury, theft, keeping pigeons, and selling their victuals to strangers.[99] The Royal Hospital at Greenwich was to offer a refuge to the superannuated seaman until 1869, when it was decided that it would be more economical for the pensioners to live in their own homes, and in 1873 the buildings were leased to the Royal Naval College.[100]

The Royal Naval Hospital at Greenwich, with all its magnificence, was not the hospital for the sick and wounded that doctors, reformers, and other public figures had argued for since the middle of the seventeenth century, when the need for a permanent hospital for casualties from the sustained periods of war at sea had become a pressing matter. Yet many contemporaries would have argued that a home for pensioned-off mariners was perhaps more important, since the welfare of the aged and disabled sailor was a perennial problem, whereas a naval hospital would only have been of vital importance in time of war when there were a large number of casualties being landed, and the resultant pressure on local resources under the contract system threatened to overwhelm local surgeons and lodging-house keepers. When naval hospitals for the sick and wounded were at last established in England in the mid eighteenth century, it was to be as a result of problems and pressures which also led to a raft of other changes in naval medicine. However, that time was still a long way off, although the need for them did not diminish.

# CHAPTER FOUR

# *Plague of the Sea*

IT WAS ONE of the most glorious of the voyages of the eighteenth century and one of the most notorious. George Anson's circumnavigation of the globe between 1740 and 1744 was a triumph of British naval might but it was a disaster for its crew. The death rate among the sailors was deplorable: as they sailed around the world, they succumbed to epidemics, they sickened, and they died. Commodore Anson's orders from the Admiralty were to raid and plunder the Spanish colonies on the Pacific coast of South America, encourage rebellion by the colonists against the King of Spain, and capture the annual 'galleon' bringing gold and silver back to Spain. The preparations for the voyage were protracted and, when the squadron did finally set sail in September 1740, the troops making up the landing force were mainly newly-recruited marines and pensioners from the Royal Hospital at Chelsea, many of them aged over sixty and some of them too immobile to desert. Their voyage round the Horn commenced during the worst possible season for beginning their expedition when, according to the purser Lawrence Millechamp onboard the sloop *Tryal*, 'the weather was still stormy with huge deep, hollow seas that frequently broke quite over us, with constant rain, frost or snow. Our decks were always full of water, and our men constantly falling ill with the scurvy; and the allowance of water being but small reduced us to a most deplorable condition.'[1] That rounding of the Horn was an epic of endurance but had otherwise been a naval disaster. Of the six warships in his squadron only the *Centurion, Gloucester* and *Tryal* remained, together with one of the two supply ships; but scurvy, cold and privation had left Anson with too few men to man even one of the ships properly. The unfortunate Chelsea pensioners had been among the first to die. By this time none of his objectives could be considered at all feasible, but Anson courageously continued with his mission and, emulating Francis Drake, set sail across the Pacific on the homeward voyage. Despite having lost two more ships and being barely able to man the *Centurion*, on 20 June 1743 Anson at last achieved a morale-boosting and profitable success in taking the galleon *Nuestra Señora de*

*Covadonga,* carrying 1,313,843 pieces of eight and 35,682 ounces of virgin silver. Anson, who had shared the privations of his men, helped to carry the sick, and was prepared to turn his hand to carpentry or whatever manual task was necessary, was feted as a hero on his return home, but his achievement had been at an enormous cost. More than 1,300 members of the original expedition had perished, and only 145 men returned home after a voyage of three years and nine months.[2]

It may have been presented as a national triumph but it was equally a medical disgrace. Most of the deaths were from scurvy, now known to be caused by a deficiency of vitamin C, and characterised by 'large discoloured spots dispersed over the whole surface of the body; swelled legs; putrid gums; and, above all, an extraordinary lassitude of the whole body especially after any exercise, however inconsiderable; and this lassitude at last degenerates into a proneness to swoon on the least exertion of strength, or even the least motion'.[3] The skin became dry and rough, the flesh flaccid, teeth loosened as the gums became purple and swollen, and wounds failed to heal. The disease had first become a problem for mariners in the fifteenth century, when ships began to stay at sea for longer periods of time, as Atlantic voyages became more common, and developments in shipbuilding and navigation made such sea passages for trade and war more viable. In 1498 Vasco da Gama reported incidences of scurvy on his voyage to India. The poet Luis Vaz de Camōes in the Portuguese national epic *The Lusiads*, immortalising the voyage of da Gama with whom he had sailed, wrote of how 'from a disease more cruel and loathsome than I ever before witnessed, many slipped from life . . . it attacked the mouth. The gums swelled horribly and the flesh alongside turned tumid and soon after putrefied. Putrefied with a foetid stench which poisoned the surrounding air'. In the absence of a physician or experienced surgeon, though not of a poet, 'some, with some little knowledge of this art, cut away the rotting meat as if they were corpses, for, as we said, if it remained they were as good as dead.'[4] Magellan also reported cases of scurvy during fifteen weeks at sea in 1519. As with that other disease new to the Renaissance, syphilis, classically-trained physicians searched in vain for references to the disease in the writings of Hippocrates and Galen, since the conventional wisdom was that if a disease were not known to the ancients, it could not exist. More practically-minded ship's doctors and their captains preferred to treat it as a new disease and find a new way of treating it.

William Clowes believed in 1593 that 'this infection, as I gathered by enquiry, was reputed principally unto their rotten and unwholesome victuals, for they said their bread was musty and mouldy biscuit, their beer sharp and sour like vinegar, their water corrupt and stinking ... By means hereof and likewise lack of convenient exercise, clean keeping and shift of apparel, and again, being in an ill-disposed climate, and want of good air, these causes and suchlike were the only means they fell into the scurvy'.[5] Richard Hawkins had noticed in 1593 that citrus fruits were an effective treatment for scurvy which he termed 'the plague of the sea'; and Sir James Lancaster's ship was the only one to escape the ravages of scurvy during an East India Company expedition to Sumatra in 1601 because 'he brought to sea with him certain bottles of the juice of lemons, which he gave to each one, as long as it would last, three spoonful every morning fasting: not suffering them to eat anything after it till noon. The juice worketh much the better if the party keep a short diet and wholly refrain salt meat, which salt meat and long being at sea is the only cause of this disease.'[6] Influenced by such observations, John Woodall wrote in his classic manual *The Surgions Mate* that 'the use of the juice of lemons is a precious medicine and well tried', but he also recommended a few drops of cinnamon in barley water and a concoction of wine, spices, sugar and egg yolk as being just as effective as lemon juice against scurvy. He was also aware that what lemons may have been aboard ship were more likely to be used as the basis of a 'good sauce at meat' on the officers' table, and of the possibility that 'the chef in the ships waste it in the great cabins to save vinegar.'[7] Woodall was open to most of the various theories put forward to explain scurvy; though he believed the 'chief cause is the continuance of salt diet, whether fish or flesh, as pork and the like, which is not to be avoided at sea, as I suppose by the wit of man', he conceded that this and 'long being at sea, without touch of land' might not be the sole causes of scurvy, but rehearsed the whole range of theories about the origin of the illness:

> Another cause of the disease to the ordinary sort of poor man is want of fresh apparel to shift them with ... partly also by the not keeping their apparel sweet and dry, and the not cleansing and keeping their cabins sweet, this also engendreth and increaseth the infection. Some charge biscuit as a cause of the scurvy, but I am not of their opinion. Some say inordinate watchings are cause thereof. Some say extreme labour wanting due nourishment. Some also affirm cares and grief to be some cause thereof, others affirm the very heat of the air, resolving the spirits and vapours, and engrossing the thick humours, causeth the scurvy; but what

shall I amplify further, for it is also true that they which have all
the helps that can be had for money, and take as much care as
men can devise are even by the evil disposition of the air, and the
cause of nature, struck with the scurvy, yea and die thereof at sea
and land both.[8]

These ideas on scurvy were to dominate thought about the disease well
into the eighteenth century. As for Woodall himself, he honestly
accepted that 'the causes of this disease are so infinite and unsearch-
able, as they far pass my capacity to search them all out'.[9] He was not
alone in this.

Anson was interviewed soon after his return to London in 1742 by
Richard Mead, physician to George II. Keen to learn from Anson's
experiences, Mead came to the conclusion that the scurvy which had
afflicted the men was caused by putrid air at sea. Anson had told him
that one of the sailors when rowing from ship to shore was 'so weak
that he fell down at the oar almost dead; when landed, the poor man
desired of his mates that they would cut a piece of turf out of the soft
ground and put his mouth to the hole: upon doing this, he came to
himself and grew afterwards quite well'.[10] This seemed to reinforce
Mead's view that land air was healthier than that at sea. Accordingly he
advocated the use of Sutton's air pump for extracting foul air from
ships, one of a number of mechanical devices being developed at that
time to improve ventilation below deck.

Even the ships' surgeons were not free from the dreaded scurvy. In
1746 the captain of the *Superb* requested a replacement for Thomas
Lloyd, the surgeon's second mate, who was unfit for duty because he
was suffering from a combination of scurvy and rheumatism.[11] Lloyd
himself also asked to be discharged temporarily as his poor health was
linked to him having been captured by Martinique pirates in the West
Indies where he lost all his possessions.[12]

There were various approaches to the treatment of scurvy tried out
on ships. Edmund Neeler invented a medicinal belt, which he claimed
could cure scurvy, itch, and infestation by vermin. His claims were
taken seriously and trials of the belt were undertaken on several ships
in 1746.[13] Unfortunately, these rolls of canvas filled with a dried herbal
mixture proved slow to cure the itch and were useless for scurvy or
anything else. Men wearing them got caught in the rigging and went
down with colds when they took the belts off, despite a request from
Captain Robert Harland for some, 'being glad to use every expedient to
preserve the health of my people.'[14] William Cockburn, physician to

the Royal Hospital at Greenwich, was a believer in the use of elixir of vitriol as a treatment for scurvy and had recommended its inclusion in surgeon's sea chests in 1732. However, he thought that it was more important to look for a method of preventing scurvy rather than one that would cure it.[15] Spinach was suggested as a preventative and Cockburn was involved in discussions as to whether 'spinach would be useful in scorbutic cases', and tastings of the vegetable, but the general opinion was against its adoption. In 1757 a portable soup was introduced, made of beef and mutton leftovers from the salted naval rations, formed into small cakes that could be mixed with boiling water. It was acclaimed as something that 'every British seafaring man in His Majesty's Navy ought to be thankful for this great refreshing benefit.'[16] In 1771 the Society of Arts sent the Admiralty a recipe for a carrot marmalade as a cure for scurvy sent to them by Baron Stosch, one of their corresponding members from Berlin, which was tried out on Cook's *Resolution* and *Adventure*.[17]

The problem of scurvy was picked up by the naval physician James Lind, who sought the patronage of George Anson to whom he dedicated his book on the subject. In his *Treatise of the Scurvy*, Lind considered the disease to be the result of faulty digestion and excretion, which require a reasonably varied diet to function efficiently. If this does not happen 'these excrementitious humours naturally destined for this evacuation, when retained long in the body, are capable of acquiring the most poisonous and noxious qualities, and a very high degree of putre-faction'.[18] On long sea voyages in wet, humid weather, the healthy seaman was unable to properly digest his diet of ship's biscuit and salted meat, with the result that he developed scurvy. The implication was that it was the conditions onboard ship that were responsible for this, rather than a monotonous, fruit- and vegetable-free diet on its own, since Lind acknowledged that 'it appears, I think, very plainly, that such hard dry food as a ship's provisions, or the sea-diet, is extremely wholesome; and that no better nourishment could be well contrived for labouring people, or any person in perfect health, using proper exercise in a dry pure air; and that, in such circumstances, seamen will live upon it for several years without inconvenience.'[19] For Lind, diet appears to take a secondary role in the prevention of scurvy compared to the improve-ment of the general conditions in which the seaman lived. Ideally, he should be cheerful and free from melancholy, which meant that he should be at sea by choice rather than through the actions of the press gang. He should be issued with warm clothing and clean bedding. The forecastle in which the men lived should be kept warm and dry and be regularly fumigated. His diet should include 'plenty of recent vegetables if they can be procured'. Following all of these recommendations, 'together with moderate exercise, cleanliness of body, ease and contentment of mind, procured by agreeable and entertaining amusements, will prove sufficient to prevent this disease from rising to any great height where it is not altogether constitutional.'[20]

Lind decided to investigate the efficacy of various remedies for scurvy, using diseased seamen on board the *Salisbury*, on which he was surgeon, in May 1747. For this celebrated medical trial Lind divided twelve seamen with scurvy into six pairs. Each pair was given a different possible cure: a quart of cider, a dose of elixir of vitriol, vinegar, sea water, oranges and lemons, and electuary of garlic. After two weeks, the pair fed on oranges and lemons had made a substantial recovery, but the other couples had either progressed very little or not at all.[21] This has been hailed as the first double-blind medical trial, but Lind failed to make clear any conclusions or recommendations from this experiment when he published his account of it. Although he cited numerous references from earlier writers of the curative qualities of oranges, lemons and limes, he made no explicit recommendation that the Admiralty should supply citrus fruit to the fleet to help maintain its health. It is little wonder that the significance of the trial should have been ignored by his contemporaries and only be recognised as of importance in the twentieth century, when vitamins and vitamin deficiency were beginning to be understood.[22] Neither Thomas Trotter nor Gilbert Blane, Lind's most prominent followers, considered that any definitive conclusions had been reached by Lind or themselves as to the cause of scurvy, and Blane, who persuaded the Admiralty to issue lemon juice to sailors in 1795, even confessed that he had never been able to satisfy himself 'with any theory concerning the nature and cure of this disease, nor hardly indeed of any other.'[23]

As a result of his work on scurvy, the Admiralty wished to appoint James Lind as surgeon to the third rate *Chichester* in 1755, 'a ship suitable to his standing to make observations on the disorders incident to seamen, particularly the scurvy, on which he has written a treatise.'[24] However, it was after his appointment as physician to the newly founded naval hospital at Haslar in 1758 that Lind continued his work on scurvy, though he wrongly believed that the 'rob', or preserved juice, of lemons was as good as fresh fruit. He also continued to argue somewhat paternalistically for improved hygiene onboard ships and for the more humane if efficient treatment of the seamen. He stressed the need for regular fumigation and improved ventilation, but also for improved personal hygiene. It was for this reason that he argued strongly for the introduction of a uniform, and facilities for the men to take regular, compulsory baths. He also recommended that ships on station should be provided with regular supplies of fresh vegetables, and that the surgeon's necessaries should include shallots and garlic. He was also opposed to the ships being crewed with 'such idle fellows as are picked up from the streets or prisons', because of the contagion they might bring on board with them and the low morale that would spread to their shipmates from such reluctant recruits.[25] The drinking of strong spirits was also to be discouraged, although spruce beer was an acceptable drink. He also devised a means of distilling wholesome drinking water from the sea. In all his writings Lind tried to find 'a plan of directions for preserving the British seaman from such distempers as prove more fatal to their corps than all other calamities incident to them at sea', and was concerned that 'the number of seamen in time of war who died by shipwreck, capture, famine, fire or sword are but inconsiderable in respect of such as are destroyed by the ship diseases and the usual maladies of intemperate climates.'[26]

Lind's influence in his own time was limited by the low status doctors enjoyed in the naval service and the obscurity of some of his writings, but he was to inspire two disciples. Thomas Trotter, physician to the Channel Fleet, referred to Lind as 'the father of nautical medicine'. He followed Lind's views on the importance of improving the living conditions of the sailors and urged that the merchant navy adopt many of Lind's suggestions. An opponent of slavery and a proponent of vaccination against smallpox, the welfare of the ship's crew was his prime concern. The other foremost disciple of Lind was Gilbert Blane, who was a powerful advocate of Lind's methods in high places. Blane had been appointed Physician of the Fleet through the patronage of Admiral Rodney, whose personal physician he had been. Blane's experiences of medicine at sea convinced him that prevention was always better than cure and that 'cleanliness and discipline are the indispensable and fundamental means of health.'[27] His scientific approach to achieving this aim was heavily based on observation and statistical reporting. Each naval surgeon was expected to report on the state of health of his ship using standardised forms and logbooks. These statistics were perhaps less useful when first compiled in finding a solution to the problems of naval healthcare, but did make the surgeon more accountable for his actions when the official record would be examined at a higher level, and he would be assessed both on what he had done in a particular situation and on the efficiency of his record keeping. Blane himself believed firmly that 'important practical truths can be ascertained only by averages expressive of the comparative results of individual facts.'[28] It was Blane who in 1795 urged the issue of lemon juice to seamen, using the example of the twenty-three-week voyage of the *Suffolk* to Madras in 1794, when there was only one death and no cases of scurvy as a result of the daily issue of two to three ounces of lemon juice to the crew.[29]

Yet the treatment of scurvy continued to be hit or miss, with no real understanding of how it could be prevented or treated. In some respects little had changed since 1769, when a request by the commander of the sloop *Ferret* for the repayment of money he had spent on the purchase of orange juice for members of the ship's company who had scurvy had been disallowed, because orange juice was 'not included in the establishment of surgeon's necessaries and a precedent should not be set.'[30] Lemon juice was found to be ineffective as a means of preventing scurvy on the *Ajax* in 1800.[31] Lind recorded that men on a supply ship bringing seasonable green vegetables to the fleet off Belleisle in 1761 had suffered from scurvy through not enjoying the benefit of their cargo. They were then 'carried on shore and after being stripped of their clothes were buried in a pit dug in the earth (the head being left above the ground), their bodies were covered over with the earth and permitted to remain thus interred for several hours, until a large and profuse sweat ensued. After undergoing this operation, many who had been carried on men's shoulders to those pits were of themselves able to walk to their boats; and what was very extraordinary, two of them who had been quite disabled by this disease recovered so perfect a state of health that they soon after embarked for the West Indies recovered, and in good spirits, without once tasting any green vegetables'.[32] Buccaneers in the Caribbean were said to have used this as a treatment for scurvy. The surgeon on the *Albion* in 1799 similarly tried to cure scurvy by burying a sufferer up the neck in earth brought on the ship especially for the purpose, but to no effect.[33] However, 'the use of the lime juice had a good effect and which I allowed in considerable quantities'.[34] Peter Henry, surgeon on *Daedalus* noticed that there had been no incidence of scurvy during a voyage to Bombay in 1802, despite the crew having had only six weeks' supply of fresh meat in sixteen months, but unlimited supplies of fruit and vegetables.[35]

Scurvy has become the focus of many studies of eighteenth-century naval medicine, yet it was only on long voyages that it was a major problem. It has, nevertheless, even been suggested that a million British seamen died from it in the eighteenth century, which is probably twice the number of sailors who served in the Royal Navy in that time.[36] On normal naval operations its only effect would have been to limit the period a squadron could remain at sea. Even then this problem could be surmounted. In 1759 Sir Edward Hawke blockading Brest ensured fresh supplies of cattle, vegetables, and beer for the Western Squadron by organising a provisions transport from Plymouth. James Lind considered it remarkable 'that fourteen thousand persons, pent up in ships, should continue for seven or eight months to enjoy a better state of health upon the watery element than it can well be imagined so great a number of people would enjoy on the most healthful spot of ground in the world.'[37]

Much more widespread than scurvy, which was sometimes used as a catch-all explanation for all maritime diseases, were deaths at sea from such fevers as typhus, influenza, dysentery, malaria, and yellow fever. Typhus, otherwise known as ship fever and gaol fever, wrecked mobilisation plans in the winters of 1739–41 and 1755–6 when men were falling sick faster than new ones could be recruited. It was not until 1909 that it was established that typhus was transmitted from person to person by body lice, but in earlier times it was blamed on bad smells in confined spaces and fumigation with sulphur was seen as a way of preventing it. The British navy became notorious for its obsession with cleanliness, but this was to help reduce the incidence of typhus. In 1781 'slop-ships' were introduced where new recruits would be washed and issued with clean clothes before being drafted to their ships. When Gilbert Blane accompanied Admiral Rodney to the West Indies in 1780, he introduced a strict hygiene regime which stressed the cleanliness of ships and men, good ventilation, and fresh fruit and vegetables. He commented that 'a true seaman is in general cleanly, but the greater part of the men in a ship of war require a degree of compulsion to make them so and such is the depravity of many that it is not uncommon for them to dispose of their clothes for money to purchase spirituous liquors.'[38] After this time typhus was mainly confined to new recruits who had not yet been washed and clothed.

It was the impact of fevers and infectious diseases that was to expose the deficiencies of sick quarters, most often in public houses, and of the hospitals overseas run by contractors. An outbreak of typhus in the London prisons in 1739 spread as men were scooped up by the press gangs and the Royal Navy mobilised for the War of Jenkins's Ear against Spain. Ships carrying this 'violent and malignant' fever brought it as far afield as Gibraltar and Plymouth by the end of the year. The scale of the epidemic brought to the fore the question as to 'whether it would be more for the public good to continue the present method of town quarters and subsisting seamen by contract, or to erect hospitals at the public expense with a proper establishment of officers and servants to take care of the sick and supply them with physic, diet and necessaries from His Majesty's stores as their several cases shall require.'[39] In 1741 the Admiralty approved the construction of a permanent hospital for 632 men at Port Royal in Jamaica, and another for a thousand patients at Gibraltar, to augment the hospitals already set up in Lisbon in 1706 and the purpose-built one at Port Mahon on Minorca, built in 1711. The establishment of new hospitals at Portsmouth, Queenborough (Kent), and Plymouth was also proposed but no action was taken for a further three years, even though it was estimated that the annual cost of caring for a thousand men at Gosport would be reduced from £21,526 12s 8d under the existing contract system, to £13,879 6s 8d in a purpose-built hospital run by the navy. It was not only the saving to the public purse that interested the Commissioners of the Sick and Hurt Board. They pointed out that 'although we are persuaded so great savings in point of expense would one time with another, peace and war, arise thereby to the Crown', there were 'much weightier' benefits arising from the proposal, especially 'the great number of lives which might in all probability be saved' in the navy, and 'that nothing can be a greater motive to peoples voluntarily entering into that service and continuing in it with cheerfulness, than a thorough persuasion that whenever it happens to be their misfortune to be sick or hurt, all proper tenderness and care will be used for their recovery' in the proposed naval hospitals.[40]

By 1744 there was concern about the great numbers of sick seamen at the Fortune Hospital in Gosport, housed in a collection of wooden huts near marshy ground and run by a local merchant, Nathaniel Jackson, contracted to look after up to seven hundred sick and wounded men. It was a hospital 'so ill-attended that though some of the sick men may be in the greatest danger and extremity, there is only a youth, the surgeon's apprentice who lives at the hospital on hand to administer assistance in the night.' Amidst the scenes of 'such drunkenness' as were to be found at such hospitals, the evils of the contract system were apparent, allowing 'such abuses as are often fatal to the health of seamen, notwithstanding all the care taken to prevent it.' On 15 September 1744 the Earl of Sandwich, First Lord of the Admiralty, submitted a petition to George II in Council proposing the establishment of permanent naval hospitals, because 'the want of such hospitals is so sensibly felt, and Your Majesty's service suffers so greatly from the loss of seamen either by death or desertion, who are sent on shore for the cure of their distempers'. A hospital controlled by the navy could contain the men so that they could not desert or get drunk, which would hold back their recovery. It was stressed that 'when the folly of the poor men is considered, intoxicating themselves with strong liquors in the height of their distempers, the great numbers that are swept away by such intemperance and the desertion of great numbers who recover, both compassion to them and the interests of Your Majesty's Service require putting a speedy stop to the evil of such pernicious consequences which can in no way be effectively done, but by building hospitals.'[41] If there were not enough money to build three hospitals at Portsmouth, Plymouth and Chatham, then priority should be given to spending £38,000 on a 1,500-bed hospital at Portsmouth in preference to smaller institutions. However, an Order in Council authorised the construction of all three hospitals to be run directly by the navy; contractors were only to be used as a supplement to the system in wartime or in areas remote from the naval hospitals. The Chatham hospital was not to be built for another century but new hospitals were established at Gosport and Plymouth.[42]

At Portsmouth the possibility of converting the ruinous Portchester Castle into a hospital, first proposed during the Commonwealth when Daniel Whistler had urged the need for a naval hospital, was again considered as early as 1740 because 'it is situated in a wholesome air and has good waters within its walls and can be come to at any time of tide and that being walled in, the seamen could not have it in their power to straggle about and commit such disorders as they often do.'[43] Portchester was being used to house prisoners of war and so was seen as suitable for a naval hospital. Problems with negotiating a lease on Portchester Castle meant that the idea of converting a medieval castle into a major naval hospital was finally abandoned, and in 1745 a new site entirely was found at Haslar, near Gosport. The site on the tip of the Gosport peninsular was isolated and most accessible from Portsmouth Sound, with the majority of the patients having to be ferried to the hospital from their ships anchored off Spithead. Access by land was not so easy, which was seen as a great deterrent to desertion. The plan was to build 'a strong, durable plain building consisting of three stories; the same to form a quadrangle with a spacious piazza within, the out fronts to be decent but not expensive', with attention given to 'the disposition, situation and dimensions of the wards for sick men, the convenience of light and air; to avoid narrowness as also crowding the beds too close together.'[44] Theodore Jacobsen, architect of the new Foundling Hospital in London, was appointed as architect, and construction work began in 1746 though it was not to be completed until 1761, by which time only three sides of the proposed quadrangle had been built as a result of pressure to economise. The only ornamentation was a pediment of Portland stone, displaying the arms of George II and personifications of Commerce and Navigation. Commerce, seated among bales and chests, distributes money, fruit and flowers. Navigation, with the North Star above her head and a compass at her feet, leans on a rudder and pours oil onto a sailor's wounds. Another sailor in distress is depicted being succoured by the serpent of Aesculapius carried in the beak of a bird. The iconography clearly points to the importance of the health of the seaman, under the auspices of the British Crown, for the prosperity of the country. The wards housed all types of patient, including surgical, medical, fever, flux, smallpox, consumptive, scorbutic, and convalescent cases, as well as there being a number of cells for lunatics. Within the high walls of the hospital were houses for the officers of the institution, storehouses, workshops, a chapel dedicated to St Luke, and a burial ground.[45] Haslar was built to house 1,500 patients in 114 wards, but by 1755 there were as many as 1,800 and in 1790 2,100 crowded together in cramped conditions.[46] It may have been one of the largest hospitals in Europe but Haslar, for all its solid and sober magnificence, was not always able to meet easily the demands placed upon it.

The Royal Naval Hospital at Plymouth was not begun until 1758 during the Seven Years War, but was relatively quickly completed in 1762, with accommodation for 1,200 patients in sixty wards in detached blocks arranged around a courtyard and connected by a single-storey Tuscan colonnade, on the roof of which convalescents could take exercise and enjoy the fresh air. John Howard, the prison and hospital reformer, praised the Plymouth hospital for having detached ward blocks 'for the purpose of admitting freer circulation of air, as also of classing the several disorders in such manner as may best prevent the spread of contagion.'[47] This had also been reported upon as an admirable feature by Jacques Tenon and Charles-Augustin Coulomb when they visited Plymouth in July 1787 on behalf of a French Royal Commission to investigate foreign hospitals, and declared that 'in not one of the hospitals of France and England, we would say in the whole of Europe, except the Plymouth Hospital are the individual buildings destined to receive patients as well ventilated and as completely isolated.'[48]

The naval hospitals were designed to a certain extent to be like prisons, to prevent the recovered seaman from deserting. Roderick Forbes, the Lisbon Agent of the Sick and Hurt Board, in 1745 wanted to rebuild the house he was using as a hospital with a fence to prevent his charges from getting 'up in the country' to drink bad wine and relapse.[49] The overseas hospitals were still run by agents under the contract system, but Haslar and Plymouth could be controlled much more easily because they were under the direct control of the navy. Haslar was isolated from Gosport by marshes and was only accessible by an often impassable cart-track or by ferry. In 1755 the Admiralty had to issue 'Protections' to the ferrymen to safeguard them against the press gangs active in the area, just as it had earlier had to protect from impressment the carpenters, bricklayers and labourers employed to build the hospital.[50] The patients themselves were brought over from their ships anchored off Spithead to a specially constructed jetty and then taken to the hospital in 'cradles on wheels'; in the nineteenth century rails were constructed to facilitate the pushing of these carts, and these rails could still be seen in the main arcade and entrance vestibule of the hospital after its closure in 2009. Tall walls surrounded the hospital to keep men in rather than intruders out, walls which were not entirely breached until after the closure of the site. Lamps were 'placed on the outside wall of the Hospital, and sentinels fixed around the same by which means if the latter do their duty, the patients may be as effectually secured as on board an hospital ship and their cure sooner completed.'[51] The patients were also made more conspicuous if they did manage to escape from the hospital by the issue of a 'Hospital Dress which would greatly tend to the people's recovery.' A hospital uniform would have been cleaner than the men's own clothing in the days before uniforms were issued to sailors, but would also enable the staff to control their movements. On arrival patients were bathed in hot soapy water, issued with clean hospital clothing, and had their own clothes fumigated before they were admitted. Since these hospital uniforms were 'to be taken into the nurses' cabins when the men are in bed and delivered to them in the morning, they could not then escape but in their shirts.'[52] That did not stop men trying to escape down the latrines and through the sewers, which were also used for smuggling in liquor, by the nurses as well as the patients.[53]

The naval hospitals, unlike contemporary civil ones which often refused to admit chronic illnesses or fever cases, had to admit all types of medical case, both sailors and marines, who were 'to be received and taken care of upon the same footing with seamen', just as at sea 'marines, sick or wounded are to be taken the same care of, by the surgeon of the ship, that the seamen are.'[54] In accordance with James Lind's belief that 'certain types of contagion automatically dissipate when patients are well separated', and that when this was done 'their range of infection is limited', patients at Haslar were separated according to their diagnosis. Patients recovering from measles, scabies, syphilis, gonorrhoea and smallpox had their own galleries for walking in. Sufferers from smallpox and measles had the name of the disease written on the back of their hospital dress in case they thought about trying to escape. Scurvy cases were also set apart, not because they were considered contagious, but because they were under a special therapeutic regime of vegetables, citrus fruit, wine, malt, and 'land air', since sea rations and sea air were considered responsible for their illness. Men suffering particularly malignant fevers and fluxes were isolated in fever wards at the far ends of the wings, so as 'to cut off communications with other patients'.[55] The most contagious patients were assigned to wards on the top floors of the buildings, the less infectious to the middle wards, and the convalescents to the ground floor convenient for their promenades.[56] At Plymouth, too, particular cases were assigned to particular ward blocks with the most infectious again on the upper floors. The insane were also segregated at both hospitals before being despatched to Bethlem Hospital in London.[57]

In a hospital of the size of Haslar or Plymouth it was not always easy to maintain the expected standards. Members of the medical staff were allowed to conduct their own private practices and were often absent from their duties. At Plymouth, there was such neglect of the hospital by medical officers that a wounded man could not be admitted to the hospital because there was no one there to open the gate, admit him, or treat him, since the surgeon was away attending a 'gentleman of great fortune' in Cornwall, causing Thomas Trotter, Physician to the Fleet, to ponder that 'by an irresistible impulse of imagination, the ghosts of so many thousands of brave men rise to my view, who have fallen into premature death by unprincipled neglect.'[58] Even when they were present, the surgeons were not always competent. Stephen Love Hammick was accused of 'unskilfully performing several operations' at the Royal Hospital in Plymouth. He dismissed charges of having misdiagnosed 'a black man named Cook' with the comment that 'whether the tumour was or was not subelavian aneurysm is merely a matter of conjecture', with little concern for the unfortunate patient's suffering. In another case, that of Charles Marriner, whose leg he had amputated, he attributed Marriner's subsequent medical problems not to the operation but that 'in getting about he fell down, injured it and broke it up again.' He resented the slur on his competence brought against him by Mr Veitch, second surgeon to the hospital, and wondered 'what opinion must be formed of a man capable of entertaining the idea that any professional man could be so base and lost to feeling as to suppose I gave an opinion to mislead, is nothing more or less than the charge of wishing to commit murder on a fellow creature, the very insinuation makes me shudder.'[59]

Arguments amongst the medical officers or with the nurses were common. Mr Parker, the assistant dispenser at Haslar, accused the steward, Mr Trotman, of having purloined the butter intended for the patients in 1760, and it was alleged that the resultant quarrel caused Mrs Trotman to have a miscarriage. Mr Parker had also had an argument with one of the nurses, Mrs Cooper, who had called him 'a saucy impertinent fellow' after he insulted her by calling her 'a saucy slut' and accusing her of being the mother of a child that had been found murdered in Gosport. The Physician and Council in charge of Haslar investigated the dispute and resolved that 'it would be right to leave the parties to make it up between themselves.'[60] In 1780, Admiral Barrington was appointed to inspect the abuses at Haslar and recommended that control of the hospital be vested in a senior naval officer, 'used to command and well versed in the management of seamen', rather than in a physician because 'the patients at Haslar are too numerous and ungovernable, the character and authority of the present officers are without dignity or respect.'[61] After Lind's retirement in 1783, the administrative control of the hospital was transferred to a naval officer and the medical governance to Lind's son John, but it was not until 1795 that the real control of the hospitals at both Haslar and Plymouth passed out of medical control to a governor with the rank of post captain, and it was not until 1870 that medical officers again took charge of the naval hospitals. From 1795 naval discipline became paramount. The previous year an inspection of Haslar had found that 'the patients were in general well satisfied with the attendance given them, and also with respect to change of clean shirts, which they have twice a week'. However, they were less happy that their own clothes removed from them for fumigation were frequently lost and 'in many instances men, the whole of whose clothes have been lost, have been detained for weeks in the Hospital under the idea of looking for them'. Moreover, although the wards and bedding were clean, they were fumigated with inefficient fumigating lamps, and the water closets 'smell offensively, and the floors, seats and walls are constantly wet'. The dispensing of medicine was left to the nurses, many of whom were illiterate, with the result that 'the medicines prescribed for one man may be given to another or indeed not given at all.'[62]

The nursing staff was at first recruited from the wives and widows of sailors and marines. Despite it being stipulated that they should be 'the most sober, careful and diligent that can be had', at Haslar they had a reputation for stealing from their patients, forging wills, and smuggling gin 'tied around their waists and under their stays in bladders'. One nurse, Jane Brown, was dismissed in 1756 'for going to bed with four or five patients and infecting one of them with the foul disease.'[63] They were forbidden to undertake any duties which were considered the preserve of the surgeon. In 1805, nurse Mary Bill was threatened with dismissal by one of the surgeons, Mr Delhuntry, who 'flew into a great passion at me', when he found her about to dress the ulcer of one of her patients, who 'complained to me of being in great pain', at a time when neither of the surgeons were in the hospital.[64] Both she and Sarah Perrott, who had also fallen foul of Mr Delhuntry's temper when he forbade her to dress wounds, preferred the other surgeon, Mr Tompson, 'who treats the patients with great tenderness and attention.'[65] The patients themselves were not always so certain that the nurses would show kindness to them, and in 1761 some of the patients at Haslar complained of Nancy Armitage who 'has treated us in such a manner that we were afraid of our lives. We have neglected taking our medicine from her less she should poison us, we never thought it was in the power of any woman to so behave and shew herself in the manner as she has done to us, and we were not able to help ourselves. She strove all she could to hurt us, she broke the poker striving to kill some of us and threatened us with drawing her knife.'[66]

Officers were spared the indignities of treatment in the large naval hospitals until the beginning of the nineteenth century, but tended to be quartered in private houses and visited there by medical doctors. Conditions for those placed in private asylums were not so good. At 'the house of Messrs Miles and Co. at Hoxton for the cure of mental derangement' in 1812, naval officers shared a small sitting room 'indiscriminately with other maniacs, some of whom have been common maniacs and were now only rendered qualified for admission by payment having been insured to the proprietors of the concern for their accommodation.' Some patients were quiet and placid but were mixed with others 'raging with inconceivable fury.' Some of the inmates were chained to their seats and others were handcuffed, such men 'frequently answering the calls of nature in the very room they are sitting in.' There was only one servant to keep twenty men clean, comb their hair, and dress them. Some of the officers had been in the establishment for two years without receiving any medication, and their diet of tea, beef, mutton, veal, cheese, and small beer was considered too stimulating for their mental condition. Perhaps one of the greatest faults of the establishment was the 'impropriety of mixing officers indiscriminately with others', such as civilians, ordinary seamen, and marines, since 'in all our naval hospitals, officers are not put in the same ward or cabin together unless they have been accustomed to mess or associate with each other on board ship, or unless they enjoy similar rank'.[67]

Status was important in naval hospitals as much as onboard ship. The appointment of a serving naval officer as governor of a naval hospital after 1795 resulted in friction between the executive and medical officers. Captain Richard Creyke was appointed governor at Plymouth in 1795 to prevent 'in the most effective manner the inconveniences which have frequently been felt by the want of proper discipline and subordination.'[68] Restrictions were placed on private practice by the medical staff, attendance at chapel was more strictly enforced, and a partition erected in the chapel to separate the nurses from the men. When the medical assistants protested about Creyke's handling of the resignation of an assistant dispenser, he read to them a letter from the Sick and Hurt Board threatening them with dismissal if they ever again questioned the authority of the governor or showed him any signs of insolence or disrespect. Creyke was unhappy when 'they showed no signs of sorrow for their improper conduct, made no apology for their contumacious behaviour', and continued to act like 'inconsiderate young men.'[69] Discipline in the hospital was to be as tight as on a ship, with the captain's actions going unchallenged. This was to continue long after the system had become well established. At Haslar, Captain Charles Craven felt that his authority was being challenged by the irregular arrivals and departures of a Lieutenant Gullifer, serving in the Channel Fleet, to visit his wife who kept house for her father Jacob Silver, who supervised the wing for lunatics. Gullifer disregarded Craven's rule that no one should enter or leave the hospital gates after ten in the evening, and was forbidden to live with his wife, or even enter the hospital site. On two separate occasions in July 1817 and September 1818 Craven had to give way and allow Gullifer entry to see his wife after she gave birth, the couple having seen each other away from Haslar between times, though 'the conduct of Lieutenant Gullifer by no means merits the least indulgence from me and it is his own fault that his wife lives separately from him.'[70]

The hospitals were used to try out new ideas in medicine, though some of the innovations were not always considered wise. In 1743 the Sick and Hurt Board rejected a request from the Admiralty to try out the use of burnt wine to cure fluxes, because this was in their view 'an old woman's remedy.' Moreover, if it were introduced at the hospital at Plymouth, it was feared that the nurses would drink more than the patients. Instead, the cures used by surgeons at sea, burnt hartshorn and cinnamon water or rice gruel mixed with cinnamon, was considered preferable.[71] The interest in research into sea diseases and the devastating mortality during Anson's voyage had also prompted the foundation of the Association of Surgeons of the Royal Navy in 1746 to advance knowledge of sea diseases. This group met in rooms in Covent Garden with the eminent surgeon William Hunter as one of their lecturers. It followed in the tradition established in the Dutch Wars of some surgeons holding shipboard clinical meetings after each engagement. William Cockburn had proposed in 1702 that such informal meetings should be put onto an official basis and that postgraduate teaching should be conducted in the hospital ships, but the Admiralty rejected his proposals for reform. Informally organised meetings of naval surgeons continued to take place in the ports, and in 1732 John Atkins devised a scheme for a postgraduate medical centre in the Portsmouth Naval Academy.[72] In this the Royal Navy was behind the French navy, where since 1689 port physicians and surgeons had been given the task of holding annual lecture courses for ship's surgeons, and an official training school for naval surgeons had been established at Rochefort in 1722, followed by others in 1725 in Toulon and in 1740 in Brest. The availability of corpses for dissection from the galleys was a bonus for such training schools. The brothers Pierre-Isaac and Antoine Poissonier-Desperrières, inspectors of navy hospitals, believed in combating scurvy with fresh citrus fruits *à la Lind.*[73]

However, the training of the surgeon in Britain very much remained as it had been in the previous century, and was to be satirised by Tobias Smollett in his novel *The Adventures of Roderick Random.* Smollett had himself been a naval surgeon and wrote from bitter experience. He had studied medicine at Glasgow University before seeking his fortune in London, where he had sought employment as second surgeon's mate on the *Chichester*, sailing with Admiral Vernon to the West Indies in 1740.[74] His experiences were to be the inspiration for his first novel published in 1748. The eponymous hero of the novel, like his creator, faced an examination at Surgeon's Hall where the grim-faced examiners told him that 'it was a shame and a scandal to send such raw boys into the world as surgeons', before asking him the almost farcical question 'If during an engagement at sea, a man should be brought to you with his head shot off, how would you behave?'[75] Before he can go to purchase his chest of drugs at Apothecaries' Hall, having already had to pay bribes to the doorkeeper, cleaner, examiners and secretary at the Surgeon's Hall, Random is unlucky enough to fall into the hands of a press gang on Tower Hill, and is appointed second surgeon's mate on the ship the *Thunder* to which he is taken by force. There, he is shocked by the sick berth where 'I was much less surprised that people should die on board than that any sick person should recover.' In a confined space are fifty 'miserable distempered wretches', who are 'breathing nothing but a noisome atmosphere of the morbid steams exhaling from their own excrements and diseased bodies, devoured with vermin hatched in the filth that surrounded them, and destitute of every convenience necessary for people in that helpless condition.'[76] The sick are summoned to have their sores dressed by a loblolly boy banging a pestle and mortar, and found fit by the doctor because he wishes to please the captain's desire to have no sick people on board.[77] When Random falls sick with yellow fever, he refuses to swallow one of his colleague's 'diaphoretic boluses', and instead has a blister applied to his neck.[78] He is also witness to naval surgery in battle. The surgeon, 'supported with several glasses of rum', sets to work and 'arms and legs were hewn down without mercy'. Meanwhile, the ship's chaplain assisting in the cockpit 'had the fumes of the liquor mounting in his brain and became quite delirious; he stripped himself to his skin and besmirching his body with blood could scarce be withheld from running on the deck in that condition.' [79]

Smollett's caricature of the naval surgeon may have been overdrawn, but it was based on some reality. Nevertheless in the year of the publication of Smollett's novel, the Sick and Hurt Board could state that 'those who enter the Naval service at an early age have excellent opportunities to gain more experience which means they have no difficulty in finding employment outside the Service once they leave the Navy.'[80] The surgeon James Ker was not overworked on a healthy passage on the *Elizabeth* to the West Indies in 1778. He rose at seven, saw his patients at nine for an hour at most, then had time to read in his cabin, before taking a walk on deck and reporting to the captain on the health of the ship. Between dinner and supper he amused himself 'variously in reading, writing, card-playing, backgammon, walking or conversation as humour leads', and after supper his time was 'spent in chitchat over our grog drinking.'[81] Many of the surgeons objected to the oversight of their instruments by the Surgeons' Hall and the monopoly on their medicine chest by Apothecaries' Hall: William Dymer, surgeon on the *Centurion*, pointed out in 1746 that his 'instruments are all clean and in good order and made peculiarly to my own practice ready for anyone's inspection here.'[82] He refused not only 'to send up his instruments to be viewed but also his medicine chest to be surveyed.'[83] Yet a well and properly stocked medicine chest was essential on a ship. The *Centurion*'s epic voyage a few years earlier had shown the importance of that.

A great contrast in shipboard health with Anson's circumnavigation of 1740–44 was made by the three voyages of James Cook to the Pacific and around the world between 1768 and 1780. He returned from his first voyage on the *Endeavour* after a voyage of three years and eighteen days with the loss of not one man to scurvy, though three others died of tuberculosis which they had contracted before the start of the voyage, thirty-one of dysentery, one from alcoholism, two froze to death, one died after an epileptic fit, and three drowned. He congratulated himself on having few men on the sick list by the time he reached Tahiti in April 1769, and that 'the ship's company had in general been very healthy owing in great measure to the sour krout, portable soup and malt', and to the 'care and vigilance of Mr Monkhouse the surgeon'. The sauerkraut and portable soup were served to the men on alternate beef and banyan days, and the malt was given to any men showing the first signs of scurvy. At first the crew had been reluctant to eat the sauerkraut until Cook had made it a luxury on the captain's table, 'for such are the tempers and dispositions of seamen in general that whatever you give them out of the common way, although it be ever so much for their good, yet it will not go down well with them and you will hear nothing but murmurings against the men who first invented it; but the moment they see their superiors set a value upon it, it becomes the finest stuff in the world and the inventor a damn'd honest fellow.'[84] The botanist Joseph Banks, sailing on the *Endeavour,* was less enamoured of sauerkraut or malt wort, which had no effect on him when he began to show the symptoms of scurvy, but when he made 'every kind of liquor which I used ... sour with the lemon juice', he was surprised to find that 'in less than a week my gums became as firm as ever, and at this time I am troubled with nothing but a few pimples on my face.'[85] It was dysentery, not scurvy, that spoiled the health record of the voyage when the only man not to fall ill with it at Batavia was a seventy- or eighty-year-old sailmaker who was 'generally more or less drunk every day.' The ship had arrived at Batavia 'as healthy a ship's company as need go to sea and after a stay of not quite three months left it in the condition of a hospital ship.'[86] Among the dead was the surgeon William Monkhouse, whose mate William Perry now took on his duties.

Cook's second voyage was an even better demonstration of the role that a high standard of hygiene could make on the health of a ship. During a voyage of seventy thousand miles lasting over three years, there were only three deaths from accidents and one from consumption on the *Adventure* and *Resolution.* He felt great satisfaction that 'our having discovered the possibility of preserving health amongst a ship's company, for such a long time in such varieties of climate and amid such hardship and fatigue will make this voyage remarkable in the opinion of every benevolent person, when the dispute about a southern continent shall have ceased to engage the attention and to divide the judgement of the philosophers.'[87] Cook was amazingly successful in preventing scurvy because he only had small crews and could put into land whenever he needed. He realised the curative potential of green vegetables and regularly foraged ashore when his ships were at anchor. Although aware of the importance of oranges and lemons, he was not overly concerned with providing his ships with them, but instead laid more emphasis on malt, from which was made sweet wort, which Cook considered 'without doubt, one of the best anti-scorbutic sea medicines then discovered, when used in time.'[88] Cook's views were to be used as an argument against the issue of lemon or lime juice to the navy.

Perhaps it was in the example he set from his close attention to naval hygiene that Cook made a real impact on medicine at sea. On his third and final voyage, the *Resolution* only lost five men from sickness and the *Discovery* none. The expedition had lost its leader when Cook was killed in a dispute with natives in Hawaii in 1779. His successor in command of the *Discovery*, James King, congratulated himself that at the end of the voyage he had left the whole crew in perfect health thanks to 'an unremitting attention to the regulations established by Captain Cook ... under the blessing of Divine Providence.'[89] William Bligh, who had sailed with Cook as master of the *Resolution* on Cook's third voyage, was a firm believer in maintaining a strict discipline in hygiene, as in everything else on his ships. He had accepted not only Cook's views of the efficacy of dried malt, sauerkraut, and portable soup, but also on the importance of 'cheerfulness with exercise and a sufficiency of rest' as preventing scurvy.[90] Following Cook, he also believed in working co-operatively with the ship's surgeon; though his surgeon on the *Bounty* in 1787, Thomas Huggan, died of alcoholism in Tahiti, despite the confiscation of his liquor supplies and the compulsory cleaning of the filthy sick berth, Bligh had taken the precaution of signing on a young surgeon, Thomas Ledward, as an able-bodied seaman, and he was among the crew set adrift with Bligh when Fletcher Christian led the famed mutiny against Bligh, although his medicine chest was left on the ship. Bligh, however, took a lead in maintaining the spirits and health of the men in the longboat, not allowing them to 'expose themselves to the heat of the sun', and noting that 'the general complaints among us were dizziness in the head, great weakness of the joints . . . most of us having had no evacuation by stool since we left the ship.'[91]

The real beneficiary of all this greater attention to hygiene at sea, and research into the causes and treatment of sea diseases, was the British sailor, whose health, general well-being, diet and conditions of service were all influenced by medically-inspired initiatives and forward-looking captains. The effects of the advances were to assume ever greater importance during the Revolutionary and Napoleonic Wars.

## CHAPTER FIVE

# *England's Expectations*

ONE OF THE most iconic moments in British history is the death of Nelson at Trafalgar. For the majority of us, the mental picture conjured up is one based on the most famous representation of all, that painted by Arthur Devis and first exhibited in 1807.[1] Wrapped in a shroud-like sheet and the focus of the light in the painting, Nelson is at the centre of the canvas, surrounded by a sorrowing group of his associates and surgeons. His wounded left shoulder is covered, and his bloody white shirt and uniform coat with its braid and decorations lie abandoned in front of him, a symbol of the redundancy of his worldly glory. His chaplain Alexander Scott rubs Nelson's chest trying to relieve the pain, his purser Walter Burke supports his pillow, and his Neapolitan valet Gaetano Spedillo holds the glass from which Nelson took his last sips of water. Liberties have been taken with what actually happened and Captain Hardy, who was not present when Nelson died, is shown standing behind him, which would have been impossible for a man six feet tall even had he actually been there. Prominent in the painting, however, is the kneeling figure of the surgeon William Beatty in the full dress uniform of a naval surgeon, feeling Nelson's pulse and about to pronounce him dead, with Nelson's steward William Chevailler looking intently at Beatty. Among the other figures can be seen the dazed and wounded Lieutenant George Miller Bligh and the assistant surgeon Neil Smith. In its resemblance to Old Master paintings of the deposition of Christ from the Cross, it is worthy of the death of a national hero, although Benjamin West, who painted a rival version of the death of Nelson, considered that Devis with his factual approach did not 'excite awe and admiration', and that it was unsuitable for the heroic Nelson to 'be represented dying in the gloomy hold of a ship, like a sick man in a prison hole.'[2]

Yet it was indeed in the cockpit of the *Victory,* used for the treatment of casualties in battle, that Nelson, a man who took a great interest in the health of his fleet, died like many another wounded mariner, after being struck down on his quarterdeck by a French musket ball at a quarter past one in the afternoon of 21 October 1805. Despite the myth that he was wearing his gold-encrusted full dress uniform and his many decorations, his vanity making him a ready target, he was actually wearing a rather threadbare undress uniform with very little gold braid and only small wire-and-sequin facsimiles of his stars.[3] He collapsed on the same spot at which his secretary John Scott had been cut in two by enemy shot an hour earlier, Scott's blood still staining the sleeve and tails of Nelson's coat. He was carried down to the cockpit, a very confined, poorly ventilated, damp, and dimly-lit space, described by Alexander Scott as resembling 'a butcher's shambles.'[4] Usually the living space of the midshipmen, master's mates and assistant surgeons, it was close to the dispensary and the hatchway down which the casualties were brought to be treated on mess tables or chests lashed together. On those makeshift operating tables, Beatty and his two assistant surgeons performed eleven amputations during the battle, all without benefit of anaesthetics other than brandy, and while the hull was shaken by the impact of enemy shot and the concussion of the ship's own gunfire. At hand were his surgical instruments in a portable wooden case, including long and short blade knives, a fine-toothed bone saw, a screw tourniquet, two trephines, forceps, probes and scissors.[5] His medical stores also included fifteen tourniquets, splints of various lengths, 120 yards of linen, and eight pounds of lint for dressing wounds and injuries. Laudanum was available to relieve pain, while olive or linseed oil mixed with ceruse was used to treat burns. Vinegar was used for disinfection and barrels stood around filled with water for rinsing the instruments, sponges and swabs. It was here that Nelson was examined by Beatty, who could do little for him, as Nelson himself realised. His first words to the surgeon were 'Ah, Mr Beatty, you can do nothing for me. I have but a short time to live . . . my back is shot through.'[6]

Beatty gently probed the wound with his right finger and Nelson told him that 'he felt a gush of blood every minute within his breast: that he had no feeling in the lower part of his body: and that his breathing was difficult and attended with very severe pain about that part of the spine where he was confident that the ball had struck', and that 'I felt it break my back.'[7] Beatty soon gave up on trying to probe for the musket ball and, when Hardy came down with news of the battle, was ordered by Nelson to attend to the other wounded. Leaving the Admiral to the ministrations of the purser Burke and the chaplain Scott, Beatty went off to amputate the leg of a midshipman. He returned in time to witness Nelson giving Hardy his last message for his mistress, Lady Hamilton, and to hear his satisfaction at the outcome of the battle, 'Now I am satisfied. Thank God I have done my duty.' In his last moments he asked the chaplain for water and air: 'Drink, drink, fan, fan, rub, rub.' He died at half past four, two hours and forty-five minutes since he had been shot, and at the moment of victory.[8]

The following day Beatty placed the dead hero's body into a large water cask filled with brandy to preserve it for the voyage home, so that he could be buried in England. Soon after arriving back in Portsmouth, Beatty performed a post-mortem examination and removed the fatal musket ball. His cold, clinical report emphasises the horrific nature of the wound and hints at the agony Nelson must have suffered in his last hours:

> The ball struck the forepart of his Lordship's epaulette and entered the left shoulder . . . it then descended obliquely into the thorax, fracturing the second and third ribs, and after penetrating the left lobe of the lungs and dividing in its passage a large branch of the pulmonary artery, it entered the spine and lodged therein.[9]

Strangely enough there is no record of Nelson's death in the surgeon's journal for the *Victory*, where it might have been expected to form a major part of the surgeon's report on Trafalgar. It could be that Beatty wanted to save the details so that he could publish them for his own benefit. His account of Nelson's death was published in 1807, and was instrumental in forging the cult of Nelson as well as bringing reflected glory on Beatty himself. Born in Londonderry in 1773, Beatty had joined the Navy in 1791 and had served on ten warships before being warranted to Nelson's flagship in December 1804. He had been court-martialled for disrespectful conduct towards the captain of the *Pomona* but exonerated in 1795. His central role during Nelson's last hours was to bring him the fame and boost to his career that his own merits alone may not have achieved, including appointment as Physician of the Fleet in 1806 and Physician to Greenwich Hospital in 1822. His best quality as a naval surgeon was his ability to keep calm and cool under fire. In many ways a typical competent naval surgeon of his time, he owed his success to his association with Nelson.[10]

Horatio Nelson was outstanding in his concern for safeguarding the health of the seamen under his command. He may famously have declared before the battle of Trafalgar that 'England expects every man to do his duty', but on him rested the national expectation that he would do his utmost to maintain the fleet as a healthy, effective fighting force. Nelson's own experiences may have been responsible for his interest in, and appreciation of, the role medicine played in warfare. He had been a sickly child but had overcome all his illnesses with fortitude, later commenting after being wounded in the eye at Corsica in July 1794 that, 'We have a thousand sick and the rest are no better than phantoms: myself, I am here a reed among oaks: I have all the diseases that are, but there is not enough in my frame for them to fasten on.'[11] Sent to sea at the age of twelve in 1771, Nelson was only sixteen when, as a midshipman, he was invalided from his ship in 1775 suffering from malaria, an illness which was to recur throughout his life. Soon back at sea, he fell seriously ill with yellow fever during the Nicaraguan campaign to capture Fort St Juan in 1780 and, declaring that 'it is the climate that has destroyed my health and crushed my spirit', requested a passage home where he spent his convalescence at the fashionable spa town of Bath.[12] Further service in the West Indies laid him low with another tropical fever in 1787.[13]

Wounds were to prove even more serious than fevers for Nelson, whereas at that time generally it was disease which killed more men at sea than injuries from battle.[14] 'A very slight scratch towards my right eye which has not been the slightest inconvenience', suffered during the siege of Calvi in Corsica on 12 July 1794, soon proved more serious and within four days of the injury he had lost the sight in his eye, though he characteristically dismissed it with the comment that 'the blemish is not to be perceived unless told.'[15] In later years he wore a green eye-shade, but the strain on his left eye convinced Beatty that he would have gone blind had he not been killed.[16] He received an internal injury in 1797 which left him with future digestion problems. Grape-shot shattered his right elbow during an unsuccessful landing at Santa Cruz, Tenerife, on 24 July 1797, and he would have lost his life had his stepson Josiah Nisbet not applied an improvised tourniquet to the wound.[17] His right arm was amputated[18] and, when asked if he wanted the amputated limb to be embalmed, he told the surgeon to 'throw it in the hammock with the brave fellow that was killed beside me.'[19] He was again badly wounded in the head at the battle of the Nile on 1 August 1798 when a piece of langridge (rough metal fired as anti-personnel shot) tore open his forehead, leaving a flap of skin hanging down over his good eye.[20] A painting was made of him going back on deck to see the French flagship explode, with his head bandaged and his hand on his heart, probably as a gift for Emma Hamilton during his convalescence in Naples.[21] There is also an aquatint of Nelson having his head wound dressed by a surgeon's mate in the cockpit of the Vanguard, while the surgeon Michael Jefferson attends a leg wound with his chest of surgical instruments beside him, a rare contemporary representation of a cockpit in action.[22]

The cockpit was the scene of intense activity during a battle. The surgeon Robert Young had no mates to assist him during the battle of Camperdown on 11 October 1797 because the recent naval mutinies had driven many out of the service. He was 'employed in operating and dressing till near four in the morning, the action beginning about one in the afternoon.' During the battle over ninety wounded were brought down to the cockpit, and 'the whole cockpit deck, cabins wing berths and part of the cable tier, together with my platform, and my preparation for the dressings, were covered with them. So that for a time, they were laid on each other at the foot of the ladder, where they were brought down.' He was assailed with 'melancholy cries for assistance . . . from every side by wounded and dying, and piteous moans and bewailing from pain and despair.' Young felt overwhelmed, and 'so great was my fatigue that I began several amputations under a dread of sinking before I should have secured the blood vessels.' However, he had to 'preserve myself firm and collected, and embracing in my mind the whole of the situation, to direct my attention to where the greatest and most essential services could be performed.' He had to distinguish between men who needed more urgent attention, but who were not as clamorous as 'some with wounds, bad indeed and painful, but slight in comparison to the dreadful condition of others', who were 'most vociferous for my assistance.' As well as using his surgical skills, he also needed to maintain morale, and 'I cheered and commended the patient fortitude of others, and sometimes extorted a smile of satisfaction from the mangled sufferers, and succeeded to throw momentary gleams of cheerfulness amidst so many horrors.' Among his patients were men whose thighs had been taken off by cannon shot and others blackened by the explosion of a salt box. When the battle was over, fifteen or sixteen dead bodies had to be removed before Young could get to the operating and dressing materials he had prepared before the action. Yet he could congratulate himself when his surviving patients were 'conveyed on shore in good spirits, cheering the ship at going away, smoking their pipes and jesting as they sailed along, and answering the cheers of the thousands of the populace who received them on Yarmouth key.'[23]

Morale was not always so good and in some cases it was shock rather than wounds that the surgeon might be faced with. On the *Revenge* in action against the French in 1809, a lieutenant was taken down to the cockpit covered with blood. He had been struck on the breast by shot which had 'knocked a man's head completely from his shoulders', and he had then been 'knocked down by the force of the head striking him.' It was assumed that he had also been wounded as he was 'very much besmeared with the blood from the man's head', but when the surgeon unbuttoned his waistcoat and examined him he could find no injury. The only treatment possible was to leave the lieutenant to compose himself before returning to his duties, but 'it was some time before that fit of composure went off, for he very prudently had no notion of going on deck again, while men's heads were flying about, and doing so much mischief.'[24]

Some surgeons attempted to assess the severity of the wounds that were coming down to the cockpit and deal with the most serious cases first, but usually there was little time to do this and, in the chaos of battle, it was a case of men being treated in order of arrival. William Robinson, also known as 'Jack Nastyface', serving on the *Revenge* at Trafalgar, wrote that 'the rule is, as order is requisite, that every person shall be dressed in rotation as they are brought down wounded, and in many instances some have bled to death.'[25] At the battle of Camperdown, George Magrath, surgeon on the *Russell*, had to juggle priorities. Henry Spence, a 25-year-old seaman, was injured when 'a large cannonball from the opponent's ship struck him a little above the ankle joints and carried away both legs.' Magrath was interrupted by another urgent case while he examined Spence's legs when 'another man came to the cockpit with profuse haemorrhages from a large artery that was divided by a splinter. I was therefore necessitated to leave Spence (previously applying the tourniquet) to staunch the man's bleeding.' Spence was then laid on the operating table to have his legs amputated, and 'lucky it was that he bore it so well, as a shot at this time came into the cockpit and passed the operating table, close, this startled all the women who formed the chief of my assistance.' The operation over, Spence was bandaged up, given a cordial and laid on a platform erected for the accommodation of wounded men in the cable tier, and then when the action was over put into a cot. He had seemed a hopeless case when first brought into the cockpit, Magrath commenting that 'the man's legs were amputated in the heat of action, which I am happy to say did not retard the case, indeed when he was first carried to the cockpit there were little hopes of success.'[26]

Not all amputations were as successful. A shipmate of William Robinson had the calves of both his legs shot away in an unsuccessful attack on the French fleet in the Basque Roads in 1809. One of his legs was amputated and he begged the surgeon to leave him the other and 'very coolly observed that he should like one leg left to wear his shoes out.' When the second leg was amputated he exclaimed, 'now to the devil with all the shoe-makers, I have done with them.' Despite his humour, fortitude and his apparent good progress, 'from lying in one position for such a length of time, his back mortified, and he breathed his last, much regretted by all his shipmates'.[27] In a battle between the frigates HMS *Macedonian* and USS *United States* in 1812, Samuel Leech, a boy seaman, described the surgeon and his mate as 'smeared with blood from head to foot: they looked more like butchers than doctors.'[28] One of their patients, John Wells, had his arm amputated and observed that 'I have lost my arm in the service of my country; but I don't mind it, doctor, it's the fortune of war.' He remained 'cheerful and gay', acting as if he had received only a slight injury, but was given too much rum by his messmates, developed a fever and died; in Leech's opinion 'his messmates actually killed him with kindness.'[29]

The success of a surgeon was not only seen during battle but in the survival of his patients after the conflict was over. On the *Victory* at Trafalgar, Beatty and his assistant surgeons, Neil Smith and William Westenburg, dealt with about a hundred officers and men wounded during the battle, examining wounds, locating and removing splinters and other foreign bodies, performing amputations and tying arteries. Beatty himself amputated nine legs and two arms.[30] The rows of shattered men lying on the orlop deck were so overwhelming that the surgeon of the schooner *Pickle,* Simon Gage Britton, was brought aboard to help with the casualties and remained for three days.[31] On the way to Gibraltar, the *Victory* was caught in a storm; wounded men lying on the deck were rolled along the ship, those in hammocks were pitched against each other and the bulwarks, some were thrown down to the decks, and wounds were reopened. Yet the high survival rate of the casualties was remarkable and reflects an impressive quality of care by the surgeons. When the *Victory* was decommissioned in early January 1806, Beatty reported that no more than six of the 102 convalescents had died, five on board and one in the hospital at Gibraltar. All the others recovered from their wounds while under his charge, apart from five who were left at Gibraltar and five who were transferred to the hospital ship *Sussex.* Remarkably, eight of the eleven amputees survived. Of the men who died after their amputations, loss of blood was the cause of death for two of them and only the 22-year-old seaman William Smith died from infection after his leg was taken off at the thigh. There were indeed very few deaths from infected wounds among the other casualties who did not suffer amputation; Alexander Palmer, 21-year-old midshipman, died of tetanus after being struck in the thigh by a musket ball, and 22-year-old landsman Henry Cramwell died of gangrene after suffering severe contusions from splinters.[32]

The cockpit below the waterline was the scene of medical and surgical action during an engagement, but the usual theatre of activity for the ship's surgeon was the sick berth. On the *Victory* this was located in a wing berth on the starboard side of the upper gun deck beneath the forecastle. It had a skylight to allow in daylight for the examination of patients and for good ventilation. There was an internal toilet in the roundhouse and good access to the heads. The sick berth was separated from the rest of the deck by moveable canvas bulkheads stretched across wooden frames and contained twenty-two cots for convalescents, two urinals, three bedpans, and fourteen spitting-pots. It also had its own stove for the preparation by the loblolly boys of such invalid foods as oatmeal porridge and mutton broth. Vinegar and a nitre fumigant powder were used for disinfection. There was a small dispensary in the sick berth, but the main dispensary was located in the relative safety of the orlop deck where the surgeon had his own cabin adjoining it. He also had a portable medicine chest for treating officers in their cabins. Nelson, conscious of his own health problems, had his own personal medicine chest, which he carried with him always.[33] The sick berth may seem too small for a ship carrying a crew of 820 men but in normal conditions all of its beds were rarely needed. Daily numbers on the sick list averaged between ten and fifteen. On 21 April 1805 there were only ten occupants, four of them having been involved in accidents, two were cases of ulcers, one man was suffering from dysentery, another case had a venereal disease, and two men were sick with 'other complaints'.[34]

Other sick berths were not so well managed. On the *Gloucester*, the sick berth appalled the chaplain Edward Mangin in 1812 and he characterised it as 'less than six feet high, narrow noisome and wet; the writhings, sighs and moans of acute pain; the pale countenance, which looks like resignation, but is despair; bandages soaked in blood and matter; the foetor of sores, and the vermin from which it is impossible to preserve the invalid entirely free.' Its location near the heads, rather than being convenient for sick men, made it smell all the more, and 'whenever it blows fresh, the sea, defiled by a thousand horrible intermixtures, comes more or less into the hospital.' Yet, he acknowledged that being put on the sick list was 'considered an indulgence; as it exempts the sick man from that more dreaded state of toil and servitude to which, when fit for duty, he is necessarily exposed.'[35] Robert Young on the *Ardent* pointed out that 'the surgeon has every necessary article for his practice, but no conveniences for applying them with facility to use.' The storeroom for his lime juice and surgeon's necessaries was usually far too small, and that 'for making up and keeping at hand a regular formula of extemporaneous medicines, for having everything he may want ready of access, his instruments, lint, needles, his lotions, dressings, pills he has no convenience whatever.'[36]

Much depended on the attitude of the captain of the ship towards the maintenance of health. On the *Victory* there were only five deaths and two hospital cases between 29 December 1804 and the battle of Trafalgar on 21 October 1805. Of those who died, one man died of fever, three of consumption, and one from a spinal injury. All the men sent to hospital in Gibraltar were consumptive.[37] Beatty believed that Captain Thomas Hardy had been instrumental in maintaining the health of the crew, especially in the avoidance of catarrhal coughs and rheumatic fevers during the winter: 'and this is attributable solely to Captain Hardy's attention to their subordination, temperance, warm clothing, and cleanliness, together with the measures daily adopted to obviate the effects of moisture and to ensure the thorough ventilation of every part of the ship.'[38] Strict discipline was necessary to achieve this. John Snipe, physician to the Mediterranean fleet, urged that close attention should be paid to naval hygiene, ensuring that the seamen were adequately clothed, that the ships were well-ventilated, clean and dry, that sick berths should be fit for their purpose and that there should be 'as nourishing a diet as situation and local circumstances will permit, composed of fresh meat and succulent vegetables.' All of this was only attainable with the co-operation of the naval officers and 'nearly the whole of this is hinged on the improved mode of discipline, which at this moment enables the British fleet to ride triumphant on the seas, and bid defiance to the hostile bands of our combined foes.'[39] Nelson, too, was determined to do everything possible to safeguard the health and fitness of his fleet, declaring that 'the health of our seamen is invaluable, and to purchase that, no expense ought to be spared.'[40]

Hygiene and cleanliness on ships had improved during the eighteenth century. Gilbert Blane had persuaded Admiral St Vincent to order the first general issue of soap to the Mediterranean Fleet for the personal use of sailors and for washing their clothes in 1797. However, these official supplies were not always promptly delivered and John Snipe had to meet demand for it by purchasing soap locally when supplies from England were delayed.[41] However, whilst washing of clothes, hammocks and the decks was important for combating the spread of infectious disease, the water used could contribute to the problems of rheumatism, tuberculosis and respiratory diseases caused by the dampness of the ship. If water from leaks accumulated in the bilges and became contaminated by decaying matter there, the resultant bad odours were seen as responsible for the miasmas that could cause disease. Care had to be taken to ensure that the decks were quickly dried and Gilbert Blane, following the example of James Lind, advised that the decks should be cleaned by scouring with hot sand or dry rubbing rather than with water. It was also important that fresh dry air should be circulated to reduce the build up of miasmas. Windsails, cylinder shaped canvas tubes, were used to direct air from the upper decks to the hatchways and lower regions of the ship. Portable stoves were used to reduce the humidity and dry out the lower decks.[42] Nelson imposed restrictions on the washing of the middle and lower decks with water to try to overcome the problem of dampness, and suggested the use of such stoves and ventilation devices to overcome the problem of humidity and increase the air flow.[43]

Adequate clothing was also needed if the men were to stay healthy and avoid such complaints as influenza, rheumatism, and other fevers. John Snipe complained that 'much of this deplorable waste of men to the service was occasioned by the want of proper warm clothing'. Like Lind earlier, he urged the Admiralty to provide free uniforms, including long trousers, flannel-lined waistcoats, warm stockings and strong shoes, since this 'would prevent many from being sent to the hospital, a number of which either die or are invalided.'[44] Blane also believed that it would be for the benefit of the service that a uniform should be established 'for the common man as for the officers,' who had possessed one since 1748.[45] Thomas Trotter was in favour of 'a blue jacket with a sleeve and cape of the same . . . a waistcoat of white cloth trimmed with blue tape, blue trousers or pantaloons of the same cloth with the jacket for winter and linen or cotton trousers, either striped blue and white, or all white for the summer, check shirt, and black silk neckcloth.' He believed that 'a uniform in all situations contributes so much to personal delicacy and cleanliness.'[46] Yet it was not until 1857 that a uniform for the seamen was introduced. Nelson took an interest in ensuring that his men were warmly clad, and designed cotton frocks and trousers to be supplied by a Maltese shopkeeper Nathaniel Taylor, which were cheaper and of better quality than those provided from an Admiralty supply ship.[47] He also declared that warm, thick Guernsey jackets 'certainly would be the best and most valuable slops that ever were introduced into the service and be the means of saving many a good seaman's life', and that 'perhaps the Guernsey jacket, in its present state, might answer the largest of the boys.'[48]

Nelson was even more interested in the quality of provisions than in that of the slops. Not only did he issue orders about the inspection of provisions and the purchase of fresh vegetables and fruit whenever circumstances permitted, but he also took account of the tastes of his men, pointing out in 1804 that there would be grumbles over the replacement of cheese with rice.[49] Thomas Trotter considered that victualling had improved considerably in the course of the French wars and that 'the salted beef and pork are excellent, and the bread, till the high price of corn rendered a mixture necessary, was as good as can be desired.'[50] The men were divided into messes and each of them took a daily or weekly turn as 'mess cook', which involved collecting food from the steward, preparing the food, taking it to the galley to be cooked, bringing the cooked food to his messmates, and cleaning the mess utensils and equipment. Breakfast was usually at eight o'clock and consisted of burgoo, a gruel or porridge made from coarse oatmeal, and Scotch coffee, made by boiling burnt bread in water and sweetening the mixture with sugar. Dinner was at midday and was a mixture of ship's biscuit or bread, meat, and pease pudding. Mondays, Wednesdays, and Fridays were meatless 'banyan' days. Supper at four in the afternoon was a cold meal of biscuit, bread and cheese or leftovers from dinner.[51] The sick were supplied with medical comforts by the surgeon, but Trotter thought these could have been better and that 'a little mutton broth is so nourishing under debility and so desirable in many cases after a long cruise that to grant it would be the *ne plus ultra* of our improvements. Our officers have kindly shared their stock with the sick; but look at their pay! Alas! They cannot afford it.'[52]

With a fairly monotonous diet and poor quality drinking water, the seamen found solace in alcohol. Gilbert Blane accepted that 'there is a great propensity in seamen to intoxicating liquors, which is probably owing to the hardships they undergo, and to the variety and irregularity of sea life. But there is reason to think that all sorts of fermented liquors, except distilled spirits, are conducive to health at sea.' This was because 'as the solid part of sea diet is very dry and hard, and as the salt it contains is apt to excite thirst, a freer use of liquids than at land is necessary, particularly in a hot climate.'[53] He especially recommended porter and spruce beer for their anti-scorbutic qualities, and wine because it seemed to preserve the French fleet from scurvy, but he considered that 'the abuse of spirituous liquors is extremely pernicious everywhere, both as an interruption to duty, and as it is injurious to health.' He was especially opposed to the drinking of rum in the West Indies, 'both because the rum is of a bad and unwholesome quality, and because this species of debauchery is more hurtful in a hot than a cold climate.'[54] Originally, the men had been served their daily half pint of spirits undiluted, but in August 1740 Admiral Edward Vernon, appalled by 'that formidable Dagon, drunkenness', had ordered that, 'whereas the pernicious custom of the seamen drinking their allowance of rum in drams, and often at once, is attended by many fatal effects to their morals as well as their health, which are visibly impaired thereby ... besides the ill consequences arising from stupefying their rational qualities, which make them heedlessly slaves to every passion,' the daily allowance of half a pint for each man was to be mixed with a quart of water in 'one scuttled but kept for that purpose and to be done upon the deck'.[55] This was to be served twice a day to prevent the men from downing their allowance in one go. It was known as 'grog', in reference to Vernon's nickname of 'Old Grogram', given to him for his habit of wearing an old grogram boat cloak. The rum ration was reduced in 1824, fixed at an eighth of a pint of rum mixed in a quarter of a pint of water in 1937, and abolished completely on 1 August 1970. Alcohol was responsible for the many accidents at sea which took up so much of the daily routine of many surgeons, such as falls from the high rigging or through open hatchways. Doctors also associated intemperance with the destruction of the digestive system and liver, and with the development of scurvy and malignant diseases.[56] The penalty for drunkenness onboard ship was thirty-six lashes, with persistent offenders being given forty-eight or sixty lashes. Hardy on the *Victory* made a determined attempt to control immoderate alcohol consumption with 135 out of a total of 225 floggings in 1805 being for drunkenness.[57]

Nelson liked neither drunkards nor women aboard his ships and declared that 'every man became a bachelor after passing the rock of the Gibraltar',[58] but many wives did accompany their husbands to sea, some smuggled aboard without the knowledge of the officers, and others the wives of warrant officers, such as the gunner, carpenter and purser, allowed privileges not enjoyed by the ratings. A woman, Sarah Pitt, even claimed to have been employed with other sailors' wives on the *Victory* at Trafalgar carrying powder from the magazine.[59] Some of the women acted as nurses during the battles. At Camperdown George Magrath relied on 'the women who formed the chief of my assistance.'[60]

However, some men smuggled prostitutes on board as well as consorting with them ashore, with the inevitable result that they went down with syphilis or gonorrhoea. At Spithead in May 1798 the surgeon of the *Russell* reported that the captain of marines 'has a girl on board, the same that communicated this disease, and, although he is well aware that she is injured, he still continues to sleep with her, notwithstanding I have put him in remembrance of what mischief she may do him.'[61] A similar situation had been noted by the surgeon Lionel Gillespie on the *Racehorse* where there were 'four prostitutes who have affected three or four persons, two with gonorrhoea and the rest with chancres – yet these women are seemingly well in health, are in good spirits and having been turned over from their first paramours are entertained by others who seem to remain unaffected by any syphilitic complaints.'[62] Mercury was the only treatment for this, the great pox, and until 1795 men reporting to the ship's surgeon for treatment were fined 15s for their cure. As a result many men resorted to quack cures, shared medicines with their messmates, and only reported to the surgeon when 'the most excruciating and dangerous symptoms had supervened.' Thomas Trotter's recommendation that this fee should be abolished was put into practice, and 'thus terminated a perquisite illiberal from its institution, inhuman in its practice and impolitic from its continuance. It forms an epoch in naval improvements, for hundreds of seamen have annually fallen victims to its effects.'[63]

Another innovation was the speedy adoption of Edward Jenner's vaccine against smallpox. This disease was not as common at sea as it was on land, but this in itself made the sailor more vulnerable when he was exposed to it, since he had had little opportunity to develop any natural immunity. Thomas Trotter, physician to the Channel fleet, was one of the earliest supporters of Jenner's method of inducing immunity by vaccinating with cowpox. He even suggested that 'some of the Gloucestershire cows should be transferred to the navy farm that surrounds the walls of Haslar Hospital for the purpose of inoculating the whole seamen of Spithead and thus prevent any return to that infection into our ships of war that we are now employed to defeat.'[64] He tried to persuade the Admiralty to issue an order for voluntary vaccination since 'there is scarcely a village that has not long shared its blessing', but it was not until September 1800, two years after the publication of Jenner's paper on vaccination, that he secured agreement to this – although this was indeed remarkably quick action for any government department.[65] Joseph Marshall and John Walker were sent to join the Mediterranean fleet with a supply of Jenner's cowpox vaccine and vaccinated eleven men on *Endymion* at Gibraltar that summer, the first naval vaccination.[66] Marshall and Walker then proceeded to Minorca, Malta, Sicily and Naples, where they continued with their programme of vaccination of the fleet.[67] Vaccination was also tried out in the Channel fleet and in September 1800 all marines joining at Chatham were vaccinated.[68] There was a prejudice against compulsory vaccination, and whether or not to be vaccinated was left up to the individual. Even Nelson could not persuade Emma Hamilton to have their small daughter Horatia vaccinated.[69]

Nelson had more authority in preventing scurvy from ravaging his fleet than he had over his mistress. He pronounced that 'it is necessary in order to remove an inveterate scurvy to give each man so afflicted six ounces of lemon juice, and two ounces of sugar, daily.'[70] As a result of the lobbying of Gilbert Blane, lemon juice had been issued to the fleet since 1795 'as the best substitute for fresh fruit and vegetables, and the most powerful corrective of the scorbutic qualities of their common diet.' Lemon juice was much easier to store and ship than fresh vegetables and live oxen, and so could be considered a dietary substitute as 'it is also well ascertained that a certain proportion of lemon juice taken daily, as an article of seamen's diet, will prevent the possibility of their being tainted with the scurvy, let the other articles of their diet consist of what they will.'[71] When there was a temporary disruption to the provision of fresh supplies of citrus fruits and vegetables in the winter of 1804–5 caused by the Spanish entry into the war, Nelson made sure that supplies of lemons and oranges from Sicily were available. Gillespie reported that 'several of the ship's companies appear to be slightly affected with scurvy indicating the want of fresh meat and vegetables, it is probable that this disposition would have been much more manifest had it not been for the supply of lemons and oranges lately furnished, the use of which has been attended with the most salutary effects.'[72] This lemon juice from Sicily was judged to be 'of the first quality.'[73]

High standards of hygiene were essential to prevent disease getting a hold on a man-of-war. New sailors and marines were inspected by the surgeon, washed, and issued with clean clothes to avoid typhus being brought on board.[74] When an epidemic of yellow fever broke out in southern Spain at the end of 1804, Nelson forbade his men to board any ships coming from Gibraltar, Cadiz, Malaga, Alicante and Cartagena to stop the infection affecting his fleet. French and Spanish prisoners were segregated when imprisoned on British ships to prevent them from passing on diseases to their captors. Believing that impure air was the source of infection, John Snipe recommended that all wood brought on to a ship should be smoked to remove the noxious effluvia contained in green wood. He also laid it down that only the purest water should be taken from the head of springs and water casks should be carefully maintained to avoid contamination. Seamen and marines who went ashore in places where there was a danger of tropical diseases were prescribed Peruvian bark, which contained quinine, mixed with spirits or wine and water, before they left the ship and on their return to protect them against malaria.[75] On the *Spencer* seven gallons of spirits and two gallons of wine were mixed with Peruvian bark, and issued over five days in October 1804 to the 272 men sent ashore on the coast of Sardinia.[76]

As well as being concerned about preventative medicine, Nelson also showed concern regarding the hospitals to which his sick and wounded men were sent. He took an interest in the management of the naval hospitals in Malta and Gibraltar, advising the governor of the Gibraltar Hospital, Lieutenant William Pemberton to give 'very strict and particular attention to the cleanliness and comfort of the patients.'[77] Stress was laid on hygiene, a nutritious diet, and a generous staffing ratio of one nurse to ten patients. Patients were allowed a pint of broth, a pound of mutton, and a pound of fresh vegetables and fruit each day.[78] The surgeon of the Malta Hospital John Gray was instructed to 'supply the necessary quantity of milk to the patients in their tea morning and afternoon' regardless of any additional costs that might imply.[79] The purser at Malta proved unsatisfactory and was dismissed, as was a dishonest dispenser at Gibraltar whom Nelson considered to be 'a character so dangerous, not only to the individual, but also to the public service', and someone who had tried to advance his own interests by 'sacrificing the upright and honest man'.[80] Nelson's interventions into hospital management demonstrated his humane concern for the men under his command.

In Malta Nelson was particularly interested in the establishment of a permanent naval hospital. The island had been captured from the French in September 1800, two years after the French had taken it from the Order of the Knights of St John, and had a strategic importance at the crossroads of the Mediterranean which made it an ideal location for a British naval base. A temporary naval hospital had been set up at the Armeria in Vittoriosa, a building with long corridors close to the ships at anchor in the Grand Harbour. It had been built as an armoury and later served as a civil hospital in the time of the Knights of Malta. Nelson considered the building to be totally unsuitable for a hospital and told

John Snipe, whom he sent to Malta in 1803 to investigate possible sites for a permanent hospital, that 'the situation of the former Hospital at Malta was particularly unhealthy, it is my directions that you do not suffer that house to be received as an Hospital, or any other which, from situation, you may judge improper; but endeavour to procure a convenient and well appointed house, in an airy and healthy situation for a Naval Hospital *pro tempore*.'[81] Snipe believed that he had found the perfect spot in 'the Palace of Bighay which is a most desirable situation for a naval hospital, in summer it is cooled by a refreshing sea breeze, and in winter perfectly dry.' As well as there being a convenient landing place for patients to be brought over from their ships, the building also had 'sufficient ground belonging to it, in a high state of cultivation, to produce abundance of vegetables for the use of the sick, and if lemon and orange trees were planted, the Fleet, on this station, might be amply supplied with those anti-scorbutic fruit.'[82] The villa at Bighi had been built in 1675 as a country residence for Giovanni Bichi, Knight of St John and nephew of Pope Alexander VII, and was located on an impressive promontory overlooking the Grand Harbour, which Napoleon was said to have boasted as being suitable for his palace once Europe, Asia and Africa had all been subjugated to his Empire.[83] While Snipe had 'carefully examined every spot in and about the Harbour of Malta, and there is no situation so well calculated for a naval hospital as Bighay, it being nearly insulated, and some distance from any other houses', the existing buildings were inadequate for receiving five hundred patients, and two wings would have to be built on either side of the main palace buildings as well as other buildings for a dispensary, kitchen, storehouses, and wash houses. He reminded Nelson that 'there is no part of the service that requires more to be regarded than the choice of a proper situation for a hospital, and the right management of it, on which the health and strength of a fleet so much depends, for in wet and unwholesome seasons, if any infectious diseases get into the hospital, which probably might have been prevented by proper care, they often weaken a fleet more than the sword of the enemy.'[84] Nelson did not need convincing and agreed that adjacent land was needed to extend the buildings and provide gardens in which convalescent sailors and marines could enjoy exercise and fresh air, 'for with the ground it is the most healthy and eligible situation in Valetta Harbour; without it, confined within four bare walls, it would be the worst place in the place, for the heat would be intolerable.'[85]

While Nelson was urging the establishment of a permanent hospital, though he conceded that 'if we give up Malta it will be unnecessary to make a naval hospital',[86] the former Slaves' Prison in Valletta was converted into a naval hospital; the Armeria was again reoccupied in 1819, although it would have been no more suitable than it had been when Nelson had condemned it in 1803. However, Nelson's plans for Bighi were not forgotten and in 1829 it was finally decided that the villa should be converted into a naval hospital. Snipe's recommendations for the construction of two pavilions on either side of the villa were also followed, and two wings with capacious balconies were built in the Doric style and the original villa was modified to harmonise architecturally with the new buildings.[87] Under the whole building ran a wide and high passage used during the building for transporting construction materials by mule, and later offering convenient communication links for the staff. The passages are very reminiscent in style of the entrance lobby at Haslar, though externally the classical grandeur of Bighi is very different from the austerity of the naval hospital at Gosport.[88] Opened in 1832 and continuing to be the main British naval hospital in the Mediterranean until 1970, the Royal Naval Hospital at Bighi, in its commanding position with its grandiose buildings overlooking the Grand Harbour, was very much Nelson's in its inspiration and formed a fitting memorial to his interest in naval hospitals.

For Nelson, the health and morale of his men were closely intertwined. Those men serving under him were convinced that his concern for their welfare was sincere. It was not only in regard to provisioning, clothing, and healthcare, but also in ensuring that their morale and spirits remained high, that he showed the importance he placed on mental as well as physical health. In 1804, rather than maintaining a long blockade of Toulon, he changed 'the cruising ground' in the Western Mediterranean so that he would avoid 'the sameness of prospect to satiate the mind'.[89] He also made positive attempts to keep the men happy, and 'the promoting cheerfulness amongst the men was encouraged by music, dancing and theatrical amusements; the example of which was given by the Commander-in-Chief in the *Victory*, and may with reason be reckoned among the causes of the preservation of the health of the men.'[90] This was a contrast with the low morale aboard the ships involved in the Spithead Mutiny of April 1797. The surgeon Peter Cullen said that 'the sick themselves showed something of a mutinous spirit and at first were rather insolent.'[91] On the *Sandwich*, this was linked to the overcrowding of the ship with its sick crew, 'in general very dirty, almost naked, and in general without beds', whose recovery was hampered by 'their own bad habits, but oftener to the foul air they breathe between decks; besides being frequently trod upon in the night from their crowded state.'[92] The attitude of the officers towards the health of their crew was the important factor in maintaining a healthy and happy ship. Some them gloried in it and in their own aids to health, such as Admiral Peter Rainier, who chose to have himself painted by Arthur Devis wearing an ungainly-looking pair of spectacles of moulded iron with straight sides and tortoiseshell 'Martin's margins' around the lenses to protect against sideways glare, a sign of the importance of good eyesight at sea.[93] The ship's surgeons were conscious of the role of their commanders in promoting health. James Campbell on the *Aetna* in 1808 recognized that 'from the very great attention observed by the captain and officers to cleanliness, ventilation, may be attributed the general good health of the *Aetna's* ship's company.'[94]

The naval officers could not have achieved so much without the co-operation and initiative of their surgeons. Many of the naval surgeons in the French Revolutionary and Napoleonic Wars had taken advantage of wartime service as an opportunity to advance themselves professionally and acquire the tastes and manners of a gentleman, in a service whose social prestige had risen since George III had sent his son the Duke of Clarence, the future William IV, to sea as a midshipman in 1779. Three-quarters of the surgeons warranted between 1793 and 1815 came from Scotland, Ireland, and Wales, and were the sons of merchants, tradesmen, and farmers. Their decision to begin their careers at sea owed more to their relatively socially disadvantaged origins than to any intellectual inferiority.[95] Peter Cullen from Scotland was relieved when he passed the examinations of the College of Surgeons in 1789, having been questioned on his knowledge of anatomy, physiology and surgery in a much more professional manner that Smollett's Roderick Random had been examined, since he 'had been led to believe that the Faculty of London were not so well disposed to candidates from Edinburgh from a spirit of envy.'[96] During the wars the position of the naval surgeon was improved to bring his pay and conditions of service into line with that of army doctors. In 1805 they were given increased status and the rank of an officer commensurate to those in the army although they were to remain subordinate to the lieutenant of the ship on which they served. They were now issued with free supplies of drugs, though they still had to supply their own instruments. The surgeon's mate was promoted to the position of assistant surgeon. The newly elevated status of the surgeon was visibly expressed with the introduction of a uniform, consisting of the captain's undress uniform with a stand-up collar. Physicians were allowed gold lace on their sleeves.[97] Their status as gentlemen was recognized. In 1813 Jane Austen, whose brothers were naval officers, described a naval surgeon, a minor character in *Mansfield Park*, as 'a very well behaved young man.'[98] After retirement from the navy on half pay like other officers, many of the surgeons who had served in it during the wars went on to enjoy successful civilian practices. One of the most distinguished of them was James Clark, the son of the Earl of Findlater's butler, who went on from service at sea to treating the dying John Keats in Rome, and appointment as physician to Queen Victoria and Prince Albert.[99] Thomas Trotter judged that 'taking the surgeons of the navy list collectively, they may be justly compared to any other body of professional men, some very capable, and others perhaps not. There are many of the number well qualified for the duties of the station, liberally educated and equal to the exercise of the art in any situation.'[100]

British naval surgeons were often horrified when they saw the results of the work of their counterparts in the French and Spanish navies. William Shoveller, the surgeon on *Leviathan* at Trafalgar, was not impressed by the condition of Spanish prisoners taken aboard, many of them 'with tourniquets on their different extremities, and which had been applied since the action, four or five days elapsing, consequently most of the limbs in a state of mortification or approaching it.'[101] Shoveller had to try to do something for these men to save their lives. The seaman William Robinson was also scathing about the 'the scene of carnage horrid to behold' on a captured Spanish ship, with the dead bodies 'in a wounded or a mutilated state' piled up in the hold, and 'the heart-rending cries of the wounded' on a French ship, where the doctor, 'having lost or mislaid some of his instruments, was reduced to the necessity of resorting to the use of the carpenter's fine saw, where amputation was needful.'[102] Gilbert Blane castigated the French for the filthy state of the hold, since the custom was that 'the blood, the mangled limbs, and even whole bodies of men, were cast into the orlop or hold and lay there putrefying for some time . . . When, therefore, the ballast or other contents of the holds of these ships came to be stirred, and the putrid effluvia thereby let loose, there was then a visible increase of sickness.'[103] Not surprisingly, dysentery and typhus were rampant. Moreover, the French and Spanish fleets did not have in place any effective measures against scurvy, and suffered a loss of experienced mariners as a result of the epidemic of yellow fever that was raging through southern Spain. When Villeneuve sailed to meet Nelson at Trafalgar, there were 1,731 sick in the Combined Fleets of France and Spain.[104]

It was this superiority in medicine and concern for the welfare of the seaman that gave the Royal Navy the advantage in the French Wars between 1793 and 1815. The advances made then had built on developments during the eighteenth century, and contributed to the foundations of British naval supremacy during the *Pax Britannica* of the nineteenth century. As Nelson had said, 'the great thing in all military service is health and it is easier for an officer to keep men healthy than for a physician to cure them'.[105]

# CHAPTER SIX

# *Middle Passage*

IT WAS HIS experiences as a surgeon on board the slave ship *Brooks* in 1783–4 that made Thomas Trotter, later Physician of the Channel Fleet 1795–1802, such an ardent opponent of the slave trade, and indeed of colonialism in general. He deplored the conditions in which naval ratings lived and worked as being little better than those endured by slaves on the notorious Middle Passage from Africa to the American and West Indian colonies. Moreover, he believed that long periods of service in the colonies, especially in the West Indies, would result in the degeneration of Europeans, as their bodies were ill-adapted to service in a hot climate.[1] At the end of the American War of Independence, Trotter had been demobilised from the Royal Navy and had signed aboard a slaver simply because he needed a job. What he witnessed horrified him. The slaves were 'locked spoonways, according to the technical phrase', below deck, and Trotter was unable to 'walk amongst them without treading upon them.'[2] In such crowded conditions they gasped for breath and lived 'in dread of suffocation.' In such a foetid environment the 'effluvium conveyed by the air in and about the vessel' attracted 'voracious fish' to follow the ship, though 'in Guineamen, this is said to be from a kind of instinct that teaches them to watch for dead bodies.'[3] Using 'gesture and motion', as well as interpreters, Trotter learned from the still-living enslaved men, women and children that most of them had been kidnapped from their homes by black African slave traders, and he was woken in the night by 'a howling melancholy kind of noise, something expressive of extreme anguish', made by the slaves waking from their own dreams of home and family only to find themselves in the hell of the slaver.[4]

Trotter's evidence before a House of Commons Select Committee in May 1790 did not go unchallenged.[5] Clement Noble, captain of the *Brooks* when Trotter had served on her, was a veteran of nine voyages to transport slaves, and was as staunch a defender of the trade as Trotter was its opponent. He claimed that on the voyage in question only fifty-eight slaves had died, and implied that this may have been because Dr Trotter was 'very inattentive to his duty' and 'spent a great deal too much time in dress.'[6] None of the slaves had died because of 'correction', and indeed he himself had disciplined a seaman 'for abusing the slaves and being very insolent to myself – I believe it was the only time that any of the seamen were flogged that voyage.'[7] He also asserted that the slaves 'always had plenty of room to lay down in, and had they three times as much room they would all lay jammed up close together; they always do that before the room is half full.'[8] The slaves, who were 'very fond of dancing' and did not need to be coerced into dancing in their chains,[9] were 'in general in very good spirits during the time they are on board the ships'.[10] Trotter was in no doubt that the sailors as well as the African captives were oppressed by the captain, 'whose character was perfectly congenial to the trade'. He had heard Noble boast to a group of fellow slaver captains, 'with a degree of triumph and satisfaction that would have disgraced an Indian scalper', of how he had punished a black seaman from Philadelphia whom he suspected of having killed some exotic birds that the captain was carrying on his own behalf from Africa to the West Indies. The man was lashed and chained to one of the masts for twelve days, and fed on nothing but the small dead birds he had been accused of killing. The other captains 'applauded his invention for the novelty of the punishment', but Trotter was revolted by such a 'wanton piece of barbarity'.[11]

The Atlantic slave trade had grown into a major maritime and commercial venture since the discovery by Europeans of the New World. However, the trade in human beings was nothing new and had continued uninterruptedly since classical antiquity. Portuguese navigators in the second half of the fifteenth century had started trading with Arab merchants along the Mauritanian coast and beyond Cape Verde, carrying slaves along the coast for their trading partners, as well as returning to Lisbon with gold, ivory, and spices. As the Portuguese empire grew, and sugar plantations were established in the Azores, Canaries and Cape Verde, slaves were also taken as a cheap source of labour to the new colonies. The Spaniards followed suit as they built up their empire in the Indies and South America to be followed by the Dutch, French and English. John Hawkins, enjoying the backing of Elizabeth I, broke into the Iberian monopoly in 1562 when he shipped a cargo of slaves to Hispaniola (Haiti). Royal approval of the trade was given by Charles II in 1662 with the issue of a charter to the Royal Adventurers of England Trading into Africa, a joint-stock company with exclusive rights to ship slaves from West Africa to the English sugar plantations in the West Indies. The riches brought by this trade inspired Charles II to name a new coin worth twenty-one shillings the 'guinea', after the Guinea coast with which the new company traded. However, the Royal Adventurers soon ran into financial difficulties as a result of the capture of the Company's forts and trading posts by the Dutch, and relinquished its royal charter. In 1689 it was reincorporated as the Royal African Assiento Company, but its monopoly soon came under attack as independent ship owners realised the profits to be made from slavery, and they were allowed to trade under licence from the Royal African Company. Established slaving nations already used the 'triangular trade' which England now adopted. Manufactured goods were taken to the Guinea coast where they were exchanged for slaves. In the Middle Passage the slaves were shipped across the Atlantic and sold to Caribbean sugar planters or American cotton and tobacco planters, whose products were then carried back to Europe. In London, Bristol and Liverpool, merchants made their fortunes on this human cargo which had to be kept healthy to command a good price.[12]

African slave traders brought their captives to the factories or stockade trading posts set up by the European slave trading companies on the coast of West Africa. Linked by chains or leather thongs, the slaves formed a caravan, or coffle, which might be force-marched for up to six hundred miles through the jungle to the coast, driven on by overseers with hippopotamus hide whips. During the many months it took the coffle to reach the sea, many slaves succumbed to exhaustion, exposure, despair, dysentery, or fevers, and were left to die where they fell. Others committed suicide by eating earth rather than prolong their ordeal. Yet they could still sympathise with the suffering of others. The explorer Mungo Park accompanied a coffle through the upper valley of the River Senegal in 1796, and was touched that 'during a wearisome peregrination of more than five hundred British miles, exposed to the burning rays of a tropical sun, these poor slaves, amidst their own infinitely greater sufferings, could commiserate mine; and frequently, of their own accord, bring water to quench my thirst and, at night, collect branches and leaves to prepare me a bed in the wilderness.' He left with regret 'my unfortunate fellow travellers, doomed as I knew most of them to be to a life of captivity and slavery in a foreign land.'[13] Once at the factory the survivors of the march were penned into the baracoon, the factory stockade, to await shipment. In an attempt to make their skin look healthy, they were polished with palm oil before being paraded in front of the slaver captains and surgeons, who advised on whether or not a purchase should be made.[14] Only the healthiest were even considered after the surgeon had examined 'them well in all kinds to see that they were sound in wind and limb, making them jump, stretch out their arms swiftly, look into their mouths to judge of their age', and had taken care to 'buy none that are pox'd lest they should infect the rest', which meant that 'the surgeon is forc'd to examine the privities of both men and women with the nicest scrutiny which is a great slavery.' In 1721 John Atkins noted that these slaves were 'examined by us in like manner as our brother traders do beasts in Smithfield.'[15]

Branded on the breast or buttock and thrust over the slavers' gunwales, the unfortunate slave now began the even greater ordeal of an ocean voyage that could last from five weeks to three months, in which up to a quarter of the human cargo might die. Olaudah Equiano, who claimed to have been kidnapped as an eleven-year-old by African traders in 1754, was astonished by his first sight of a ship, *Ogden*, and of white men so that 'I was now persuaded that I had got into a world of bad spirits, and that they were going to kill me.' He fainted, 'overpowered with horror and anguish', when he saw a large copper boiling pot in a corner of the deck, and 'a multitude of black people of every description chained together, everyone of their countenances expressing dejection and sorrow', believing that he had fallen into the hands of cannibals, 'those white men with horrible looks, red faces and long hair.'[16] Worse horrors faced him when he was taken to the lower deck. He was greeted with 'such a salutation in my nostrils as I had never experienced in my life; so that with the loathsomeness of the stench, and crying together, I became so sick and low that I was not able to eat, nor had I the least desire to taste anything.'[17] That stench became 'pestilential when the ship put out to sea', while 'the closeness of the place, and the heat of the climate, added to the number in the ship, which was so crowded that each had scarcely room to turn himself, almost suffocated.' Sweat, vomit, urine, blood, and tubs full of excrement, coupled with the heat and poor ventilation, made the atmosphere below deck intolerable, and many of the slaves died 'falling victims to the improvident avarice, as I may call it, of their purchasers.'[18] Equiano was relieved that as a sickly child he was allowed to spend much of his time at sea on deck and unfettered, where the women slaves mothered him. He was, nevertheless, jealous of the dead who were thrown overboard as 'I envied them the freedom they enjoyed and as often wished I could change my condition for theirs.'[19]

The ships were small and confined, ranging from fifty to five hundred tons, with between one hundred and seven hundred slaves stowed as carefully and economically as cargo, in the least possible space. Each male slave was manacled hand and foot to another slave, and packed into the main slave deck just over the waterline and not much more than five feet high. Around its edge ran a shelf which halved the already limited headroom and made space for a second layer of human merchandise. Each man had no more than sixteen or eighteen inches in which to lie. Women and children were allocated even less space, but were not manacled together. Thomas Clarkson, one of the most prominent of the abolitionists, was told by one sailor of 'the misery which the slaves endure in consequence of too close a stowage', and that he had 'heard them frequently complaining of heat and have seen them fainting, almost dying for want of water.'[20] The more merciful of the seamen would 'get them immediately onto deck, fearing lest they would otherwise have fainted away and died.' They were far too valuable to be allowed to die. Every slave lost represented a debit in the ledger, but even had a third of the cargo died there would still be a handsome profit to be made. There were suggestions that losses could be reduced by decreasing the overcrowding in the ships in which the slaves were transported. In 1681, the Cape Town factors of the Royal African Company suggested that 'if Your Honours would be pleased to beat them down in their number though you gave them 5s per head extraordinary, Your Honours would be considerable gainers at the year's end.'[21] The directors of the Company remained unconvinced and tight-packing continued to result in unnecessary deaths. The Dolben Slave Carrying Act of 1788 recognised the importance of allowing more space for each slave and only allowed five slaves to be carried for every three tons of cargo capacity. It also required all British slave ships to carry a surgeon who was to keep full records of sickness mortality for each voyage. Plans of the *Brooks* were published by the anti-slavery movement to demonstrate the overcrowding on slave ships, and showed the stowage of slaves under the provisions of the Dolben Act rather than the even more cramped conditions that had previously been the norm; they were horrific enough to the British public.[22]

After about eight days at sea, when the vessel was distant from land and the possibility of escape, the slaves were allowed on deck for the sake of their health and the hygiene of the ship. They were taken on deck for their meals and exercise. The morning meal usually consisted of African food appropriate to the origins of the slaves, such as rice for those from Senegambia and the Windward Coast, yams for those from Benin and Biafra, and corn for those from the Gold Coast. The afternoon food was European in style, such as beans and peas with salt meat and fish or 'dad-a-dab', a concoction of salt meat, pepper, and palm oil. If a slave refused to eat from sickness, depression, or as an act of defiance, he or she would first be threatened with the cat-o'-nine-tails, and if that failed to persuade them they were forced to eat by the application of hot coals or a mouth speculum.[23] Men confined in irons 'were ordered to stand up and make what motion they could', in a macabre dance to the wail of a sailor's bagpipes or the strumming of a fellow slave's banjo to give them exercise, though some of them 'refused to do it, even with this mode of a punishment in a severe degree' when they were lashed to make them obey.[24] While the slaves were on deck, the seamen would go below to empty the tubs of urine and excrement, scrub the decks and beams with sand to remove the dried filth, vomit and mucus, and, once every couple of weeks, fumigate the area with sand, tobacco fumes, and vinegar.[25] The seamen resented such duties and took out their frustrations on the more helpless of the slaves. When a group of sick slaves were brought on deck on the *Young Hero* and covered with a sail, they contaminated it 'with blood and mucus, which involuntarily issued from them'. The seamen who had to clean the sail punished them with a beating which drove the fearful slaves to the tub where 'they sat straining and straining.' The surgeon Ecroyde Claxton believed that this caused 'prolapsus ani, which it was entirely impossible to cure.'

Nothing could prevent outbreaks of contagious disease. Dysentery, the bloody flux, was one of the major causes of death on slaving vessels. Alexander Falconbridge, a surgeon on a slaver, declared that 'it is not in the power of the human imagination to picture to itself a situation more dreadful or disgusting',[26] yet found the words to describe the horrific conditions he witnessed on his visits to his slave charges: 'The deck was covered with blood and mucous, and approached nearer to the resemblance of a slaughter-house than anything I can compare it to, the stench and foul air were likewise intolerable.'[27]

Dysentery could be controlled to a certain extent by the regular cleaning of decks, and the washing and shaving of the slaves. Native West Indians had partial immunity to malaria and yellow fever, but fevers in general were the second biggest killers. Scurvy was a problem where there were no fresh provisions or citrus fruits on board. Measles, smallpox and influenza could devastate a ship.[28]

Smallpox was the most feared since it could halve the value of cargo and also threaten the European crew. Inoculation against smallpox was being carried out by surgeons on British slavers by the 1720s, not many years after its popularisation by Lady Mary Wortley Montagu, and was common on French ships and on British and French plantations by the 1770s.[29] However, one way of stopping the contagion, practised by many captains, was to isolate and throw overboard the sick slave in order to save the rest. In 1781 Captain Luke Collingwood of the *Zong* jettisoned 132 sick slaves, their hands bound, after sixty Africans and seven of the crew had died on a voyage from West Africa to Jamaica. He told the crew that 'if the slaves died a natural death, it would be the loss of the owners of the ship; but if they were thrown alive into the sea, it would be the loss of the underwriters.'[30] In 1819 all the slaves and most of the crew of the French slaver *Rodeur* were blinded with ophthalmia: one survivor said, 'we were blind, stone blind, drifting like a wreck upon the ocean, and rolling like a cloud before the wind'. When it reached Guadeloupe, having been refused aid by the Spanish ship *San Leone* which was itself in need of help, the thirty-nine slaves who were completely blind were thrown overboard to claim on the insurance.[31]

Once the voyage was over the survivors of the Middle Passage were paraded like cattle before prospective buyers. They were fattened up during their last days at sea, their sores and abscesses were disguised with rust and gunpowder, and even their anuses were stuffed with oakum to hide signs that they had suffered from the flux. Grey hair was plucked or dyed black as buyers preferred slaves with ebony complexions and short black curly hair. Their bodies were rubbed down with palm olive to make them glisten and glow with healthiness. The buyers were familiar with such stratagems to enhance the value of the human commodity, and took care to examine in intimate detail the slaves they were interested in purchasing. Doctors were often brought along to inspect the slaves to check that they were in good health, and estimate the likely length of their working life and their predilection to illness.[32] Mortality was high among slaves in the West Indies since slave owners often calculated whether it would be cheaper to buy a new slave or pay for treatment of a sick one. Young adults, house slaves and craftsmen were more likely to receive medical care and survive than the less valuable elderly and unskilled. Doctors were contracted to visit plantations once or twice a week and had little incentive to check the health of all the slaves there. The medicine they did administer was European medicine which many slaves distrusted.[33] Back at the slave market, sick slaves or ones who attracted no interest from buyers were often abandoned and left to die unattended on the quayside. They no longer had any commercial value and were expendable.[34]

The job of the ship's surgeon was to keep mortality down and profits up. Some surgeons on slave ships were strong supporters of the system. James Irving was twenty-three when he first went to sea as a surgeon on a slaver in 1783, and by 1789 had become captain of the *Anna,* a vessel carrying eighty slaves, which was shipwrecked in May 1789 off the coat of Morocco only twenty-four days out of Liverpool. Irving and his crew were captured by 'Arabs and Moors' and sold into slavery. He found this situation intolerable since 'I could have died rather than devote my life to be spent in so abject a state, bereft of all Christian society, a slave to a savage race who despised and hated me for my belief', and was relieved when his freedom was negotiated by the British consuls at Mogador and Tangier to whom he had appealed for help.[35] Yet he had no sympathy for his own 'black cattle' whom he found disagreeable, and felt 'almost melted in the midst of five or six hundred of them'.[36] Despite having been enslaved himself, he could not see the black slaves he tended as a surgeon as anything but goods whose saleability was to be maintained by his medical skills.

The seaman, however, was not as valuable a commodity as the slave. Many ships' surgeons took no interest in the health of the sailors. The surgeon on the slave ship *Albion* 'neglected the sick seamen, alleging that he was only paid for attending the slaves.'[37] Alexander Falconbridge considered that 'the sufferings of the seamen employed in the slave trade from the unwholesomeness of the climate, the inconveniences of the voyage, the brutal severity of the commanders and other causes, fall very little short, nor prove in proportion to the numbers, less destructive to the sailors than the negroes.'[38] One slaver captain described his sick seamen in 1721 as 'walking ghosts'. In 1770 the entire crew of the brig *Elizabeth* died in the Gambia, leaving behind them a ghost ship. In 1796 Captain Cooke of Baltimore 'lost all his hands, except a negro man and boy.' It was little wonder that slave ships were referred to as 'marine lazar houses'. Dead sailors were often thrown overboard at night to conceal their deaths from the slaves who might, seeing the crews depleted by death, consider rising against their captors.[39] If rations were short, the slaves were often fed before the sailors because they had a greater monetary value. Flogging was the norm. Equiano witnessed a white sailor 'flogged so unmercifully with a large rope near the foremast that he died in consequence of it; and they tossed him over the side as they would have done a brute.' It was a warning not only to the other sailors, but also to the slaves of the consequences of disobedience, which Equiano took to heart as 'this made me fear these people the more; and I expected nothing less than to be treated in the same manner.'[40]

It was the plight of the sailor on the slavery ships which aroused the indignation of the evangelical abolitionist Thomas Clarkson, when, aged twenty-seven but still innocent of the world, he set about gathering evidence against the slave trade in the sailors' haunts, characterised by 'music, dancing rioting, drunkenness and profane swearing', in Bristol and Liverpool in 1787; he was often accompanied by the athletic and resolute Alexander Falconbridge for physical protection and the backup arguments of a man who could speak from experience as a surgeon on a slaver. He was impressed by seven young seamen from the slaver *Africa* whom he met in Bristol and considered to be 'pillars of the state':

> I am sure no one can describe my feelings when I considered that some of them were devoted, and whatever might be their spirits now, would never see their native home more. I considered also how much the glory of the British flag was diminishing by the destruction of such noble fellows, who appeared so strong, robust and hardy, and at the same time so spirited, as to enable us to bid defiance to the marine of our enemies the French.[41]

The men serving on slave ships, like other merchant seamen, were to be pressed into the navy during the French Wars. Their good health was of concern to a patriot like Clarkson but their sufferings distressed the humanitarian in him. He took up the cause of a surgeon's mate called Thomas who had been beaten so often by Captain Edward Robe of the slave ship *Alfred* that he had tried to commit suicide by leaping into shark-infested waters. Thomas had been rescued by his shipmates but the captain had him chained to the deck and beaten repeatedly. When Clarkson met him, shortly before the seaman's death, Thomas was bedridden with his wounds and had been driven mad by his experiences. Witnessing the results of such brutal treatment stirred 'a fire of indignation within me.'[42] It was not only the testimony that he obtained from the sailors which he was to marshal in support of the cause of the abolition of the slave trade, but also the sight of the physical condition to which many of his witnesses had been reduced, since 'I have also had ocular demonstration, as far as a sight of their mangled bodies will be admitted as a proof.'[43]

Towards the end of the Middle Passage some captains would deliberately make the lives of the sailors unbearable, especially those of the sick and disabled, in the hope that they would desert and not only save the masters their pay, but also of the expense of taking them back to England. Admiral Rodney believed that in the West Indies 'there have been many instances of harsh treatment in captains of those ships to get rid of their men.'[44] James Towne was 'left on shore at Charles Town, South Carolina, with two others, without either money or friends. The two died.'[45] Many of these men were stricken with malaria, ophthalmia, ulcers, and Guinea worms. In Barbados in 1788 there were 'several Guinea seamen in great distress, and in want of the common necessities of life, with their legs in an ulcerated state . . . and their toes rotting off, without any person to give them any assistance or to take them in.'[46] The workhouse at Barbados was crowded with slaver sailors. In Jamaica in 1791, 'a very great proportion of those who are in Kingston Hospital are Guineamen.' This dumping of the 'lame, ulcerated and sick seamen' was 'a very great nuisance and expense to the community at Kingston', which in future required shipmasters to deposit money as a security against them abandoning their sick in port.[47]

Around half of all Europeans who travelled to West Africa in the eighteenth century died of microbial infections within a year of arriving there, many of them from mosquito-borne malaria and yellow fever, as well as from dysentery and smallpox. Europeans were already familiar with malaria, but now encountered a more virulent form of the ague, or intermittent fever, than they had hitherto known. James Lind warned that 'the recent examples of the great mortality in hot climates, ought to draw the attention of all the commercial nations of Europe towards the important object of preserving the health of their countrymen, whose business carries them beyond seas', and stressed that 'unhealthy settlements require a constant supply of people, and of course drain their mother country of an incredible number, and some of its most useful inhabitants.'[48] Thomas Trotter believed not only that Europeans were congenitally unsuited to life in hot climates, but that their health would degenerate and their manliness be undermined by laziness, dissipation, and an addiction to luxury and leisure induced by the tropics.[49] Other doctors, such as John Hunter, believed that Europeans would adapt to such climates, becoming resistant to disease and even darkening in complexion over a number of generations.[50] They had already adapted their customs to suit the new environments that they were colonising, however dangerous to health the heat and humidity may have been deemed. Clothing was lighter. Houses were built with better ventilation and settlements were located on hills rather than on the coast. Marshes were drained and attempts made to make the environment more congenial to Europeans. Lind accepted that 'if any tract of land in Guinea was as well improved as the island of Barbados, and as perfectly freed from trees, shrubs, marshes, etc the air would be rendered equally healthful there, as in that pleasant West Indian island.' However, he still advised that 'the best preservative against the mischievous impressions of a putrid fog, a swampy, or of a marshy exhalation, is a close, sheltered and covered place; such as the lower apartments in a ship, or a house in which there are no doors or windows facing these swamps.'[51] By the 1790s it had become accepted that Europeans were unsuited to labouring in the tropics and could only form a class of overseers there, whereas Africans were much more resilient in the heat and suitable as labourers. Such beliefs could be used to defend the shipment of slaves across the Atlantic in pursuit of trade and colonial development.

It was not only sources of labour accustomed to working in hot climates that the slave trade carried unwillingly across the world to new homes. Just as in the sixteenth century smallpox had been taken to South America, where it had led to the destruction of great empires by striking at virgin populations, supposedly first introduced at Yucatan in 1519 by an African slave of the Spanish conquistadores, the slave trade brought new diseases to areas where they had previously been unknown. The slave trade may be connected with later smallpox outbreaks in colonial Brazil, with a strong correlation between epidemics in the parts of Africa from which the Portuguese got their slaves with those in Brazil. Drought and war between rival African tribes, the sale of captives in those wars to the Portuguese slave traders, and overcrowding on the voyages to Brazil all fostered the spread of the disease to the Portuguese colony.[52]

The mosquito was responsible for two of the diseases which especially hit tropical colonial areas hard, yellow fever and malaria, and which the slave trade probably brought to the New World. Malaria had long been thought to be the result of exposure to marshy air, which had an effect on the nervous system causing fever, vomiting and nausea. In 1846 the naval surgeon John Wilson described how a traveller might wander without fear of illness through the forests of Africa and America during the day but everything was different once night fell when 'death then, in the form of fever or miasm lurks in every corner, hovers around every bush, to the constitution that is unassimilated or the newcomer. Miasm, condensed and concentrated through the absence of light and heat, rises emanating from the debris and decomposition around, but, like the morning dew, through the influence of the sun, the great purgatory, the air and winds, which on anything aeriform or miasmal act, soon passes away, reduced to its original nothing.'[53] Until 1880, when the French army surgeon Alphonse Laveran identified the parasites *Plasmodium vivax* and *Plasmodium falciparum* which cause malaria, the disease was generally believed, like most fevers, to be caused by bad air. Only once its cause was understood and the role of the mosquito in its transmission demonstrated in 1898 by Ronald Ross, an officer in the Indian Medical Service, could it plausibly be linked with the exchange of diseases from the Old World to the New. There is no real evidence of it having been present in the Americas before European contact and colonisation. However, by the 1650s it was recorded along the eastern coasts of South and Central America, and by the 1680s it was being reported by English settlers in North America. Conditions in the plantations were especially favourable to the spread of malaria with slave labourers, cotton or tobacco plants, and animals settled in low-lying, poorly-drained areas that offered breeding-grounds for the mosquitoes which transmitted the disease. Negro slaves were considered to be less susceptible to malaria, but, despite popular beliefs, only some people of African descent have the sickle cell characteristics that protect against liver disease or death from malaria, and even fewer have the Duffy negative factor in their blood which confers immunity to *Plasmodium vivax*.[54]

The Old World may have imported malaria to the New, but it was the New World that provided the first effective remedy for the disease, when cuttings from the cinchona bark were taken from a Peruvian tree and carried back to Europe in 1632. This bark was soon found to provide relief from certain intermittent fevers. It was promoted by the Jesuits, and for a time there was the inevitable Protestant reaction against a Catholic cure, though it very quickly came into demand as a powerful remedy for the ague and was soon a standard in pharmacopoeia. By 1808 Peruvian bark in wine was widely used as a prophylactic against malaria in maritime medicine, but many doctors believed that 'blood letting is the best general practice in tropical fevers', since cinchona tasted bitter and its side effects included vomiting and diarrhoea.[55] It was not until 1820 that quinine was isolated from cinchona bark by the French physiologist François Magendie in collaboration with the pharmacist Pierre-Joseph Pelletier. Its value as a preventative measure became apparent during the Niger expedition of 1854, when quinine was described by the naval surgeon W B Baikie as 'the mainstay of the sufferer' since 'it not only cures, but . . . it actually prevents, and . . . by taking this invaluable drug while in unhealthy localities, persons may escape totally unscathed.' He recommended that it should be taken in the form of quinine wine taken twice daily.[56] Quinine remained the standard prophylactic for malaria until the introduction of mepacrine in 1932.

Yellow fever, a viral disease transmitted by mosquitoes, was probably another legacy brought from Africa, where it was endemic, by the slave trade to the colonies of the New World. Known variously as 'Barbados distemper', 'bleeding fever', and 'yellow jack' after the quarantine flag flown by ships, it is first documented outside Africa in Barbados in 1647, when there were five thousand deaths from a 'new distemper' characterised by black vomit and jaundice. This was at a time when Barbados was developing an economy based on sugar plantations in moist low-lying areas in which mosquitoes could breed and feed on the sucrose from cane syrup. These sugar plantations were worked by slaves, and in the 1640s there had been an acceleration in the import of slaves to Barbados. From the Caribbean, yellow fever moved northwards to New York in 1668, Philadelphia and Charleston in 1690 and Boston in 1691, as well as southwards to the ports of Columbia, Ecuador, and Peru. Although brought from Africa, it was Europeans who were most susceptible to yellow fever, possibly because the slaves already had acquired some immunity. From the Caribbean it reached the colonial powers of Spain and Portugal where there were several epidemics during the eighteenth and nineteenth centuries. However, it was in the Caribbean that it was most feared by Europeans who, unlike the black slaves and local white planters, had no immunity to it. The English attack on Martinique in 1693 collapsed in the face of yellow fever, and in 1741 Admiral Edward Vernon's abortive action at Cartagena resulted in the loss of almost half of his nineteen thousand men to yellow fever.[57] During an epidemic, yellow fever could be highly contagious, as on HMS *Termagant* where it broke out in 1856 after two men were taken on board in the West Indies after sleeping outside the barracks at Port Royal where there had been an outbreak; on the ship 'every sentry whose post was near the hospital, all the nurses and the men who were about the sick invariably took the disease.' The surgeon treated it by administering alcohol: 'champagne appeared to be very beneficial occasionally, but warm port was more generally serviceable. Brandy was generally disliked. Quinine wine was tried . . . with very little benefit.'[58]

Even more than the West Indies, West Africa remained unhealthy for the British seaman. After the abolition of the British slave trade in

1807, followed by the abolition of slavery in the British Empire in 1833, the Royal Navy maintained a squadron of ships off the west coast of Africa to suppress illegal slave trading. In 1847 Alexander Bryson described the West African Squadron as 'the most disagreeable, arduous and unhealthy service that falls to the lot of British officers and seamen, without, it is to be feared, much prospect of its coming to a speedy termination.'[59] The Squadron's principal base was the barren rocky island of Ascension which offered rest and refreshment after months of patrolling in the Gulf of Guinea and the Bight of Benin. There was a permanent hospital and a supply of fresh water. Futile attempts were made to establish other bases on the islands of St Thomas', Prince's and Fernando Po, which offered strategic positions for the interception of slavers, being close to the slaving ports of Lagos and Whydah and the outlets of the river slave routes of the Bonny, Calabar, Cameroons and Niger. The explorer Sir Richard Burton had recommended the erection of a naval hospital on Fernando Po, but this scenic island could be a death trap where 'officers and men are frequently tempted to wander both too far and too long by the shaded brooks which intersect the bush, forgetting that they may encounter the latent principles of fever in every step they take.'[60]

At sea yellow fever took its toll of the officers and ratings of the West African Squadron. On the *Eden,* 110 of the 160 men on board died between May and December 1829:

> The whole of the officers with the exception of the First Lieutenant and the gunner are either dead or confined to bed; the men are dying almost daily amidst incessant rain and frequent tornadoes accompanied with much thunder and lightning; the main deck is crowded with sick and constantly wet. The moral effect of these scenes became palpable in every countenance; while for want of medical attendance, the surgeon and two assistant surgeons having died, it was impossible to pay attention to the ventilation of the ship, or even to the personal comfort of the sick.[61]

Another surgeon was taken on board at Fernando Po, but before the ship could reach the cooler clime of St Helena the 'Lieutenant and Master held a survey on the Surgeon by the Captain's orders and found his intellect deranged, so that it was considered imprudent to interest him with the charge of the medicines or the sick.'[62] Only when the ship reached Ascension did the daily death roll come to a sudden stop.

Alexander Bryson suggested various ways of improving the health of the West African Squadron. He recommended the banning of shore leave in Freetown, capital of Sierra Leone, noted for its high rates of fever and the temptations it offered to the crews who forgot their sorrows in the raw native spirits. He also wished to limit the number of expeditions along the rivers by small boats, although these were popular with the men as a relief from the monotony of cruising along the coast. He advocated that the bilges be pumped out more frequently and washed with chloride of zinc, and that the decks should be washed less often in order to reduce humidity. Tarpaulins and awnings should be used to keep the ship dry, there should be a change of clothing for every sailor sent out in the patrol boats, and they should be given tea or coffee on their return to the ship. The result of these changes, according to Bryson himself in 1856, was that at Sierra Leone 'the orgies of the barn, which lowered the character of the white man in the eyes of the black, have long since ceased', and the general health of the squadron had improved.[63] Yet conditions on the slavers had perhaps worsened since the trade had become illegal, because the slavers were so anxious to escape interception that they no longer separated sick from healthy slaves, allowed them the minimum of rest or recreation, and tried to accomplish the Middle Passage as quickly as possible. The stench from them could be detected a mile away according to witnesses, and when the Squadron boarded a slaver they found horrific squalor. Bryson considered that 'there is perhaps not any condition in which human nature may be viewed in a more revolting aspect than in that of a crowded slave vessel with dysentery on board', which 'of all the horrors attending the Middle Passage, with the exception perhaps of smallpox, is the worst', and that 'the effluvium which issues from her decks, or rather prisons, is peculiar and sickening beyond conception, and is generally perceptible at a great distance to leeward.'[64]

James Cook, no opponent of slavery, was fully aware of the effects of Western colonialism during his exploration of the Pacific in 1773:

We debauch their morals already prone to vice and we introduce among them wants and perhaps diseases which they never before knew and which serves only to disturb that happy tranquillity they and their forefathers had enjoyed. If anyone denies the truth of this assertion let him tell me what the natives of the whole extent of America have gained from the commerce they have had with Europeans.[65]

1. The quarantine system at the harbour in Malta, at the crossroads of the eastern and western Mediterranean, was central to the control of seaborne infection and offered a model for quarantine elsewhere. (© National Maritime Museum, Greenwich, London, PU1723)

2. The surgeon's chest on the *Mary Rose,* with its syringes, pharmaceutical jars and medical instruments, offers a glimpse into medicine in the reign of Henry VIII. (*Mary Rose* Museum)

3. After the battle of Schoonevelt in 1673, the wounded were removed from the *Royal Prince* or treatment on a hospital ship or ashore. (© National Maritime Museum, Greenwich, London, PW6875)

4. The Royal Hospitals at Chelsea and Greenwich were founded for pensioners rather than wounded soldiers and sailors, but some of the pensioners from the rival institutions were able to compare military and naval injuries over a drink and smoke. (George Cruickshank cartoon, © National Maritime Museum, Greenwich, London, PAD8531)

5. The Sailor's Return might result in long term health problems in 1750 for the young fresh-faced sailor tempted by women and drink as he landed on shore. (© National Maritime Museum, Greenwich, London, PW3801)

. Haslar Naval Hospital was the
largest hospital and largest brick
building in the United Kingdom when
founded in the eighteenth century and
played a major part in naval medicine
until its closure in the twenty-first
century. (© National Maritime
Museum, Greenwich, London, PU1074)

A

# TREATISE

ON THE

# SCURVY.

## IN THREE PARTS.

CONTAINING

An Inquiry into the Nature, Caufes,
and Cure, of that Difeafe.

Together with

A Critical and Chronological View of what
has been publifhed on the Subject.

By *JAMES LIND*, M.D.

Fellow of the Royal College of Phyficians in *Edinburgh*,

The SECOND EDITION corrected, with Additions
and Improvements.

*L O N D O N:*

Printed for A. MILLAR in the *Strand*.

MDCCLVII.

. James Lind's 1757 *Treatise on Scurvy*
soon became a classic of naval
medicine and launched his reputation
as the father of naval medicine.
© National Maritime Museum,
Greenwich, London, D8264)

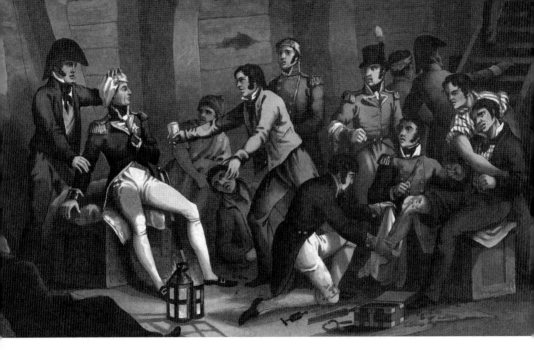

8. Horatio Nelson was treated with other casualties in the cockpit of the *Vanguard* after the battle of the Nile. (Charles Heath, © National Maritime Museum, Greenwich, London, PAD5574)
9. Wounded tars celebrated with a bandaged Nelson the victory of the battle of the Nile. (Thomas Rowlandson, © National Maritime Museum, Greenwich, London, PW3892)

He might equally have been writing of the lessons of the slave trade, from which in terms of health and happiness, neither the enslaved nor the seamen transporting this human freight, never mind the sailors charged with suppressing this inhuman trade, ever gained anything but misery.

# CHAPTER SEVEN

# *Huddled Masses*

IT TOOK COURAGE to decide to make a new life on an unfamiliar continent, but for the nineteenth-century emigrant the voyage could be hazardous enough in itself, even before the task of building a new life in an unknown land could begin, especially for those travelling in the horrors of steerage. Many of them lay huddled together, described by the pioneer historian of American immigration Oscar Handlin as 'seafaring adventurers out to discover new continents, amidst the retching noisome stench, the stomach-turning filth of hundreds of bodies confined in close quarters.'[1] Passage from Europe to America in the days of sail could take six weeks if sailing conditions were good and even up to a hundred days if the winds were adverse or the weather stormy. Hundreds of steerage passengers were crammed together indiscriminately in cramped, dimly-lit, ill-ventilated, un-hygienic compartments. The voyage to Australia, lasting around twenty-two weeks, took even longer. For the emigrant, the voyage was not to be undertaken lightly.

Between the end of the French Wars in 1815 and the outbreak of the American Civil War in 1860, the bulk of European emigration was from the British Isles, Germany and Scandinavia, areas where changes from agrarian to industrial economies had given an impetus to movement from the countryside to towns and to other countries in search of new livelihoods and greater opportunities. By the end of the nineteenth century most emigration to the United States came from southern and eastern Europe. Emigrants from the Austro-Hungarian Empire, Greece and southern Italy were often unskilled labourers seeking an escape from the breakdown of peasant economies, whereas those from the Russian and the Ottoman Empires were also in search of political and religious freedom. Emigration also offered an escape from such natural disasters as earthquakes and famine. The British government was quick to see the value of emigration as a remedy for social distress and a safety-valve for economic discontent, encouraging the Irish to seek refuge from the potato famine of the 1840s in other continents rather than flock to England.[2] Australia was first seen as a dumping ground for convicts and later as a continent ripe for colonisation. Emigration to Australia was government-sponsored. People who wished to go to North America did so of their own volition and through their own efforts. Emigrants cannot easily be characterised but were mostly young, economically active, and ambitious to build a better life, prepared for the hardship of a sea journey to what they hoped was a land of promise.

Convicts being transported to Australia had few hopes of anything but the unknown when they left their native shores. The conditions facing the early travellers on the convict ships, which began to transport prisoners to Australia in 1787, were worse than those on slave ships, where the master of the ship at least had a financial interest in ensuring that his valuable human cargo arrived intact. On convict ships it may even have been commercially profitable if some of the men, women and children being transported were to die, since the master could then sell their victuals at inflated prices in the new colony at Botany Bay. Private contractors were paid £18 for each convict they carried, whether dead or alive. In order to ensure that more care would be taken of the convicts during the voyage, the British Government began to pay a bonus of £4 10s 6d for each convict landed in good health. Even such a generous financial incentive did not stop the master of the *Atlas* and those of other ships from carrying so much private cargo for sale in Australia that the scuttles could not be opened, with the result that the atmosphere below deck was so foul that candles were extinguished by it.[3] The first convict fleet of 1787 took on board 568 male and 191 female convicts in a squalid, semi-naked state. Sixteen of them died of gaol fever (typhus) before they even left Portsmouth, and twenty more died during the 250-day voyage, with a further ninety-three being landed sick. Typhus had spread at sea and each night the women convicts had to be battened down in their foetid quarters, since 'the hatches over the places where they lay could not be suffered to be laid off, during the night, without a promiscuous intercourse immediately taking place between them and the seamen and marines.'[4] Of the 6,634 convicts transported between 1787 and 1800, one in 8.57 of the men and one in 28.2 of the women died.[5]

The scandal of the convict ships came to a head in 1814 when fifty-four men on board the *Surrey* died of typhus on the voyage to Sydney, including the master, both mates and the surgeon. The remaining crew were unable to bring the ship into harbour. Typhus had appeared within a fortnight of the ship's sailing. The ship was fumigated, but the convicts had not been issued with soap, in order that it could be sold for a profit on arrival; their wine rations had been similarly withheld. Only twenty convicts were allowed to exercise at any one time, because the master was afraid that they might mutiny. Lachlan Macquarie, Governor of New South Wales, immediately asked William Redfern, an Assistant Colonial Surgeon, to report on what had happened. Redfern had himself been transported in 1801 for his part in the Nore mutinies of 1797 when, as the nineteen-year-old surgeon's mate on the *Standard,* he had urged the mutineers to unite. His sentence of death had been commuted to transportation on account of his youth and he had then worked as an assistant surgeon at the Norfolk Island penal settlement. After being pardoned in 1803, he had continued to practise as a surgeon and in 1808 joined the Colonial Medical Establishment at Sydney, where one of his achievements had been the building of a new general hospital. Redfern had the ideal background to investigate the conditions on the *Surrey* and make recommendations for the better medical treatment of prisoners. He considered it 'only to be wondered at that so few died', but saw the voyage of the *Surrey* as 'an awful and useful lesson'. His recommendations were that there should be a more generous allowance of wine and lemon juice to prevent scurvy, better and cleaner clothing, regular exercise, and that the spread of 'the most subtle poison' of typhus should be prevented by 'an effusion of cold water over the body.' By far the most important of his recommendations was that the surgeon should be given the authority to challenge brutal, incompetent, or drunken captains and to enforce strict standards of sanitation and hygiene.[6] These recommendations were accepted and the surgeon-superintendent was to play a part in maintaining the health of the convict ships until the end of transportation in 1868.

The surgeon-superintendent on a convict ship, appointed by the Admiralty from naval surgeons on half pay, had the power to make recommendations on when the convicts should be unfettered and allowed to take exercise and enjoy the fresh air on deck, the issue of rations, the punishment of offences, and even the placing of guards. Convicts were now medically examined by the surgeon before embarking and anyone suffering from an infectious disease was not allowed on board the ship. Those allowed to embark were washed, shaved, and given a clean uniform. The decks were holy-stoned and scrubbed regularly during the voyage and the quarters of the convicts fumigated. Conditions were now better for the convicts but that did not make them any easier to deal with. After the suppression of a mutiny by the convicts on board the *Chapman,* the surgeon was afraid to go below deck to dress the wounds inflicted on the prisoners by the guards because of the vicious character of the mutineers, a defence accepted by Governor Macquarie of New South Wales when he arrested the surgeon and captain for their callous behaviour towards their charges.[7] In 1823 Surgeon Hall complained that 'six women conspired to murder me', spurred on by the offer of a bottle of rum from the mate, 'and did actually form a mutiny of an alarming nature, in which I was knocked down in the prison, beaten and kicked.'[8] Nevertheless, the surgeon did help to civilise the convicts, sometimes even organising church services and school classes for them, all of which significantly improved the health and morals of the people transported to Australia.

James Mitchell, the surgeon-superintendent on the convict ship *Guildford*, could congratulate himself on arrival in New South Wales in July 1822 on the 'healthy state' in which the convicts were landed and that

> the number of sick on this voyage was comparatively small when it is taken into account the number of guards and convicts (in all 232) cooped up within a small place and for such a length of time, and that for the safety of the ship the prisoners were only allowed on deck in divisions, added to this the greater part of them were ones who had led a rustic life and were accustomed to a vegetable diet.[9]

His successor on the *Guildford* Charles Linton considered the victuals to be 'without exception of excellent quality', and that the convicts' quarters were well-ventilated, but was more critical of the ventilation of the hospital because it was below the forecastle. However, he considered exercise to be even more vital than ventilation, urging that 'the whole of the prisoners, except such as it may be found necessary to retain in irons as a punishment for crimes or refractory conduct committed on board, ought to be released from their fetters at a very early period' to get exercise and fresh air as much as possible, avoiding 'the intense heat of the day'.[10] The success of the system of control of health and hygiene on convict ships is summed up by the comments of William McDowell, surgeon on the *Lady East* in 1825, that his charges 'were not sufficiently ill to be considered worthy of giving a minute description of' in his medical journal, 'with the exception of a considerable number of trifling cases such as constipation of their bowels or requiring cathartics and medicine occasionally'.[11]

The health and dietary systems used on convict ships offered a model for maintaining health on the government-assisted emigrant passages to Australia which started in 1831 and were funded by the sale of land in the colony to wealthy settlers. The ships on which these emigrants sailed were tightly regulated by the Colonial Land and Emigration Commission from 1840 and had to carry a qualified surgeon. At first naval surgeons were employed, many of them with experience on the convict ships although with little familiarity with pregnant mothers, children and babies. After 1840 the Emigration Commission preferred to employ civilian doctors. These doctors were to play an important role in maintaining the health of the emigrants, from the first medical inspection at the medical depot to screen out the unfit and sick to arrival in New South Wales. Not all of them were as concerned about their charges as they ought to have been. Samuel Archer, the 21-year-old surgeon on SS *Great Britain* in 1857, was more interested in natural history than in his passengers, and had to be recalled to the ship from the beach, where he was searching for shells during a stop at Mindelo, in order to treat a coaler who had fractured his skull when struck by a winch handle; he was perhaps as concerned that the previous day his white trousers had been soaked and caked with sand so that he 'much resembled a bricklayer' more than a surgeon.[12] The surgeon was responsible not only for dispensing medicine and dealing with injuries but ensuring that 'the between decks were kept perfectly dry during the whole period of the voyage' through daily dry scraping and sanding of the decks, and occasional fumigation 'by pouring hot vinegar over the chloride of lime, which at all times had the effect of destroying any latent or unpleasant effluvia.'[13]

Many of the diseases with which the surgeon had to deal were minor, such as diarrhoea, constipation, and seasickness, for which the cure on the emigrant ship *Adam Lodge* in 1839 was the issue of a gill of wine daily to each adult.[14] When a more serious infectious illness struck, the surgeon had to act swiftly. Scarlatina presented itself on board the *Maitland* two days out from England on 26 June 1838. John Smith, the surgeon, immediately examined all the children as soon as he had diagnosed the first case, and ordered every sufferer to be sent to the hospital. However, 'there was a great reluctance evinced by some parents to the admitting of their children into the hospital', and the parents succeeded in thwarting the efforts of the surgeon, 'all remonstrance having been unavailing, and all attempts at coercion were interdicted'.[15] Children, not surprisingly, formed the majority of the passengers who died on the assisted passages to Australia. Three-quarters of all the assisted migrants dying at sea were under the age of six.[16] In 1838, Sarah Brunskill, sailing from Plymouth, lost her son from diarrhoea and her daughter from measles in the course of one day, two weeks into the voyage: 'two little angels they looked, so beautiful in death'.[17] Death also became a commonplace for Ellen Moger in 1839. She lost three children, even though at first her husband 'Edward and the children suffered but little from sickness'. As the voyage went on the 'dear children' were 'gradually getting weaker and, for want of proper nourishment, became at last sorrowful spectacles to behold.' The loss of her children 'overpowered me and from the weakness of my frame, reduced me to such a low nervous state that, for many weeks, I was not expected to survive.' Sarah Brunskill witnessed twenty burials at sea and Ellen Moger thirty, mainly of children. Mrs Moger was disturbed by 'the sad tolling of a bell informing you some poor victim to sickness and privation was about to be launched to a watery grave; such events are not uncommon, but the mind, I assure you, soon becomes hardened and callous on board a ship.'[18]

The passengers also suffered if the ship proved unfit to be at sea. In 1846 the *Robert Isaacs* had to put back to the Azores after six weeks at sea and was 'condemned as unseaworthy'. The passengers were returned to Southampton, rather than Liverpool from whence they had first sailed, and the Colonial Land and Emigration Officer dispatched an official 'to afford any assistance in his power to the distressed emigrants', but it was the inhabitants of Southampton who had risen to the occasion with 'the prompt and efficient charity displayed by them' in the provision of accommodation, clothing, medical care, and assistance in returning them to their original homes.[19] The people of Belfast showed similar concern for typhus patients on the *Swatara*, when it put into that port in March 1847 with a sick passenger who was admitted to the local hospital through the efforts of Lieutenant Starke, the local Emigration Agent. By early April there were twenty such cases on the ship, and the Roman Catholic bishop assisted Lieutenant Starke in persuading all the passengers to disembark, so that the ship could be properly cleaned and fumigated, while the public authorities of Belfast made available empty buildings for the sick passengers. By this time the passengers were using up their own stores of provisions and had no money to restock them. Lieutenant Starke raised a subscription to help them and the people of Belfast responded generously. On 17 April the *Swatara* sailed for Australia, leaving behind all passengers showing any signs of typhus although 'the misfortune of the sick was that they lost their passage and had no right to demand a return of their passage money.' The only aid they had was that the captain of the ship had filled the vacant berths with new emigrants from Belfast, and had left the proceeds for the benefit of the sick passengers left behind.[20] Yet, despite all the problems facing the emigrant to Australia, the regulatory framework of assisted passages meant a higher chance of survival than on the shorter, unregulated crossing to North America.[21]

In the early nineteenth century the cheapest passages, costing as little as thirty shillings from Ireland to Quebec, were on board leaky timber ships, castigated by an official enquiry into shipwrecks in 1839 as 'some of the worst kinds of ship afloat'. Much more expensive and relatively safer were the American merchant ships of the Black Ball and Red Swallowtail lines sailing from Liverpool. Yet even these well-built, fast packets were ill-suited for the transport of passengers, being designed primarily for the carriage of cargo. The textiles and iron they carried westwards to the United States took up less space than the raw cotton or tobacco that they brought to Britain, allowing thrifty ship owners to lay temporary decks over the cargo in the lower hold. Fitted out with rough pine berths and stocked with sufficient provisions and water for the voyage, these temporary decks allowed for the transport of passengers as yet another lucrative form of freight. Here hundreds of passengers were berthed together without regard to any distinction of sex or age, since it was the custom of many shipowners to 'leave the whole deck on which emigrants were berthed undivided in any way'.[22] Even when berths were divided up, they were only separated from each other by a nine-inch plank, which meant that when the berths were filled with bedding the division was no longer apparent, leaving 'men, women and children in one promiscuous heap'.[23] Robert Whyte, travelling on a ship from Ireland to Quebec, felt that 'the Black Hole of Calcutta was a mercy compared to the holds of these vessels. Yet simultaneously foreigners, Germans from Hamburg and Bremen are arriving, all healthy robust and cheerful.'[24]

Such overcrowding raised concern about morality rather than about the spread of disease. Proposals were put forward for the sake of decency that the steerage should be divided into three distinct compartments. Single men would be forward and single women aft, with married couples travelling amidships to separate the two. Government-sponsored emigrants to Australia were divided up in this way, but paying travellers themselves opposed such a scheme, preferring to travel in family groups or with people they knew. Parents especially 'feared the contamination of their daughters, if removed from under their own eye, by improper characters among the single women who might be on board'.[25] The 1852 British Passengers' Act contented itself with separating single men from the other passengers, but that did not stop one cabin passenger, William Hancock, from observing that sexual activities seemed to be the main diversion of those in steerage, with 'most of the arrangements, or lack of such, being such as to permit of the most unrestricted intercourse and placing modesty and decency at a discount'.[26]

Immorality was a lesser consideration for ship owners in opposing the partition of steerage than the problems of ventilation that it could cause. The only way of ventilating steerage had originally been by means of the hatches which had to be battened down in rough seas. It was little wonder that in Canada 'the harbour master's boatman had no difficulty at the distance of gunshot . . . in distinguishing by the odour alone a crowded emigrant ship.'[27] The 1848 American Passenger Act laid down that every steerage compartment should have at least two ventilators and that hatchways should be able to be left permanently open. Many of the new packet ships after this date were fitted with iron ventilating tubes capable of functioning in all weathers, though many of these were blocked up by the passengers to keep out the cold. The Act also laid down a legal minimum of space for each passenger. As a consequence of this, new three-decker ships were built with two steerage compartments stacked one above the other, with the result that the lowest deck was now darker and more airless than before, and the upper steerage passengers suffered from the stench and effluvium rising from below.

Conditions on the iron-screw steamships which gradually took over the transatlantic routes were an improvement on those faced by passengers on the sailing ships, but infectious disease remained the scourge of steerage. Although steamships were beginning to carry mail, freight, and a small number of cabin passengers from the 1840s, it was only in the 1852 that the Inman Line regularly began to carry steerage passengers in large numbers. Soon even the more prestigious Cunard, National and Collins Lines followed suit in the hope of profiting from the large numbers of emigrants leaving Europe for North America. Even though the fare of six guineas for passage in steamship steerage was double the cost of travel on a sailing ship, crossings were now taking less than fourteen days and so were preferred by the majority of emigrants.[28] Seasonal migration across the Atlantic became a realistic option, and skilled workmen moved backwards and forwards in search of work, or to make their fortunes in America so as to establish themselves more securely at home. The Lancet reported that now for the vast majority of passengers on such ships 'the middle passage has very few horrors'.[29] Steerage passengers were all accommodated in compartments containing about twenty berths, with single men, single women and married couples separated from each other for the sake of decency. Joseph Chamberlain at the Board of Trade urged that every emigrant ship with a significant number of single women should have 'a woman of character and experience in the position of a matron'.[30] Nevertheless, the berths were only two feet wide and passengers had to provide their own straw mattresses that were thrown overboard at the end of the voyage. On many ships there was little room for luggage and all but the essentials went into the hold, with the result that many men wore their one suit of clothing, stained by rain, seawater, food, urine and vomit, throughout the whole passage with little opportunity of cleaning either themselves or their garments. After a few days, according to the Italian medical inspector Teodorico Rosati, the dormitories were 'reduced to a dog kennel'.[31] On one British ship in 1888 there were sixteen people in one cabin that was so narrow that there was no room for a 'stout man to pass', and the cabins were soon 'fouled with vomit.'[32] The Board of Trade found that steerage conditions for poorly-clad and rough-mannered passengers in 1881 were such as to elicit 'feelings both of pity and disgust', although they were no worse than 'the crowded cottage of an English labourer, the close, narrow garret of the workman, or the cabin of the Connemara peasant'.[33] Moreover, any improvement in these conditions would mean a rise in fares beyond the means of most emigrants.

Food and water were frequently as foul as the environment in which they were consumed. Since 1815 there had been a legal requirement for emigrant ships to carry provisions for their passengers and an official scale of victuals was laid down. Many emigrants, however, preferred to take their own food rather than buy food from the shipping company. Irish emigrants, in particular, would take with them a bag of potatoes, a sack of oatmeal and a few dried herrings, but rarely had enough to last the whole journey. When provisions ran low, some passengers were reduced to stealing from each other's stores, and eventually most were forced into buying food at exorbitant prices from the ship's captain. In 1842 the British Government introduced regulations for the issue of provisions by the ship, though the scale only provided for seven pounds of food for each person a week, half of it in bread or ship's biscuit and the other half in potatoes. Gradually the scale was extended to include pork, beef, flour, rice, tea, sugar and molasses, but this was not often of the highest quality. William Mure, the British consul at New Orleans, had reported to the Colonial Office that on most ships arriving from Liverpool, 'the bread is mostly condemned bread, ground over with a little fresh flour, sugar and saleratus[34] and re-baked. It would kill a horse.' He attributed an outbreak of fever on the *Blanche* in 1850 to the poor quality of the pork. Unscrupulous captains were using the provisioning system for their personal gain. The master of the *Blanche* charged grossly inflated prices for necessities, practising 'a most disgraceful system of extortion.'[35] In October 1850, the officers of the Black Star liner *Washington* did not issue anything but water to the passengers on the first two days of the voyage, and when food was distributed the emigrants receiving it were 'cursed and abused, cuffed and kicked by the mates' as they waited for their provisions. Passengers who bribed the cook with money or whisky were treated to five or six cooked meals a day, but less favoured passengers were lucky to get a hot dinner on alternate days. As a result twelve children died from dysentery 'brought on by want of nourishing food.'[36] The captain of the *Bache McEver,* sailing to New Orleans from Cork, had gone even further in so far as he had 'conducted himself harshly and in an improper manner to some of the female passengers ... having held out the inducement of better rations to two who were almost starving in the hope that they would accede to his infamous designs.'[37]

Even when they were issued with sufficient provisions without any attempts by the ship's crew to take advantage of their passengers, seasickness often prevented many voyagers from cooking for themselves the food necessary to their health. After 1852 all emigrant ships leaving the ports of the United Kingdom were required to carry cooked rather than raw food. The American Passenger Act of 1855 also adopted this regulation, which now became standard on all emigrant ships. Such legislation, however, could not improve the quality of the food. Emigrants, 'squatting on the decks near the stairs, with a plate between the legs and a piece of bread between the feet, ate their pasta like beggars at the doors of convents' on some Italian vessels as late as 1908.[38] By this time many of the better ships now had dining rooms in which steerage passengers could eat in more comfort than on deck or at their berths.

Water was stored in wooden casks that might previously have contained oil, vinegar, turpentine, molasses or wine with the result that it was often tainted by the container. The Reverend William Bell, travelling from Leith to Quebec on board the *Rothiemurchus* in 1817, complained that 'our water for some time past has been very bad' and that 'when it was drawn out of the casks was no cleaner than that of a dirty kennel after a shower of rain, so that its appearance alone was sufficient to sicken one.' He also found that 'it had such a rancid smell that to be in the same neighbourhood was enough to turn the stomach.'[39] By 1848, little had changed and this 'want of pure water was sensibly felt by the afflicted creatures.'[40] Within a few years, though, the problem of contaminated water was solved once it began to be stored in iron tanks.

Effluence was a perennial problem. On the better ships there were separate lavatories for men and women, fitted with washbasins and provided with both cold and hot water, 'essential to the comfort of the passengers and conducive to health.'[41] Generally, there were never enough water closets for the large number of passengers carried. The *Angelo,* carrying emigrants from Sweden to England for subsequent passage to America in 1881, had small, cramped lavatories with no water for flushing which were condemned as 'more evil-smelling, unsatisfactory places it is difficult to imagine.'[42] One ship in 1888 had toilets consisting of five seats over a trough without any partitions to give even a minimum of privacy; this facility was on the same deck as the ship's hospital, which did nothing to improve hygiene for the sick. On the same ship there were no closets below deck, and 'passengers sometimes make use of the alleyway which forms a sort of gutter around the ship.' As a result the bilge was fouled and became putrescent, producing noxious gases which travelled upwards 'compromising the health not merely of the steerage but also the first class passengers.' Public health officials commented wryly that 'there is no such thing as steerage bilge. Class distinctions cannot be maintained in what is practically the ship's sewer.'[43] A voyager on an Italian ship in the same year, E De Amicis complained that 'the place that should have been the cleanest was a horror, with only one bath for 1,500 third class passengers'.[44]

It was not surprising that in such conditions ship fever or typhus was prevalent. In 1848, 17.08 per cent of the 89,738 passengers who left the United Kingdom for Quebec died of typhus, 5,293 during their passage and a further 10,037 in Canadian hospitals. The death rate was particularly bad on the *Virginius*, sailing from Liverpool, which lost 158 of its 476 passengers during the voyage. Of the surviving passengers, 106 were unloaded at Grosse Island suffering from typhus, 'ghastly, yellow-looking spectres, unshaven and hollow-cheeked'.[45] 'Feeble and tottering' as they landed, the survivors were a reminder that 'the worst horrors of the slave trade which it is the boast or the ambition of this Empire to suppress, at any cost, have been re-enacted in the flight of British subjects from their native shores.'[46] William Smith, a

Manchester weaver, crossing from Liverpool to New York on the *India*, saw 'the tear of sympathy run down the cheek of many a hardened sailor' at hearing the 'heart-rending cries of wives at the losses of their husbands, the agonies of husbands at the sight of the corpses of their wives, and the lamentations of fatherless and motherless children; brothers and sisters dying, leaving their aged parents without means of support in their declining years'. Typhus had first struck the ship within a week of leaving Liverpool, carrying off the captain and twenty-six passengers. A further 122 passengers were stricken during the eight-week-long journey, including William Smith himself.[47]

Cholera, in which violent diarrhoea, cramps, and vomiting were usually followed by death within hours, was even more malignant and feared. It was especially prevalent on the ships taking 'coolies' (unskilled labourers) from India to the West Indies, where it was believed that Indian labourers were better suited to the climate than Europeans, just as in the days of the slave trade it had been assumed that African slaves were best suited to the temperatures and humidity. It was recognised by the Colonial Office that very little could be done to keep the emigrant ships free of cholera, since Calcutta was 'never quite free from cholera and . . . to insist on perfect health at the depot would be tantamount to stopping the emigration altogether.'[48] The problem was that, in their eagerness to find employment overseas, many of the emigrants hid any symptoms of disease when they were inspected by medical officers before boarding the ship and then, having brought the disease on board, did not seek medical help until too late. The food provided on the ships was based on European tastes and did not appeal to Indians; it was believed that the Bengali coolies suffered when fed on sea biscuit because they were more used to rice, just 'as is often the case with Irish and Scotch Emigrants who have been accustomed to potatoes.' Death rates from cholera were high among children on these coolie emigrant ships and it was thought that restricting the number of children travelling might reduce the incidence of cholera. However, if there were restrictions on the size of families allowed to emigrate from India, it was recognised that there would be labour shortages in the West Indies and that the maintenance of good health, through well-ventilated accommodation, adequate privies, nutritious food and medical care was 'so important to the future continuance of emigration and to the well-being of the West India Colonies.' The paradox was that shipboard mortality could have been kept down if there were fewer child passengers, but there would have been labour shortages if families were not allowed to emigrate together:

A large number of children, especially if under six or seven years of age, must be undesirable in a sanitary point of view in Indian as in English emigration, and it would therefore be advisable that the Emigration Officer should as far as possible exclude families having more than a certain proportion of young children. But his doing so will necessarily impede him filling his ships.'[49]

Cholera spread rapidly from India through Asia, Russia and Eastern Europe, reaching Western Europe in the 1830s. It first appeared in England in October 1831, brought to Sunderland by ship from Hamburg or Riga. By February 1832 there were epidemics in Newcastle, Edinburgh and London. The disease first crossed the Atlantic with emigrants on the brig *Carrick* sailing from Dublin in April 1832. Of the 173 passengers, forty-two died of cholera before arriving at Quebec on 3 June. By 23 June cholera had entered the United States through the ports of New York and Philadelphia. In a later epidemic in 1848, cholera again crossed the Atlantic by ship to New York and New Orleans before spreading through North America. It reached San Francisco in 1850 by ship from Panama. As with so many other infectious diseases before it, cholera spread rapidly on the ships plying the oceans.[50] Not surprisingly, it took a heavy toll on the crowded emigrant ships. The *Brutus* set sail from Liverpool on 18 May 1832 with 330 apparently healthy emigrants. On 27 May cholera broke out and by 3 June there had been so many deaths that it was decided that the ship should return to its port of origin. By the time it reached Liverpool again on 13 June there had been 117 cases of cholera and eighty-one deaths. In 1853, of the seventy-seven ships that set sail from Liverpool for New York, forty-six were stricken with cholera and 1,328 emigrants died of it. On the *Washington,* a hundred of the 898 passengers died. In 1866, the newly-built steamship *England,* carrying a thousand passengers from Liverpool to New York, lost forty passengers at sea and 227 at Halifax, where it put into port; thousands more died in port during the Hamburg cholera epidemic of 1892. Significantly, many of the passengers on the ships with outbreaks of cholera from 1853 onwards came from Germany or central European regions where cholera was already raging when they left home.[51]

Quarantine was the knee-jerk reaction of many continental European governments to the threat of infectious disease. The Habsburg Empire had long prided itself on being a cordon sanitaire against infection, literal and metaphorical, political and medical, from the East. The response of the German Empire to the 1892 cholera epidemic was to build control stations along its eastern frontiers with Russia and Austria-Hungary. Emigrants from Eastern Europe were medically examined before they could pass through Germany to any of the ports from which they could take a ship directly across the Atlantic or in transit to the British ports to begin their ocean voyage. The British tradition was more liberal and laissez faire, though the need to control infection made some coercive action a necessity. In 1849, the General Board of Health had recommended that the quarantining of ships and passengers infected with cholera, yellow fever and typhus should be suspended on the grounds that such diseases were caused by 'epidemic atmospheres' which might cover thousands of miles, though only affect unwholesome spots within them. Sir John Simon, Medical Officer of the Privy Council, in 1865 criticised the quarantine regulations as 'a mere irrational derangement of commerce', which interfered with foreign trade but could not prevent the importation of infectious diseases from abroad.[52] By the end of the nineteenth century the quarantine system, based on Acts of Parliament passed between 1710 and 1825 and administered by Customs officials, was in decline and was finally abolished by the 1896 Public Health (Ports) Act. Port Sanitary Authorities were now made responsible for the medical inspection of ships and were given the power to detain vessels carrying infectious diseases until the vessels could be disinfected and provision made for the isolation of the sick.[53]

In the United States immigrants were blamed for having brought in disease as part of a nativist Anglo-Saxon Protestant response to an influx of Roman Catholic and Jewish incomers from southern and eastern Europe. Not only were they blamed for having imported cholera, typhus, and even plague, but they were seen as reservoirs of infection which made them a threat to public health. The Irish were blamed for the cholera epidemics of 1832 and 1849. Catholicism was actually linked with poverty, corruption, and disease. The direct connection between the importation of epidemic disease and immigration was given added force by the acceptance of the germ theory of disease at the end of the nineteenth century.[54] The Marine Hospital Service, originally founded to provide medical care for merchant seamen,[55] took on the role of being 'watchdogs at the gate' charged with screening out such undesirables as 'all idiots, insane persons, paupers or persons likely to become public charges, persons suffering from a loathsome or dangerous contagious disease'.[56]

After 1892, transatlantic immigrants arriving in New York had to negotiate the obstacle of medical inspection at Ellis Island before they could enter the New World of promise, despite the words 'give me your tired, your poor, your huddled masses . . . the wretched refuse of your teeming shore' inscribed on the base of the nearby Statue of Liberty. The State of New York had established an Emigration Commission in 1847 when thousands of fevered Irish immigrants were arriving each day. The management of the Marine Hospital at Staten Island was taken over by the Emigration Commission and an Emigrant Hospital and Refuge was established on Ward's Island in the East River, but New Yorkers were hostile to the landing of any passengers suffering from any disease, and in 1858 the Marine Hospital on Staten Island was burned down by its neighbours, who feared the outbreak of typhus and smallpox. However, in 1855 an Emigrant Landing Depot had been opened at Castle Garden in Manhattan where medical inspections could take place, and the arrival of the immigrants could be handled in an orderly fashion. In 1892 the Federal Bureau of Immigration opened a new immigrant depot on Ellis Island, whose isolation made it easier to screen and keep out undesirables. Immigrants were often bullied by officials. Monsignor Giovanni Battista Scalabrini, bishop of Piacenza, witnessed in 1901 an official aim a stick at the legs of an Italian immigrant, laden with two heavy suitcases, because he was not quick enough in moving when ordered to do so; the bishop feared that the force of the blow could have broken the man's legs. The unfortunate immigrant had then put down his cases and hit the official in retaliation, swearing that 'if I had a gun I would have killed him.' Scalabrini reflected that it would be better if the officials in their treatment of new immigrants could 'instil in them a sense of confidence in their new country on arrival, instead of treating them like animals or worse', though he admitted that his fellow countrymen, in particular, were generally regarded as rough-mannered 'without any protection from the contempt of others'.[57]

Whatever their ethnic origins, for most emigrants their experience of Ellis Island was 'the nearest earthly likeness to the final Day of Judgement, when we have to prove our fitness to enter Heaven', as described by Stephen Graham who had travelled to New York with Russian immigrants in 1913.[58] On arrival in the imposing main inspection hall, the immigrants, wearing identity tags corresponding to their numbers on the ship's manifest, queued up before two United States Public Health Service doctors, the first of whom inspected them for physical or mental abnormalities. Chalk marks were put on the right shoulder of anyone suspected of a defect: 'b' for back problems, 'c' for conjunctivitis, 'g' for goitre, 'k' for hernia, 'l' for lameness, and 'x' for mental illness were among the most common marks made. The second doctor was looking for the symptoms of contagious disease. The scalp would be examined for evidence of lice or scabs that might indicate the presence of the contagious skin condition fauvus. Buttonhooks were used to inspect the linings of the eyelids for signs of trachoma, a blinding disease responsible for more than half of the detentions, although many cases went undetected because there was little time for symptoms to develop on a relatively short steamer journey between inspection on departure from Europe and on arrival at Ellis Island. Trachoma, especially prevalent in Russia and Poland, was viewed as a Jewish disease by many immigration officials.[59] Anyone failing the initial examination had to undergo a more thorough examination, including anyone suspected of mental deficiency or feeble-mindedness. Any of the detained immigrants suffering from an infectious disease was admitted to the infirmary on Ellis Island. Yet between 1890 and 1924, less than one per cent of immigrants were returned to their ports of origin on medical grounds, with never more than three per cent in any one year in that period.[60]

The low numbers of immigrants refused admission to the United States owed much to the medical checks they were compelled to undergo even before they left Europe. It was in the interest of the shipping lines to ensure that their passengers were healthy and free of any infectious diseases before they boarded ship. Any emigrants refused entry into the United States had to be returned to the port of embarkation at the expense of the shipping company. Not only was it necessary to have a doctor on board the emigrant ship to ensure the health of the passenger during the voyage, but safeguards needed to be taken in port before embarkation. At Liverpool, Cunard provided free accommodation in hotels for emigrants awaiting embarkation, which were visited daily by a company doctor to carry out medical examinations. Other European countries were more rigorous in their precautions against carrying ill or diseased passengers who might be rejected. At Rotterdam, the Holland-America Line opened a comfortable emigrant hotel, but before they could be admitted to it, newly-arrived intending emigrants had to undergo the indignity of medical examination and disinfection in an observation shed. Their clothes were disinfected, while they took an antiseptic bath and had their hair shampooed with a mixture of soft soap, carbolic acid, creolin and petroleum. The hair of the men and boys was close cropped with clippers.[61] Compulsory bathing and fumigation also faced travellers arriving at the Auswandererhallen built in 1900 by the Hamburg-

Amerika Line on the island of Veddel near Hamburg. Here the strict sanitary and medical supervision of the emigrants was a response to the 1892 cholera epidemic, which many Hamburgers had blamed on Russian emigrants passing through the port of Hamburg. Only once the passengers and their luggage had both been thoroughly disinfected were they allowed to pass to the 'clean side' of the emigrant depot, with its dormitories, hotels, shops, restaurants, and churches. Each morning trumpets heralded the beginning of the doctors' rounds and all residents were expected to undergo repeated medical checks until the final medical inspection shortly before embarkation. The disinfection facilities and sewage system were built to the latest technical standards, though allowance had to be made for those of the emigrants, 'some of them from rather uncultivated regions', a euphemism for Russians and Poles, who 'don't know how to use water closets'.[62] Doctors ensured that public health was maintained in these transient communities, deliberately isolated from the world around them.

Emigrant ships also had to carry doctors by law from the middle of the nineteenth century. Medical provision in the Royal Navy had offered the initial model for medical provision on board civilian shipping. The Admiralty had stipulated that convict ships should carry a surgeon since 1815, and from the 1830s government-chartered emigrant ships, mainly to Australia, adopted similar regulations. Other emigrant passenger ships, though not all of them, followed this model. It was not until the passage of the 1854 Merchant Shipping Act that all British ships were required to carry medical equipment and stores, and all British passenger ships with more than a hundred people on board were required to carry a qualified surgeon.[63] The 1855 Passenger Act made it mandatory for all passenger ships to have a medically-qualified doctor, proper dispensary and hospital accommodation, all of which were examined by the port authorities at the start of the voyage. Other ships were not required to carry a doctor, but were expected to have the necessary medical supplies.[64] After 1867, ships without doctors were issued with medical guides, giving plain instructions as to treatment and the dispensing of medicines, by the Board of Trade.[65] A scale of medical supplies and comforts was laid down for ships depending on the number of passengers,[66] but many shipping companies prided themselves on exceeding the regulations both in diet and medical supplies,[67] though others complained that 'the new scale is quite out of proportion with the requirements of a voyage of ten or fourteen days duration to Canada or the United States and, if insisted on, will materially add to the already long list of expenses which the steamship owners are called upon to pay.'[68] Many doctors, by contrast, considered that the government medicine chests which all ships had to carry were 'altogether antiquated', since they contained some drugs no longer required, while better modern drugs were not included.[69] The Board of Trade was quick to respond to these criticisms, and in November 1888 issued a revised scale of medicines, medical instruments and medical comforts to be carried on passenger ships, with the advice of the Royal Colleges of Physicians and Surgeons:

> We have been actuated by a desire to bring the scales to a level with the advanced position of modern medical and surgical practice in order to give to the medical officer of a ship the means of efficiently performing the duties to which he has been appointed.[70]

However, the quality of the doctor serving on the passenger ships was not always of the highest. Most of them were 'not treated as a gentleman and had no authority.'[71] A survey by *The Lancet* in 1875 found that 224 men sailing in passenger ships as surgeons were not on the Medical Register, since they only held qualifications from the Society of Apothecaries, which would not entitle them to serve as a surgeon in a hospital or the armed forces, and that fifteen of them were under the age of twenty-one, which meant that they were totally unqualified.[72] It concluded that

> The medical service of the mercantile marine has not, until very lately, occupied a specially dignified position in the profession. It has too often been a refuge for the destitute of our cloth; and some ship owners, whose only objective is to screw and pinch as to expenditure in every possible way, get a cheap article in doctors as in other things and do not care to enquire if he be qualified to kill or not.[73]

Yet the surgeon on a passenger or emigrant ship was 'called upon to exhibit more practical knowledge of surgery and midwifery than can be possessed by any unqualified person.'[74] In order to meet a shortage of suitable doctors willing to serve as ship's surgeons on merchant vessels, it was necessary to lower the qualifications required, and in 1899 colonial medical qualifications were recognised for the role.[75]

The hospital accommodation assigned to the surgeon on an emigrant ship was often unsatisfactory, and was dismissed by one MP in 1889 as 'in many cases scarcely any larger than that covered by the table' in the House of Commons.[76] Yet every British passenger ship after 1855 was supposed to have a compartment on an upper deck fitted out as a hospital, which was not to be used for any other purpose.[77] Nevertheless, many emigrant ships ignored the rules and used them for other purposes, including the accommodation of first-class passengers, ship's officers and other members of the crew. At the same time the surgeon was often given inferior quarters, sometimes being given a small, dark, badly situated cabin, and on occasion even having 'to stow himself away in the dispensary, surrounded by medicines and drugs, having no other place to sleep in.'[78] On better lines, the hospitals were not used for other purposes. On ships of the Union Line the hospital was usually fitted within the surgeon's quarters, although on one steamer it was adjacent to the surgeon's room and in another completely separate from it. Infectious cases were housed in hospitals on the upper deck where 'they are consequently more or less exposed', and accordingly well-ventilated.[79]

The crews of emigrant ships benefitted from the medical facilities provided for the passengers. Yet the health of the merchant seaman was for a long time ignored. In 1863 Dr Barnes, physician to the Dreadnought Seaman's Hospital housed in a ship moored off Greenwich, noted that half of his patients were suffering from scurvy and castigated the ship owners of Liverpool, Hamburg, and the American ports for 'exhibiting the greatest amount of disregard of the safety and health of their crews.' This he considered a matter of national concern:

> When it is remembered that the security of this country has on several occasions been imperilled by the disablement of the Royal Navy through scurvy, it may be presumed that the same cause will imperil the safety of our merchant ships. And there can be no doubt that many ships have actually floundered at sea because the crews were so prostrated from scurvy as to be unable to handle them when overtaken by severe weather.[80]

In 1830 the crew of the South Sea whaler *Ranger* was 'so crippled with scurvy, that not only had we ceased to look for whales, but feared the loss of some of them ere the products of the land rescued them from its putrid jaws.' The voyage was only saved when the ship reached Saipan and the young surgeon John Lyell was able to take on board fruit and fresh provisions, 'so powerful are limes and coconuts in dispelling this putrid malady.'[81] The Merchant Shipping Acts of 1844, 1850, and 1854 ordered ship owners to provide lemon or lime juice to protect their crews from scurvy, but many of them ignored the law until further legislation in 1867 laid down a system of inspection to stop the adulteration of the juice, and check that it was actually being supplied.

On merchant ships without a surgeon on board, the captain was responsible not only for maintaining the health of the crew but also for treating them if they fell ill or were injured. When John Wilson, a Durham coalminer turned sailor, succumbed to yellow fever in 1860 off Madagascar, the only medical care he received was from the captain of the *Ennerdale*, 'whose knowledge of medicine and its administering was very elementary and contained in some stereotyped prescriptions', and who mistakenly dosed him with calomel. When he was discharged, Wilson consulted a qualified doctor who prescribed treatment with leeches to drive the calomel out of his system. Much more important to Wilson was the care of him taken by his shipmates, who were 'the essence of kindness' and rigged up an awning for him on the quarterdeck and kept the invalid supplied with rice water. Wilson, later a convert to Primitive Methodism and strict temperance, believed that his close call with death was related to his ignoring the advice of a European doctor in Kurrarchee, India, to avoid alcohol, and his warning that 'a very large percentage of English sailors died in consequence of drinking, and especially liquor.'[82]

The standard handbook on first aid at sea had been written by the naval surgeon Thomas Spencer Wells in 1851. It contained a scale of medicines for the government medicine chest which all ships were supposed to carry, and also advice on how to keep the crew healthy. It was obvious to Wells that there were two causes of disease at sea – the ship, and the men themselves. The environment on board was unhealthy with its 'impure air, want of space in mess places and sleeping berths, dirt and wet'. The physical environment was capable of improvement with 'ventilation, improved construction and dryness', all areas which were improved through legislation in the late nineteenth and early twentieth centuries at a time of a wider concern with public and occupational health.[83] The Merchant Shipping Acts of 1867 and 1894 stipulated a minimum space requirement of 72 cubic feet and 12 feet of floor space for each seaman, increased in 1906 to 120 cubic feet. Yet the sleeping and messing accommodation in British merchant vessels remained inferior to that in ships from many other European countries, resulting in a high incidence of tuberculosis, although improvements in cooking, washing and sleeping facilities were slowly introduced after the First World War.[84]

Spencer Wells considered the crew to be the other source of disease on a ship, through their 'unwholesome food and water, intemperance, dirt, improper clothing, exposure to cold and wet and imperfect discipline, shown in a want of proper regulations of the amount of sleep and labour and of amusements for the crew.'[85] In reforming the crew there was only so much that legislation could achieve, mainly in the field of proper diet. The 1906 Merchant Shipping Act for the first time laid down a scale of victualling for merchant seamen and stipulated that vessels over one thousand tons should have a trained cook.[86] Without having passed a medical examination, it became impossible for an able bodied seaman to gain qualification as a mate. When William Cowper failed his sight test in the late nineteenth century after easily passing everything else for his second mate's certificate, he felt that 'all hope of his making a successful career at sea was now extinct.'[87] Many shipping companies also introduced their own medical examinations for new recruits, and the Essential Work (Merchant Navy) Order of 1941 established medical examination centres at large ports, with mass radiography to screen men for tuberculosis.[88]

For all the improvements in his living and working conditions, the image of the merchant seaman remained low. In 1874 the British consul in Copenhagen considered that 'when of temperate habits and under a good master he is probably the best sailor in the world, both as regards seamanship and labour capacity, but, unfortunately, temperance appears to have become the exception, insobriety the rule, and when under the influence of drink he is brutal and insubordinate, and acts totally regardless of consequences.'[89] The ship's company of the seaplane carrier HMS *Ben-my-Chree* in 1915 was recruited in Liverpool from 'mercantile ratings ... the sweepings of place after all the shipping companies had had their pick', and 'physically they were a very poor lot, but we had to take what we could get', even though many of these merchant seamen, resistant to naval discipline, 'get very bloody-minded and are liable to refuse duty.'[90]

On shore there were attempts to reform the character of the seaman by philanthropists and religious reformers. The plight of the many disabled seamen impressed for service in the French Wars and then discharged after 1815, with no claims on the naval charities such as Greenwich Hospital, aroused the concern of such evangelical reformers as William Wilberforce and Zachary Macaulay. In 1821 at the City of

London Tavern they formed the Seamen's Hospital Society for the benefit of sick seamen of all nationalities. It was supported, like most of the voluntary hospitals of the time, by public subscriptions, donations and legacies. The Admiralty donated a 50-gun ship, the *Grampus,* as a hospital with accommodation for 181 patients, which was moored in the Thames off Greenwich. This soon proved inadequate and in 1832 the Admiralty donated the *Dreadnought,* a 104-gun veteran of the battle of Trafalgar, as a new hospital. In 1870 the Seamen's Hospital Society obtained the lease of the former infirmary block of Greenwich Hospital for an annual rent of one shilling and reopened it as the Dreadnought Seamen's Hospital.[91] Further dispensaries were opened in the London docks, including the Albert Dock Hospital opened in 1890. The merchant seamen treated there often suffered from tropical diseases and offered good clinical material for Patrick Manson's studies of malaria. When the London School of Hygiene and Tropical Medicine was founded in 1899, it was attached to the Albert Dock Hospital and remained there until a new Hospital for Tropical Diseases was opened at Euston in 1920.[92]

Seamen's hospitals were founded in most of the major ports of the world, involving a mixture of colonial government and charitable initiatives. In many British colonies a hospital duty tax levied on vessels arriving in the port was used to fund the medical care of sick seamen. In Malta they were at first housed in a ward set aside for them in the Civil General Hospital in Valletta, but the sailors disturbed the other patients with their unruliness and their feigning of sickness in order to stay on shore as long as possible. As a result a separate hospital for the sole use of merchant seamen was established. Then in 1910 a new hospital for seamen, the Zammit-Clapp Hospital, was founded by two sisters, Emilia Zammit and Mary Clapp, with the Maltese Department of Health providing payments for each patient and supplying all equipment for the hospital, but the nursing being undertaken by the Little Company of Sisters. After 1923 yet another voluntary organisation took over the healthcare of visiting merchant seamen with the foundation of the King George V Hospital by the Seaman's Christian Friends Society Hospital Trust of London, as a memorial to the men of the Merchant Navy who had perished in the Great War. This pattern of hospital provision was repeated throughout the British Empire.[93]

In 1827 the Destitute Sailors' Asylum was founded by a group of philanthropists, in a converted warehouse in Whitechapel close to the London Docks, to house shipwrecked and destitute mariners, but it soon became apparent that something also needed to be done to help seamen to find decent lodgings, better than the disreputable lodging houses and brothels of the ports to which they sailed, where they were prey to the crimps and prostitutes, who would 'by their allurements, decoy the unwary sailor into some den where he was soon robbed of all his wages', and had no option but to sign up for the first ship on offer.[94] In 1835 the world's first Sailors' Home was opened in Well Street in East London through the efforts of the clergyman George Charles Smith. Agents would be sent to the docks to meet the ships on their arrival to try to persuade the crew to use the Well Street Sailors' Home with its slops shop, a sailors' bank, evening classes, and chapel. In 1893 the London School of Nautical Cookery was opened at Well Street to train cooks for the merchant navy in collaboration with the London County Council; this was enlarged when the Merchant Shipping Act of 1906 made it compulsory for all British foreign-going ships to carry a certificated cook.[95] Joseph Conrad knew the Sailors' Home from his days at sea and described it as 'a friendly place . . . quietly, unobtrusively, with a regard for the independence of the men who sought its shelter ashore, and with no other aims besides that effective friendliness.'[96] Seamen's Missions and Homes were formed throughout the world to provide rivals to the public house and brothel. They also provided an effective social welfare network for the distressed merchant seaman. During the Second World War, the crews of torpedoed merchant ships often had to depend on missions to seamen, charitable clothing depots, charities for the merchant navy, such as the Shipwrecked Mariner's Society, and the generosity of individuals for accommodation and clothing, rather than state aid.[97] When the 134 survivors of the *Aldegrove* arrived at Gibraltar in 1941, 'some of the men had to walk through the streets in bare feet', but the representative of the Ministry of War Transport had 'no funds at his disposal and could not do anything else for us other than put some of the men up at the Sailors' Home and some in a hotel'. The men had lost all their possessions, and replacement kit and 'clothing was very costly and very scarce'.[98]

The health and welfare of the crews of merchant naval vessels and the human cargo they carried on emigrant ships was as vital to the British Empire as the Royal Navy, although more neglected. It was also important in shaping the melting-pot societies of the continents to which the emigrants were travelling, as well as the shape of world trade. As more people came to travel over the sea for pleasure as well as from necessity and could afford higher expectations, standards improved for all, but that was a slow process. The Royal Navy had offered a model for how to maintain health at sea, but merchant seaman and emigrant alike merited better medical care and healthy conditions as much as Jolly Jack Tar did. Eventually they got them.

# CHAPTER EIGHT

# Sea Airs

UNTIL THE NINETEENTH CENTURY, no one considered the climate at sea to be at all healthy. On the contrary, sea airs were looked upon as the cause of sickness among seamen, particularly the scourge of scurvy. Ocean voyages were an ordeal to be undergone to get to a specific destination and were never something to be enjoyed for its own sake. Yet with the improvements in ship design during the nineteenth century, it became possible to offer more luxury for the passenger able to pay for it. Not all passengers on emigrant ships to North America, Australia, India or the colonies had travelled in steerage. Civil servants, imperial administrators, businessmen, and the wives of army officers expected a little more comfort, and were able to pay more for more luxurious and commodious conditions. Now ships began to cater solely for passengers, rather than taking on board travellers in addition to the main purpose of carrying cargo or the mail. Improved lighting, more deck space and provision for entertainment improved the quality of the voyage for voyagers. As the larger ships became floating pleasure palaces, a sea cruise was increasingly seen as health-giving and life-enhancing. As early as the 1880s the *British Medical Journal* had begun to endorse the curative value of a sea cruise and the idea of cruising for pleasure began to gain acceptance.[1]

Family doctors were used to hearing the question 'Where shall I go for a healthy holiday?' from their patients, some of them confirmed invalids. Now in the 1880s and 1890s they could recommend to them the benefits of holidays at sea.[2] They suggested that a sea voyage to Australia was the best treatment for a tall, 'overgrown' sixteen-year-old boy with a weak chest. The ideal ship for his condition would be a sailing ship in preference to a steamer but 'it is now somewhat difficult to get a good one'.[3] The humorist J K Jerome was perhaps more cynical about the medical advice to take a sea voyage as the cure for a multitude of ailments:

A sea trip does you good when you are going to have a couple of months of it, but, for a week, it is wicked. You start on Monday

144

with the idea implanted in your bosom that you are going to enjoy yourself. You wave an airy adieu to the boys on shore, light your biggest pipe, and swagger about the deck as if you were Captain Cook, Sir Francis Drake, and Christopher Columbus all rolled into one. On Tuesday, you wish you hadn't come. On Wednesday, Thursday, and Friday, you wish you were dead. On Saturday, you are able to swallow a little beef tea, and to sit up on deck, and answer with a wan, sweet smile when kind-hearted people ask you how you feel now. On Sunday, you begin to walk about again, and take solid food. And on Monday morning, as, with your bag and umbrella in your hand, you stand by the gunwale, waiting to step ashore, you begin to thoroughly like it.[4]

Jerome was not alone in thinking that sea travel was not the universal panacea that many doctors were prescribing indiscriminately. Alex Hill, Master of Downing College, Cambridge, complained in 1896 of the inappropriateness with which, on medical advice, 'dipsomaniacs are let loose in one of these floating hotels, erotic persons of both sexes are placed in an atmosphere of flirtation, and a sea voyage is prescribed for various other cases, for which it is equally unsuitable, instead of being restricted to those for whom, almost alone, it is suitable – cases of excitable or exhausted nervous system or depressed metabolism.' Hill's pleasant voyage to Ceylon had been marred by the suicide of 'a hypersensitive cultured young Oxford graduate', who had been sent on a long sea voyage to 'cure him of the blues', and had 'thrown himself with zeal into all the busy idleness of shipboard life, a heroic effort to forget his own depression in trying to make the voyage pleasant for others.' Among the crew on that voyage was also a consumptive cabin steward, 'sent by his doctor to attempt a life which is extremely trying to a robust man'.[5]

The idea of an ocean voyage being healthy had its origins in the health regime of the long-established spas, with their salubrious mineral baths, and the emerging coastal resorts. By the eighteenth century the coastal landscape was being regarded as romantic, and coastal resorts were developed as alternatives to the inland spa towns such as Bath, Cheltenham, Harrogate, and Buxton, where it was fashionable to take the waters for the sake of good health, however foul-tasting and sulphurous those waters may have been. Sea bathing, once associated with popular ideas that the spring tides had pro- phylactic powers, became fashionable as entrepreneurial doctors promoted its medicinal value, and also that of the ozone in the sea air.

The patronage of the Prince of Wales helped to transform Brighton from a small fishing village to a town devoted to pleasure and sophisticated pastimes in the late eighteenth century, but one where dissipation might be linked with the worthier pursuit of wellbeing. Sea bathing, at first the luxury of the upper classes, became popular with the professional classes in the mid nineteenth century, which led to the popularisation of the seaside resort. Better and cheaper rail transport links then brought the market for seaside holidays to the working classes.[6] Healthy seaside holidays suggested that, once the discomforts of such travel could be overcome, a sea voyage could also be health-giving.

Modern transatlantic passenger services really began in 1818 when the Black Ball Line started up a regular crossing between England and the United States on its fleet of sailing ships.[7] Steamers only started to challenge the domination of sail with the launch of Isambard Kingdom Brunel's paddle steamer *Great Western* in 1837, which reduced the Atlantic crossing to an advertised fifteen days. However, the unreliability of the early steam engines and the risk of running out of fuel meant that the early steamships continued to have sails.[8] Charles Dickens sailed on the Cunard Line's *Britannia* in 1842 and was not at all impressed with 'what may be called the domestic noises of the ship: such as the breaking of glass and crockery, the tumbling down of stewards, the gambols, overhead, of loose casks and truant dozens of bottled porter, and the very remarkable and far from exhilarating sounds raised in their various state-rooms by the seventy passengers who were too ill to get up to breakfast.'[9] He found the cabins far too small and uncomfortable, and the saloon, 'not unlike a gigantic hearse', unbefitting to the self-esteem of a bestselling novelist and journalist.[10] The ship's doctor only appeared to drink wine and brandy and play whist with the passengers.[11] Dickens preferred to return home on a sailing ship.

Brunel's second steamship, *Great Britain*, the first ocean-going, iron-hulled, screw-driven ship, similarly failed to live up to the promise of a cleaner, more hygienic journey held out at its launch by Prince Albert in 1843. Queen Victoria had been impressed that 'all the fittings and decorations are very fine and everything made as comfortable as possible, but I should not care to go to sea with such a quantity of passengers or in such a long narrow ship'.[12] The passenger accommodation did not look so alluring by the end of the maiden voyage to New York. An American journalist thought that the bed linen was 'uninviting', and 'the whole appearance of the cabins, whatever may have been their original splendor, was to us, greasy and smirchy.' What was most noticeable was 'the grease and dirt with which everything is covered'. Lady passengers were warned not to be 'particular about putting on a nice dress to appear in, if you do it will, we fancy, be the last time you wear it.'[13] The griminess of the ship remained a constant theme during its service on the routes to New York and later to Australia. Women passengers especially found the voyage trying, despite a passage connecting some of their cabins with a 'commodious boudoir', so that 'ladies who are indisposed or in negligé will be able to reach their sleeping berths without the slightest necessity for their appearing in public'.[14] A traveller complained in 1862 about passengers smoking on the starboard side of the ship because 'the practice is in itself offensive, and leads to expectoration, which, unfortunately, is swept up by our dresses'.[15] Rats were also a constant problem. On her honeymoon travelling from Melbourne to Liverpool in 1866, Mary Crompton was alarmed when a rat 'came into my cabin as I was going to bed, I jumped onto the berth and waited until Joe came down, then he and one of the stewards had a grand rat hunt but the gentleman escaped through a hole.' Another passenger was 'wakened by one biting her toe nails'.[16] On the longer voyages to Australia, the loss of infants was a commonplace even among the saloon passengers, one of whom in June 1866 had given birth to a stillborn girl, the mother having 'been ill ever since we sailed, she has one little girl though she is just twenty.' Shortly after, a child was born healthily in steerage, and an old man of eighty died there without any family with him.[17]

The ships were often cold and damp. This was to be expected aboard the liners plying the route from Liverpool to New York but, even in the summer, balmy days when passengers could walk the decks in bright sunshine were rarer than passengers anticipated. In 1888 the Inman Line warned passengers to take plenty of overcoats, wraps, and 'the thickest underclothing' with them in their cabin baggage for use in their staterooms as well as on deck, despite the 'delusion that people do not take cold at sea'.[18] Another way of keeping warm, as well as of passing the time, was to indulge in excessive amounts of food and alcohol, available in copious amounts to first-class passengers. Comfort, though, was increasing aboard ship all the time. Cabins on the port side were considered pleasanter, cooler, and healthier on vessels sailing to India, and the starboard on the return to Britain, being largely out of direct sunlight. This has given rise to the unsupported belief that the word 'posh' is an acronym of 'port out, starboard home'.[19] Even though it may not be maritime slang, 'posh' was what the ships were becoming.

By the early twentieth century many passenger liners had developed into massive, ornate floating hotels in which the discomforts of ocean travel were minimised if they could not be entirely eliminated. The comfort of the passenger was increased when the first-class cabins and saloons were moved amidships away from the vibration of the engines and where there was less motion from the action of the waves. The White Star line *Oceanic* had led the way in 1870 with its large portholes, electricity, and running water for its amidships first-class accommodation, setting new standards for ocean liners. Staterooms and cabins were now designed for comfort, and the public rooms were places of entertainment in which the wealthy traveller could relax and enjoy the voyage. Increasingly they resembled hotels rather than ship cabins. The tradition of dressing for dinner during the voyage was started onboard the Cunard Line's *Mauretania* and *Lusitania* now that life on the liner was more akin to life on shore, and finery could be worn without fear of it being soiled by the squalor of the ship or the seasickness of the passenger. The ships of the White Star Line, such as the *Olympic* and *Titanic* with their swimming pools, gymnasia and tennis courts, prided themselves on being the most luxurious ships ever.

The fate of the supposedly unsinkable *Titanic* has come to symbolise the pride, hubris and end of the optimism of the superficially idyllic Edwardian age. When the pride of the White Star line set sail on its maiden voyage in April 1912, it embodied the height of luxury for its first-class passengers, many of them society figures and millionaires, with its grand staircase, sumptuous dining salon, elegant, lounges, writing and smoking rooms, and well-appointed staterooms. After the sinking of the ship there was a suggestion that 'the provision of Turkish baths, gymnasiums and other so-called luxuries involved a sacrifice of some more essential things, the absence of which was responsible for the loss of so many lives', but there was actually enough space for lifeboats among the splendour.[20] Equally as impressive as the public rooms were the up-to-date medical facilities, which not only complied with Board of Trade regulations but even exceeded them. The medical team on board the *Titanic* was led by the 62-year-old senior surgeon, William Francis Norman O'Loughlin, who had practised medicine at sea for over forty years. He was assisted by 37-year-old John Edward Simpson, a territorial captain in the Royal Army Medical Corps who had originally gone to sea on account of his own ill health, and who had responsibility for the health of the second-and third-class passengers and of the crew. Both of these doctors had previously served together on board the *Olympic* and both were to go down with the *Titanic*. They were aided by a hospital steward, William Durnford, and two stewardesses, one acting as nurse-stewardess for the first-class passengers and the other as matron for the immigrant passengers in third class, many of whom she had to teach how to use a flush lavatory.

Hospital facilities, like everything else onboard ship, were strictly segregated. The first- and second-class passengers had their hospital wards on D-deck near the galley, where there were also two isolation rooms for infectious cases, whilst the crew had a small sick bay for their use close to their quarters, and the third class had their own hospital wards. The surgeons worked from a dispensary and surgery close to their cabin berths, though first-class ticket holders could expect to receive treatment in their own cabins. These medical facilities were little used on the ill-fated first voyage. The only recorded casualty during the voyage was when a first-class passenger fell on the grand staircase and broke her arm, but accounts differ as to whether the assistant surgeon Simpson set her arm in plaster, or whether she insisted on being treated by a fellow passenger, a New York orthopaedic surgeon Henry William Frauenthal.[21] Ironically, Dr Frauenthal was to break the ribs of a fellow passenger and knock her unconscious, when he leapt aboard a two-thirds-full lifeboat as the ship went down, in a successful attempt to save himself. Another first-class passenger, Charlotte Drake Cardeza, preferred to rely on her own medical chest, which she took on board with her luggage of fourteen trunks, four suitcases and three crates.[22] First-class passengers could also keep themselves fit in a well-equipped gymnasium, often formally dressed in suit, collar and tie, or in skirt, coat and bonnet. Thomas McCawley, the 36-year-old 'instructor ran here and there, looking the very picture of robust rosy-cheeked health and fitness in his white flannels, placing one passenger on the electric horse, another on the camel, while the laughing group of onlookers watched the inexperienced riders vigorously shaken up and down as he controlled the little motor which made the machines imitate so realistically horse and camel exercise'. As the ship was about to go down, the physical training instructor remained at his post and gave guidance on the use of the mechanical horses and parallel bars to those who sought distraction from their fate.[23]

Even after the sinking of the *Titanic* following its collision with an iceberg on 12 April 1912, class distinctions continued to govern the medical treatment of the survivors and the disposal of the bodies of the victims. When the survivors were brought aboard the *Carparthia,* the first ship to reach the site of the sinking, they were divided up according to their status aboard the *Titanic,* once their names and details had been recorded, and then sent to the relevant first-, second- or third-class dining salon for first aid by one of the three surgeons on the rescue ship. After treatment for hypothermia, shock, exposure to the elements, and minor injuries, the first- and second-class passengers were accommodated in the public salons and officers' cabins, whilst the third-class passengers were moved into steerage. Harold McBride, the *Titanic*'s junior wireless operator, was put into the hospital bay, suffering from crushed and frostbitten feet, since he was in need of continued medical attention. However, when the ship reached New York, the usual customs formalities were suspended for all passengers, and even the immigrants among them were spared the usual inspections on Ellis Island.[24] Other ships were sent to recover the bodies of the victims. First-class passengers, who could be identified from their effects or simply because they were well-dressed, were placed into coffins on the poop deck. Second- and third-class passengers were merely sewn up in canvas sacks. Many of the crew, whether identifiable or not from their effects, and some of the less obviously affluent of the passengers were immediately buried at sea. The bodies of those crew to be brought ashore for burial, however, were stored in the ice-filled holds of the ships and were not 'embalmed or even sewn up in canvas', and when they were brought ashore at Halifax it was found that 'many of the frozen limbs had to be broken', to get the bodies on to stretchers and into their coffins.[25] In the confusion, errors of classification were made and the social order subverted: some members of the crew were brought back for burial on land in Savile Row tailoring, in the coffins reserved exclusively for first-class passengers. Several of the crew, seeking warmer clothing that might help them to survive in the icy waters, had presumably helped themselves to bespoke suits and heavy overcoats from the abandoned staterooms, and, being in death well turned-out and of smart appear- ance, had been afforded the respect accorded to first-class passengers, only for their true identities to emerge when their personal effects were properly examined before their corpses were prepared for embalming and burial.[26]

White Star's rival, the Cunard line, prided itself on never having lost a ship, but this record was to be broken with the sinking of the *Lusitania*. It also prided itself on having the latest in medical facilities and on their not being needed. The writer Elbert Hubbard noted that 'a doctor is at your disposal chiefly for social purposes as it seldom happens that anyone is sick because everyone is happy'. What kept the passengers so contented was the luxury in which they found themselves, the sumptuous appointment of the public rooms and first-class staterooms and cabins, the gourmet menus, the latest technological developments in electric power and ventilation, and the gymnasia offering 'daily exercise in a great variety of beneficial forms.' Hubbard even rhapsodised that 'here is health, joy, information, education, growth, outlook, that will inspire you for the rest of your life.'[27] He and his second wife were to lose their lives, when the *Lusitania* sank within eighteen minutes of being torpedoed by a German U-boat on 7 May 1915, with the loss of 1,201 out of the 1,962 people on board. Some passengers were trapped in the lifts as the electric power suddenly failed. There was no time for doctors to treat anyone. There was a disorderly scramble for the lifeboats. The majority of the survivors were fit young men and women aged between sixteen and thirty-five who were better able to hold their own in the confusion.[28]

A career on a passenger liner was seen as being suitable for an elderly, sick, newly-qualified, or even indolent doctor, for whom the salubrious effects of a relaxing time at sea would be as beneficial as for many of their passengers. Aleck Bourne 'needed a rest and a change' in 1911, after six months as a house surgeon in a hospital and after sitting his final medical examinations, so he took a job as a ship's doctor on a slow 3,000-ton ship bound for North Africa and Alexandria. With only twelve passengers, he expected to have an easy time with little to do during the voyage, but had not expected to be prostrated with sickness for forty-eight hours. Luckily for him, the passengers were 'as sick as I was and therefore needing no more medical attention than that which was ably rendered by the steward. His treatment was champagne.'[29] Not finding the easy time he desired, Bourne returned to London, going on to become a leading gynaecologist and abortion reformer, refreshed after his brief time at sea. For other doctors, going to sea for the sake of their health was more than merely a pleasant interlude. Thomas Stanley North had qualified as a doctor in October 1922 and, like Aleck Bourne earlier, had done a six-month house job with the intention of climbing the professional ladder and becoming a specialist. However, he was not in good physical condition as a result of his war service and after finishing his job as a houseman he had taken the post of ship's surgeon on SS *Leicestershire* for the sake of his health. North was only a month into his medical studies when he joined the army as a private in November 1915. He had been seriously injured at the Battle of the Somme in July 1916 and had been invalided out of the army, returning to his medical studies in May 1917 still only aged twenty. His time as a ship's surgeon was to be equally short, and he died at sea on 31 October 1924 aged twenty-seven, as a direct result of his war wounds.[30]

Seasickness was the most common ailment to affect passengers on any ship, but it was one which the passenger was often reluctant to bother the doctor with, because it was believed that there was nothing that could be done about it. Instead, travellers often brought with them a patent remedy that was as likely to upset their stomachs as it was to do anything to relieve the *mal de mer*. The bedroom steward, if asked for advice, would recommend that the sufferer went on deck to get some fresh air, but only because he wished to clean the cabin. The more important passenger would consult the captain who 'has very clear views on the therapeutic effects of castor oil, and is frequently ready to furnish advice on the treatment of seasickness based on the authority of his Master's Ticket.'[31] The writer J K Jerome trivialised the problem when he mused on the 'curious fact, nobody ever is sea-sick – on land. At sea, you come across plenty of people very bad indeed, whole boatloads of them; but I never met a man yet, on land, who had ever known at all what it was to be sea-sick.'[32] Nevertheless, it remained a constant problem at sea. There was nothing that even the most luxurious of liners could do about stormy weather. In *Brideshead Revisited*, his elegy to aristocratic gilded youth, Evelyn Waugh described how those who had not succumbed 'seemed bound together by a camaraderie of reciprocal esteem; they did nothing except sit rather glumly in their armchairs, drink occasionally, and exchange congratulations on not being seasick.'[33]

Seasickness was not the only problem that the lone ship's surgeon might be called upon to deal with in the course of a cruise on a smaller ship. Whereas in a hospital he would have had the help of a team of nurses and anaesthetists, with all the instruments sterilised and in their right place, aboard ship he had only himself to rely upon. At sea the surgeon had to improvise and disinfect an operating theatre, sterilise the instruments and dressings, and administer the anaesthetic himself, then once the patient was unconscious keep an eye on the crew member or passenger to whom he had entrusted the ether mask or chloroform muzzle while he operated. Stuart Tidey performed an operation for appendicitis in a ship off the coast of British Columbia, helped only by a Japanese orderly who fainted twice during the operation and had to be laid out on the floor until it was all over. Once the operation was finished, the surgeon had to clear up after himself, something unthinkable in any hospital, and then nurse the patient. Essentially he was being called upon to do 'the work of five or six experts with practically the same time allowance as they employ working in co-operation, while his surgical skill is measured by the standard of hospital results.' Since major operations were a rarity, the ship's surgeon was not accustomed to them and his skills were often rusty. It was said that 'after two year's sea service the M.O. has forgotten all he ever knew about medicine – an exaggeration, no doubt, but one which expresses the tendency to rust inseparable from the professional life of the M.O. in the Merchant Service.'[34]

Injuries to the crew were commonplace. On the *Great Britain,* a sailor, 'one of the best on the ship', lost his footing while painting the anchor in 1866, fractured his skull in two places and had a cut beside his ear. The passengers collected £50 for him as he had supported his parents from his wages but considered that 'the poor young man may get well but I am afraid there is not much chance'.[35] On the same voyage a carpenter was 'ill some time in consequence of a large piece of beef tied high on the mast' falling on him.[36] On an earlier voyage to Melbourne in 1866, William Wheatley, an eighteen-year-old sailor, 'steady, honest and in every way a credit to those connected to him', was swept overboard and no trace 'could be found after nor the mop or bucket with which he was working at the time.'[37] The previous year the ship had been so crowded that the stewards had to sleep on the tables and, after one particularly rough night, one of the stewards had fallen off the table and, panicking, had run along the corridor melodramatically shouting, 'Oh I've been killed – all my ribs are broke, I'm killed, I'm killed.'[38] Engineers on Peninsular and Orient Ships were warned paternalistically against lying on their bunks in their working clothes, since 'however tired a man may be, ten minutes can always be spared to clean himself and his sleep will be thus rendered far more refreshing and beneficial.'[39]

There were different problems facing the doctor adventurous enough to join a foreign ship, where crew and passengers not only spoke a different language, but often had different cultural expectations. An English doctor serving on a pilgrim ship from Malaya to Jeddah, from which the pilgrims could each Mecca, in 1911 found that he was dependent upon the assistance of the chief officer of the ship in acting as 'interpreter, philosopher and friend.' The pilgrims all crowded closely together on the decks, as there were no cabins or bunks for them, and in such crowded, cramped conditions, infection, characterised by enlarged glands and pustular rashes, soon spread. The doctor, though, was ignorant of Eastern diseases because 'seated comfortably by the fireside, an Osler on his knee, these diseases present a vivid and unmistakeable picture, but on the gangway surrounded by perspiring hordes of dark-skinned humanity, even the newly qualified man must feel inward qualms.'[40] The ship's officers knew more about such diseases from experience than the ship's doctor ever could from his training in a London teaching hospital, or his desultory study of Sir William Osler's classic textbook *The Principles and Practice of Medicine*, and it was they who were able to guide him in the right direction. However, the pilgrims, showing a deep streak of fatalism, preferred not to consult the doctor, who only found out about their illnesses once they were dead. With treatment 'almost impossible' in such circumstances, 'the energies of the ship's surgeon are concentrated upon the detection and isolation of any infectious disease', a task not made easy by the victims of smallpox hiding inside a ventilator, or covered with cargo and then slipping ashore to avoid quarantine.[41] Such an experience, whilst frustrating, was an eye-opener into other cultures for a Western doctor, and a far cry from the gentility of most passenger liners.

The position of the doctor on a passenger ship depended to a certain extent on an ability to bluff, since 'one is expected to be an authority on all matters, moral and maritime, to be able to recognise every boat and know her line and speed, and a hundred other things.'[42] This was an accomplishment most young doctors were able to pick up in their training, in the days when a hospital consultant considered himself to be a god, and was happy to make Olympian pronouncements on subjects about which he actually knew nothing, with an air of authority that could not be brooked. For the young doctor at sea there could be disconcerting, almost humiliating, moments when passengers failed to recognise their professional status and mistook them for a steward or chief officer. Donning a uniform for the first time had been a great moment of pride for many a newly-qualified doctor, for whom 'clad in neat blue with shining brass buttons and bands of red and gold on one's sleeves, with the cap carefully adjusted at the most fetching angle on one's head, one looks in the glass, smiles and involuntarily thinks "the girls!".'[43] After that brief glimpse of glory, it was deflating for the doctor's sense of self-importance not to be immediately recognised; not yet enjoying the frock coat and striped trousers of the Harley Street specialist, he might as well have been in his best lounge suit or the short white coat of the medical student. One young man acting as medical officer on a cruise to the Mediterranean in 1910 was taken aback when a lady remarked to him that if her friends did not rally from their seasickness soon, she would have to call in the doctor, 'but I don't suppose he would do any good, do you?' The doctor politely and meekly agreed with her.[44]

The role of the ship's doctor was often as much social as it was professional, and most of the doctors were happy to join in the fun. One young doctor on a Mediterranean cruise ship in 1910 found that his time as ship's doctor passed far too quickly, and that 'if anyone wants a good holiday this is not at all a bad way to take it.'[45] He had been disappointed when the ship was ready to leave Southampton and the call 'any more for shore' was the signal for 'the bevy of beauty parading the decks to make a bolt for the gangway and leave their mothers and aunts aboard', but he was to make a hit with these very women left to take the cruise. During a stormy passage through the notorious Bay of Biscay, many of the sleeping passengers had been so alarmed that they had rushed out of their cabins and assumed that the doctor, who had stayed up late in the lounge, was fully dressed because he knew that the ship was about to sink. When reassured that this was not the case, an elderly lady naively remarked to him, 'Oh doctor, if you had only come in your pyjamas we should have been quite happy'. She and the doctor were both contented when they reached the sunny Mediterranean where 'warm weather and a full moon do much to make one forget material troubles. And then we began to amuse ourselves.'[46] Remaining correctly attired, doubtless to the secret disappointment of some of his admirers and more in keeping with the decorum expected by the other ladies, he took a full part in all the dances, deck sports, games, and shore excursions. E C Hardwicke summed up his own experiences as surgeon on a liner to Buenos Aires in 1912 as 'I strengthened my health, increased my weight, deepened my capacity for drinking cocktails, and added to my vocabulary and my stock of yarns. In short, I had an excellent time.'[47]

Glamour was the keynote of the ocean liners in the inter-war years, newsreels regularly showing members of the aristocracy, Hollywood film stars, and the celebrities of the age going on board such art deco liners as the *Queen Mary* and *Queen Elizabeth*, dressed in all their finery. There was an elaborate dress code for passengers. Dressing for dinner was almost obligatory, though dinner jackets and black tie for men were now acceptable rather than the more formal tailcoats and white tie of the years before the war. A range of lounge suits, blazers, sweaters, pullovers, plus-fours, white linen suits, evening dress, and sports clothes were all needed for the well-dressed man, a steward brushing and pressing them for him after each use. The white linen suit, in particular, was seen as the ideal clothing for a cruise in warmer climes since it was not only extremely stylish but was hard-wearing, durable and, with its ability to absorb moisture, very comfortable and healthy. Women needed an even more extensive wardrobe from evening dresses to tennis skirts and bathing suits.[48] Food remained plentiful and extravagant, and the bars were well-patronised. For American passengers in the early 1920s, the liners offered a means of beating Prohibition since alcohol was available to them at sea. Indeed, Cunard and the White Star Line began the original 'booze cruises' by offering cheap overnight trips to New Yorkers, taking them beyond the three-mile limit from the American shore on which the ban on drinking alcohol applied. It was not the healthiest of measures, but met a need for the bright young things wanting a drink but without the time or money for a full voyage, though it did give them the taste for longer pleasure cruises which many of them were to indulge in later.[49]

Exercise facilities became ever more important as the cult of keep fit got underway. Tug-of-war, deck tennis, quoits, wheelbarrow races, races with wooden horses, and physical drill could all be played on the long narrow promenades. The larger liners had the latest equipment in their gymnasia. The *Viceroy of India,* built for P&O in 1929, was the first liner to have an indoor swimming pool, albeit one filled with salt water. Before this time, pools made from canvas and wood had been rigged up on the decks.[50] The smart young international set that found its natural milieu in such a setting was described by *Harper's Bazaar* in glowing terms in 1934, equating youthful healthiness and wholesomeness with a sea-borne lifestyle: 'cruisers are gay lads with a spark of adventure in their bright clear eyes. Ozone-minded. Active, alert. Soften under the influence of beauty, moonlight, music and mixed drinks.'[51]

The ship's doctors on board the luxury liners of the 1920s and 1930s had perhaps an even better time than their counterparts had done before the First World War. The doctor enjoyed all the pleasures and privileges of a first-class passenger with use of the lounges, swimming pools, cinema, dining saloons, promenade decks, and squash and tennis courts whenever his far from arduous duties allowed. The dispensaries were well-stocked with all the essential equipment needed for an operation, but wherever possible doctors still preferred to get their patient ashore for any serious surgery. As well as having lavish equipment, the ship was also well manned with medical staff. On the larger liners there were two doctors, the senior of whom attended first-class and tourist passengers, and the junior attended to the crew and third-class passengers, as well as two male hospital attendants and two nurses. There were twelve beds in the general hospital ward and eight in an isolation ward. Compared with most hospitals on land the medical facilities were good.[52] In contrast to general practice, the work of a ship's surgeon was 'comparatively free from anxiety', offered a good salary for a young man and very good living and working conditions, but 'to set against these are the tedium, the lack of medical interest, and often the short time ashore in the home port.'[53] Alongside the luxury of the great liners went more modest cruise ships 'to meet all pockets', so that 'thousands of people have experienced the joys of ocean travel who up till recent years would never have dreamed of such an undertaking on the high seas', and 'a great many business and professional people have learned to love shipboard life and the carefree existence of an ocean voyage.'[54] So much so that some of them chose to spend as much time at sea as possible. Many retired doctors found the life of a sea-surgeon as congenial as it was to young men at the start of their careers. They even found that some passengers travelled on the same ships as much as they themselves did. Robert Blackham, who had become a ship's doctor on retirement as physician to the Viceroy of India, met one lady who had become a 'permanent passenger' on the same voyage backwards and forwards to Australia for five years, and for whom the doctor almost acted as a general practitioner.[55]

The increasing dominance of air travel after the Second World War made the great liners redundant for carrying passengers across the Atlantic, and forced them to market themselves as destinations in their own right and find new commercial opportunities. Educational cruises for school children became popular in the 1960s aboard the P&O ships *Uganda* and *Canberra*. SS *Uganda* had originally been built as a troop carrier and then was converted for use for educational cruises in 1961, when the combination of a floating schoolroom, the exposure of children to new experiences, and a bracing, healthy sea air was a selling point. These liners had teams of doctors to deal with the inevitable accidents children will have away from their parents and in a setting where even the best discipline exerted by their teachers could not keep them risk-free.[56] On other more general cruise ships the emphasis was on the fun, relaxation, and healthy image of a cruise. For some officers and passengers, romance was very actively sought; one woman purser was speaking for many of her female passengers in 1965 when she noted that 'there are lots of gorgeous, handsome, suntanned men around. I suppose the uniform helps a lot, but wow.'[57]

Shipboard medicine continued to be seen 'as a life of leisure, pleasure, sea, and sun, interrupted occasionally by the lucrative treatment of petty illnesses and ending in alcoholic debauchery.'[58] This was a widely held view, reinforced by the portrayal of the ship's doctor in such popular films as *Doctor at Sea* and *Carry on Cruising*, where the doctor, when not dealing with eccentric crew and passengers, doling out dubious concoctions for seasickness, or giving injections in embarrassing places, is more concerned with the pursuit of attractive young women passengers, or with consoling himself with alcohol for his lack of amorous success. The reality was often very different. On cheap package cruises the passengers were often elderly and unfit, but were expected to take part in the keep-fit classes, deck tennis and swimming galas organised for their entertainment during their days at sea, and the strenuous shore excursions when in port. John Carter, a doctor on a ship carrying such passengers in the early 1970s, remarked that 'I have often observed, apprehensively, purple-faced, overweight sexagenarians "keeping fit" in the morning, eating an enormous lunch, smoking away the afternoon, "doing their thing" in the discotheque at 1 a.m., and ascending the Acropolis the following morning.'[59] Not surprisingly such a regime often resulted in heart attacks, strokes, and orthopaedic injuries. Nor were the medical facilities on these smaller, often foreign-registered ships, up to the standards of the luxury liners. In many cases they only catered for minor injuries and illnesses. The sick bays were small and on one occasion John Carter had to offer a patient his own bed, which was in the surgery. Evi Kalodiki was another doctor who took a temporary job on a similar ship, and when checking the medical supplies found several that were missing or past their use-by dates. She listed everything and sent a copy to the shipping company to request replacements and to protect herself professionally and legally in case anything went wrong.[60]

Inevitably, deaths did happen at sea, especially when many passengers were elderly or on a cruise for the sake of their health, and found themselves tempted by the possibility of overindulgence. Burial at sea could only take place if there were no suspicious circumstances surrounding the death, and only after a post-mortem examination on board or at the nearest port of call. The ship's nurse was responsible for preparing the body for burial at sea, and the boatswain would sew the corpse up in a canvas bag, with the final stitch going through the nose to stop the body from slipping down inside the sack. If the relatives of the dead man or woman wished the body to be brought home, or foul play was suspected, the body would be kept in refrigerated conditions.

Modern cruise ships have mortuaries, but in the 1960s the ice room was often the only place where a body could be stored. When a member of the deck crew of the *Otranto* died after falling into an empty swimming pool, the officers suspected that the death had not been accidental and placed the man's body in the ice room, where, to prevent it from freezing to the deck, the captain and purser turned it every twelve hours. On another ship the freezer was emptied of food to accommodate a corpse.[61]

The facilities on luxury liners, by contrast, were much more extensive and even lavish. When the luxury liner *Andrea Doria* was launched in 1951, it was hailed as a symbol of Italian resurgence after the miseries of the Second World War. Instead, it was to be remembered as the last sinking of a great ocean liner on a voyage from Genoa to New York, at a time when the days of regular transatlantic crossings themselves were numbered. The medical response to the disaster in which forty-six passengers lost their lives and many others were badly injured, as well as five crew of the *Stockholm* with which it collided, was to show both the best and worst of maritime medicine. Immediately after the collision off the coast of Nantucket on 25 July 1956, the ship's doctor, Bruno Tortori-Donati, and his assistant, Lorenzo Giannini, had gone to the sickbay on A-deck to prepare for the expected casualties from those cabins that had met the full force of the impact. They soon realised that the ship was sinking and organised the evacuation of the two bedridden patients already in the sickbay, one of whom had a fractured thighbone and the other suffered from cancer. A third patient, a cabin boy suffering from an abscessed tooth, had already left his bed to find a safer place on the ship. It took two male nurses over an hour to carry the beds of the two women patients to a muster station to get a place in a lifeboat.[62] Newly-married, 25-year-old Joseph Bruno Levy had spent the evening dancing with his wife Susanna at a party in the sumptuous main lounge and was at the first-class bar when he felt the force of the impact. Having seen his wife into a lifeboat, he had been pushed in the back by a panicking fellow passenger and sent sliding down the oily, wet deck into the deck railings. He suffered hairline fractures in both legs and fainted. When he recovered consciousness he was alone except for an abandoned child, whom he managed to get into a lifeboat. They were picked up by the *Stockholm*, and Levy, still in his wet and torn tuxedo, was furious when they were put into a third-class cabin without blankets, food, or a change of clothing. When he finally saw a doctor, who did not even look at his legs, he was told to get seen to in New York. Once he arrived there and was reunited with his bride, Levy's priorities were to seek medical treatment and a change of clothes.[63] The physician on the *Stockholm* was already fully occupied with dealing with fractured skulls, arms and legs, and a man who had lost his eye. The most seriously injured were airlifted from the ship by helicopter and taken to hospital.[64] Some of the other ships coming to the aid of the survivors did not have ship's doctors. When the captain of the *Cape Ann* found out that there were two Italian doctors among the survivors that he had picked up, he turned over to them all the drugs and surgical instruments in his medical chest so that they could take charge of the casualties, many of them with fractures.[65]

Fortunately, disasters and sinkings are rare on modern ocean liners, which have not lost their attractions. On a twenty-first-century cruise ship such as the Cunard Line flagship *Queen Mary II*, good medical facilities at the highest of international standards are an essential selling point for passengers, since a high proportion of people now taking a cruise are middle-aged or elderly. There are about three or four heart attacks among the passengers on an average day at sea, most of them minor, but a member of the staff of the medical centre is always on duty with a defibrillator ready for any cardiac emergencies that will inevitably arise. The *Queen Mary II* has two hospital ward single cabins and a two-bedded high dependency unit available for any passengers who need observation or nursing. There is also a well-equipped minor operating theatre, X-ray room, and laboratories where routine diagnostic tests can be undertaken. There is a dental facility, but this is only used for very simple emergency dental repairs, often when a passenger loses a crown just before dining at the captain's table. Passengers with serious illnesses or in need of urgent surgery are landed at the nearest port, taken ashore to a hospital and then repatriated. In the most dramatic cases a passenger might be winched off the liner by helicopter, always accompanied by a nurse. Medical charges are high for each consultation and for any medicines prescribed, but most of these charges end up being paid from medical insurance policies. Although not equipped to provide continual care for the elderly, a cruise could be considered economical yet luxurious compared with the fees for residential care on land, a scenario very few cruise lines would wish to contemplate. The doctors in the ship's medical centre also have responsibility for the health of the crew, who have their own more modest sick bay. Whereas the waiting room and consultation rooms for the passengers would not disgrace a luxury hotel, with their leather sofas and deep armchairs, the crews wait to see the doctor on plastic chairs in a corridor, reminiscent of older, more run-down National Health Service hospitals ashore. As in the National Health Service compared with private practice, the quality of care received by the crew was in no way inferior to that of the passengers and, because of a doctor-patient relationship built up over a longer period of time than possible with passengers on a short cruise, sometimes may even have had the edge.[66]

There are two ship's doctors and three nurses on *Queen Mary II*, most of whom have Accident and Emergency or geriatrics experience; a generalist rather than a specialist surgeon is what is needed. The medical crew have a high status within the hierarchy of ship's officers. A nurse is a two stripe officer, a doctor is a three stripes one, and the senior doctor three and a half stripes; the Captain only has four stripes. The modern ship's doctor tends to be very self-confident and extrovert, but also needs to be versatile and adaptable in dealing with everything from minor illnesses to a major stroke.[67] When off duty the doctor and nurse are free to use all the public facilities, a privilege only extended to officers, but must be conscious of still being on duty, by not relaxing the professional image and in socialising with the passengers. One nurse considered the ship to be her 'second family', since 'being onboard ship for such long periods of time away from our families created a special bond.'[68] For the young doctor intent on seeing the world for a few years before settling down, the life of a ship's doctor has distinct attractions. South African doctors, in particular, seem to relish the opportunity for resourcefulness and independence. The social duties would also seem natural for someone educated at an English public school and traditional medical school with its rugby-playing image. The recluse and the specialist would have no place aboard.

Today the association of cruise liners and health remains strong. Brochures advertising cruises still wax lyrical about the healthiness of life onboard ship:

Opportunities for pure relaxation. The chance to rejuvenate yourself. You can take advantage of both when you travel on a holiday with P&O Cruises. On board you will find some of the most luxurious spa facilities afloat offering all the latest treatments for men and women. Then there are saunas, steam rooms and hair salons. In fact, there's everything you need to be truly pampered. If you want to get, or keep fit and healthy then our ocean-view gymnasiums, personal trainers, sports courts, swimming pools and a comprehensive well-being programme, are designed to help you do just that. The beneficial effects of a P&O Cruises holiday should be felt long after you return home.[69]

The words are from 2010; the sentiments and ideas behind them go back to the earliest days of ocean voyages undertaken for pleasure.

CHAPTER NINE

# Bright and Breezy

BY THE MIDDLE of the nineteenth century the image of the sailor and marine had undergone a sea change. No longer the dirty, diseased, drunken, rag-clad rogues of previous centuries, the 'sons of the sea' were now the object of popular admiration and affection in a way that the army never quite managed. They were the heirs of Nelson and it was on their command of the oceans that trade, the Empire, and national prosperity rested. Now they were seen as attractive and healthy representatives of the bulldog breed, 'sailing every ocean laughing foes to scorn,'[1] men who were 'bright and breezy, free and easy' in demeanour,[2] and national heroes, intrepid at sea and devil-may-care ashore. John Liddell, surgeon at the naval hospital in Malta, was able to declare in 1839 that 'the perfection of health enjoyed by the British Navy has now become a subject of such general notoriety.'[3] Impressment had ended in 1815 and after 1823 sailors now signed onto the Royal Navy for continuous service rather than to a specific ship for a single term. Even when men were still recruited 'at some tavern much frequented by sailors', they were chosen 'from the seaman's appearance or the cut of his jib', although they may not always have been as healthy as their 'physical conformation' suggested, as in the case of Royal Marine John Barton, selected at the age of twenty-two for being 'good looking' with 'nothing in his appearance indicative of ill-health', and yet who proved to be of a 'delicate and sickly constitution' neither in keeping with his appearance nor his new calling.[4] Pay was also improved and there was a new dignity to the sailor's lot. Recruiting posters for the Royal Marines in 1810 had announced that 'all men of respectable character, good countenance and robust health, who do not exceed twenty five years of age and are full five feet six inches high, can enjoy a glass of grog or are fond of a jovial life, have now the opportunity of enlisting in that gallant corps the Royal Marines.' By the end of the century the stress in recruiting was no longer on their capacity for drink but on their general health, and posters stressed that recruits 'must be of strong muscular frame, strong eye sight, sound in constitution . . . and they must possess general intelligence and be of good character.'[5]

This new-found dignity was expressed in uniform. Since its introduction in 1748 to differentiate the officers from the men under their command and give an indication of social status, officer's uniform had kept pace with changing contemporary fashions on which it was based, and by the nineteenth century emphasised the squared shoulders, understated elegance and lean silhouette of contemporary ideals of vigorous masculinity. Over the next century it continued to follow closely on contemporary fashion, often being made up for officers by the same West End tailors who measured them for their civilian clothes, while remaining very clearly a uniform, though some old-fashioned sticklers for tradition complained that now uniform was 'nothing more nor less than a civilian blue coat with the stripes on the sleeve.'[6] In turn, the naval officer's uniform was to influence the cut of the civilian suit as Savile Row tailoring set the tone for men's style, later even influencing the design of such discreet, expensive and luxurious Italian tailors as Brioni, a Rome-based outfitter which in the late twentieth century was to be honoured with dressing on film Ian Fleming's creation of the brand-conscious former naval officer and secret agent James Bond, and for whom the English style was the hallmark of the gentleman, as indeed of the healthy officer.[7] Naval officers had always been as concerned that they were correctly dressed when in mufti as they were about uniform. Midshipman Alexander Scrimgeour at the age of nineteen was very anxious about the maintenance of his wardrobe, even in the middle of the First World War, and filled his letters to his mother with instructions about sending on to him items of clothing, his need for 'two suits of mufti in London' and repairs to his uniform trousers, as his 'servant is willing but unskilled and, being a marine bandsman, wields the piccolo with more skill than the needle.'[8] A dashing appearance and a clean one had been instilled in him as virtues of his rank, and essential for an admirer of actresses and 'cocktails and fizz' at the Adelphi. Ratings were not given a uniform until 1857, and when this was introduced it was based on that worn by the sailors on the royal yacht *Victoria and Albert*.[9] First popularised by the young Albert Edward, Prince of Wales, in the 1840s, sailor suits became a popular costume for Victorian children and represented a national pride in the Navy. For the men for whom they were uniform, they represented improved hygiene and an end to the lice-infested rags many of them had previously worn, which could bring typhus or gaol fever onto many a ship.

It was not only in his garb that the nineteenth-century sailor had an advantage over his forebears. His diet was now greatly improved. In the days of sail, the staples of victualling were grog, salt meat, and ship's biscuit. In 1825 the daily issue of a pint of grog was reduced to a quarter of a pint or a gill, and in 1850 to an eighth of a pint at dinner and supper. Tea and cocoa were now more popular, but heavy drinking continued to be the norm, and many men were saving up their dinner ration of grog to consume with the suppertime issue and be incapable of duty by sundown. In the tropics grog was mixed with lemon juice, which was also added to sugar to be 'made into sherbet', as a prophylactic against scurvy.[10] However, the increasing use of West Indian limes, which were not so effective against scurvy, instead of lemons, might have caused a serious health problem without the introduction of freshly made bread in place of ship's biscuit, and of preserved meat and vegetables into the diet of the sailor. T E Lawrence thought that 'the invention of bully beef had profited us more than the invention of gun powder, but gave us strategical rather than tactical strength since ... range was more than force, space greater than the power of armies', an observation as applicable to the navy as to the army.[11] Nicholas Appert had experimented with bottled meat for the French navy in 1806, but the first canning factory was opened by Bryan Donkin and John Hall at Bermondsey in 1812. By 1831 canned meat was a regulation item in the medical comforts of a ship. The Admiralty established its own canning factory at Deptford in 1866 soon after the murder and dismemberment of Fanny Adams at Alton in Hampshire, prompting the sailors at Portsmouth to spread the rumour that her remains had been canned at Deptford, supposedly the origin of the phrase 'sweet Fanny Adams', which soon came to mean something else, and much more vulgar, in cockney rhyming slang.[12] The surgeon on the *Blossom* had reported in 1824 that 'the preserved meats have been seven years in the ship and are in the highest state of preservation.'[13] However, it is likely that men on John Franklin's expedition to the Arctic in search of the legendary North-West Passage in 1845 were poisoned by the tinned foods that should have made their diet easier and, when that ran out, may even have resorted to cannibalism, which had not been unknown among shipwrecked sailors hitherto.[14] On Franklin's first Arctic expedition of 1820–1, the surgeon John Richardson had shot an Iroquois guide Michel on suspicion of having killed and eaten up to three members of the expedition who had gone missing, and of having passed their meat off as part of a deer killed by a wolf. The idea of an Indian eating human flesh was abhorrent enough to the British public, but they could not even countenance the implication that white men on

Franklin's last expedition in 1845 could have eaten other white men, however desperate they may have been to survive.[15]

Whilst changes may have been made to the diet of the men, ventilation and overcrowding continued to be a problem as long as wooden sailing ships remained the norm. Thomas Spencer Wells, surgeon on the *Modeste* in 1852, condemned the cramming in of 130 men to sleep in a space 54 feet by 6 feet as 'less breathing space than is enjoyed by the inhabitants of the lowest lodging houses in the narrowest alleys of London; still further less than is secured to the felons condemned to imprisonment in any gaol in Britain.' Officers doing their rounds often had to rush up on deck to recover from the foetid atmosphere on the mess deck, and Wells pointed out that that the result of these conditions, as well as spreading pulmonary tuberculosis, was that 'slow poisoning by carbonic acid I believe to be very general in the navy.'[16] An expert on ventilation, D B Reid, had advised in 1844 that all new ships should have built-in air ducts and pumps to expel noxious airs, or else 'in a few minutes after the men have retired to rest, the atmosphere around them became saturated by moisture, and largely charged with carbonic acid and animal exhalations', and 'the premature old age which appears to creep insidiously upon the sailor who sleeps where such an atmosphere prevails, arises more from this cause than all the other hardships to which he is exposed.'[17]

The problem became even more acute after the construction of the first sea-going ironclad, the *Warrior,* in 1861. Condensation on metal plating was worse than on the old wooden walls, and attempts to coat the metal with wood or cork only seems to have harboured vermin. The iron hulls were conductors of both heat and cold. The engines took up so much room that free air space was minimal, and the necessity for watertight compartments separated by bulkheads further prevented the free circulation of air. Six-inch pipes run through the ceiling planking of the *Warrior,* in an attempt to provide natural vents for foul air, were useless. Only steam fans could now provide much more efficient systems of ventilating the new steamships, and these were increasingly fitted after the construction of the *Devastation,* the first of a modern generation of battleships, in 1873. Meanwhile, tuberculosis had become a greater problem than in the days of sail, as a result of the worsening of ventilation and the damp and cold of the ironclads, and by 1862 it was claimed: 'consumption is the most uniform and persistent cause of the large destruction of life in our Navy . . . in all years and nearly alike in all climates, phthisis eats its slow and inevitable fatal course into the strength of our Navy, and causes on the whole a greater amount of permanent loss to the service than any other single malady.'[18] Steam also made possible an adequate supply of drinking water by distillation to fill the iron water tanks that had been standard since 1815. Two Grant's distillers, such as those installed on the *Warrior*, could manufacture up to twenty gallons of fresh water from sea water each day, while 104 tons of fresh water could be stored in the tanks. Yet water supplies still remained limited.[19]

Disinfection, however, remained the mainstay of the maintenance of hygiene above and below deck. In the regulations issued in 1825 to medical officers serving with the fleet, the surgeon was charged to take 'when infection shall exist or there shall be cause to suspect its existence, with the captain's permission, every possible measure for checking it, bearing in mind that dryness, cleanliness and ventilation are the most effectual means to prevent disease and to remove the latter when it exists.'[20] William Burnett, in charge of the Medical Department of the Royal Navy from 1830 to 1845, made his fortune from the supply of a patented disinfectant fluid made from chloride of zinc. Chloride of lime was found effective for 'destroying unwholesome effluvia between decks', and in oppressive hot climates 'completely succeeded in removing the disagreeable close smell which always prevails when a number of persons are confined in a limited circulation of air.'[21] After 1867 carbolic acid was the preferred disinfectant because 'it may be freely sprinkled about decks or urinals . . . and no injury need be apprehended to wood, iron or clothes', and it may be 'poured into air openings or any places emitting nauseous and unpleasant odours . . . to prevent any effluvium arising from the decomposition of organic matter in the bilge water.'[22] It was also used as an antiseptic in operations. In this concern for the environment, the navy saw the stirrings of a nascent public health movement, a feature of many other naval services such as that of the United States, where naval medicine amounted to the first federal healthcare programmes because of the need for the naval authorities to keep control over the health of their men.[23] In Britain, Gavin Milroy, Board of Health Medical Inspector, believed the public health side of the naval surgeon was crucial, and 'the more the medical officers of our ships are regarded in the light of preservers of health, and not merely healers of disease, the better.'[24]

This role of the naval doctor was to be tested in the Crimean War. However, there was a shortage of suitable surgeons when war broke out in 1854. The status of the naval surgeon had been raised in 1805, but little had been done to consolidate this since the end of the French Wars.

Responsibility for the organisation of the naval medical service had been transferred to the Victualling Board of the Admiralty in 1817, and then in 1832 placed under the control of the Physician of the Fleet, renamed in 1843 Director General of the Medical Department of the Navy. This might have been seen as an improvement in the position of the naval doctor, but the surgeon continued to hold a warrant rather than a commission until 1839. The pay was lower than for equivalent ranks in the army medical service, the assistant surgeons did not have their own cabins but had to mess with the midshipmen, their juniors in age and education, and opportunities for promotion were limited with so many surgeons on half pay. Thomas Wakley, reforming and radical editor of *The Lancet,* took up the cudgels on behalf of the assistant surgeons, but there was an entrenched hostility to change within the naval establishment.[25] William Burnett, the Director General, made futile attempts to improve conditions.[26] Despite the service as naval surgeons of such distinguished scientists and clinicians as Sir John Richardson, Thomas Hooker, Thomas Huxley, and Thomas Spencer Wells, there remained a prejudice against naval careers among the staff and students of the medical schools. In 1854 there were only 201 naval surgeons on active service, yet the full complement for the 227 ships in service was 328.[27] Spencer Wells, on half pay and invalided from the naval medical services, preferred to offer his services to the army than return to the ardours and limitations of life aboard ship.[28] It was perhaps fortunate that there were no major naval actions during the war, or the deficiencies of the medical staffing might have been more obvious.

The *Belleisle,* an old 74-gun ship of the line, was converted into a 155-cot hospital ship for the Baltic Fleet, though in the opinion of its medical officer Robert Beith, 'the process of fitting out proved rather tedious.'[29] The ship had a full complement of 240 men, including a medical inspector, two surgeons, two assistant surgeons, one hospital clerk, fourteen male nurses, and three female washers. There was a small operating room. The injured and ill ratings were accommodated on the lower and orlop decks. The sick officers had their own 'small wretched dog-holes called cabins' which proved insanitary and, when the hospital ship was refitted in 1855, were replaced by 'two good sized airy and well-furnished wards'. At the same time the hospital staff was increased by five additional nurses and five dressers, but, even more valuably, a washing machine was installed which 'has enabled us to dispense with the uncertain and capricious services of some troublesome washerwomen.'[30] As well as British sailors and marines, *Belleisle* also treated Russian prisoners of war, who 'presented shocking pictures of filth and corruption; many of them swarmed with maggots.'[31] The surgeon of the steam frigate *Odin*, Edward Cree, was impressed during his visit to the *Belleisle* in August 1854 to find 'everything very nice and clean, but pretty full of our sick and wounded, beside the worst of the Russian wounded, very bad some of them are.'[32] This hospital ship gave sterling service in the Baltic, but similar ships were sorely needed in the Black Sea during the cholera epidemic of 1854, and to deal with the casualties from the battles of Alma and Balaclava. Instead, the *Bombay* and an old Turkish man-of-war moored in the Bosphorus were used, although 'by no means well adapted for their purpose.' Typhoid fever broke out on them, which was ascribed to 'the poisonous miasmata arising from the state of the bilge-water', though more likely to be the result of defective ventilation and overcrowding.[33] Regulations for ships carrying the sick and wounded stressed the need for good hygiene, the holy-stoning and scraping of decks rather than washing them, and the airing of bedding. Meanwhile, 'exposure to the invigorating sea air being most conducive to health, the convalescents must be kept on deck under its awning for such periods daily as the medical officers may think consistent with due care of their health.'[34]

The cholera epidemic in the Black Sea fleet off Varna at the beginning of the war coincided with an epidemic then raging in Marseilles and Toulon, and was probably taken to the Crimea by the French forces. The first British cases appeared in HMS *Diamond*, but the epidemic on the *Britannia* was an 'unparalleled outbreak of diseases surpassing anything in the minds of the naval service for the suddenness of its advent, the tempest violence with which it raged and the havoc it committed.' The ship was taken to sea as a quarantine measure. The consumption of fruit was forbidden and the decks washed down with chloride of zinc. In all, 139 men died.[35] Ships carrying prisoners of war thought to be suffering from cholera were careful to keep the decks awash with disinfectants. The surgeon on the *Sphinx* made sure that as soon as the Russians had been disembarked in 1855 'the whole of the ship was thoroughly scrubbed and ventilated by which prophylactic measures we escaped that disease which I consider we had every justifiable reason to anticipate would have attacked the ship's company.'[36]

The ship's surgeons did see some action during the bombardments of Sevastopol in September 1855. Many of the wounded brought aboard the *Arethusa* were 'skinned and much confused by being knocked against each other', and 'any alarm they evinced is not to be wondered at when it is remembered the stench'. All the surgeon Charles Deane Steel could do when the wounded men were brought down to him on the lower deck, where he stood at the bottom of a ladder 'with tourniquet in my hand and lint bandage', was to 'take a cursory glance to see that there was not anyone requiring immediate assistance, but most happily under all circumstances no one was so seriously wounded as to require a capital operation' on the carpenter's bench set up for him as an operating table.[37] Surgeon Sabben on the *Sphinx* was relieved that 'fortunately, I may add miraculously although in the thickest of the fight, we escaped all injury, being but one boy by the name of Edward Tracey who was drowned by the swamping of a gig at the stern.' Everything had been carefully arranged in the cockpit for him before the bombardment had commenced, with his instruments, swabs, drugs, wines and spirits, and buckets of water 'for the wounded to drink from or for other purposes', and all laid out within reach of the improvised operating table made in time-honoured fashion from chests and mess tables. Ship's beds were laid on chests and mess tables at either side of the cockpit, and were set out for the walking wounded. Two men were positioned to 'lower the wounded in a cot down the hatchway from the upper deck direct to the cockpit', and other sailors, 'whose kindness and attention would tend much to alleviate the sufferings and raise the physical depression of the wounded', were ready to assist the medical staff by offering drinks to the casualties.[38]

Even more comforting were the ministrations of the women nurses in the naval hospitals set up at Eupatoria and Therapia near Constantinople. The Royal Naval Hospital at Therapia occupied a private house and a kiosk belonging to the Sultan, which was not entirely suitable for hospital use because of the small windows, low ceilings, and the 'improper position and faulty construction of the Turkish privies, some of the doors of which opened directly into the wards', which were 'still offensive', regardless of the number of times they were disinfected.[39] Work was soon commenced to remedy the deficiencies of the sanitation, but more serious were complaints of inattention and pilfering on the part of women recruited as nurses in Malta. At first they were replaced by 'respectable' sailors, and then in January 1855 a 'number of respectable female nurses engaged in England' arrived, led by Eliza Mackenzie as matron.[40] The wife of a Church of Scotland minister, who acted as unpaid chaplain to the hospital, Mrs Mackenzie had observed the work of the nurses at the Middlesex Hospital, and ran Therapia efficiently until she had to return home suffering from exhaustion in November 1855. More tactful than the better-known Florence Nightingale working at Scutari, she established good relations with the medical staff, even being elected an honorary member of the officers' mess, and managed her nurses firmly. She had visited Scutari and 'found it in a state of confusion' and 'a frightful place to manage', with an overworked Florence Nightingale having taken to her bed.[41] She acknowledged that her own task was easier in a smaller, more efficient naval hospital. Sidney Godolphin Osborne was very impressed by that hospital where 'nothing could exceed the cleanliness, comfort and order which appeared to prevail ... the patients are as happy as sailors ever are when sick and in bed.' He was especially struck that he 'saw here none of that confusion and resort to temporary expedients which so prevailed at Scutari', and that 'it was in its management and general economy, the one English thing I saw properly conducted in the East.'[42] Until its closure in June 1856, Therapia treated 1,775 patients regarded as incurable on their own ships, including cases of smallpox, scurvy, frostbite and syphilis, as well as wounds, and only twenty-two out of 230 operations proved fatal.[43] The navy, with such a record, escaped the worst of the criticism reserved for the army medical services once the war was over, though its shortage of doctors may well have proved a scandal had it been exposed to the same strains as the medical services of the army.

The Crimean War had raised public concern about the welfare of the soldier and sailor, both physical and moral. The relationship between vice and ill-health had been made by John Liddell back in 1839, when he commented that 'there could not be devised a more fertile source of disease than the habits to which a growing stripling is at once necessarily introduced on his admission to the marines, for besides the fatigue of frequent drills, the broken sleep and the exposure to inclemencies of the weather at night, he is freely fed on rich animal food, his blood is heated by intoxicating liquors, and his system is destroyed by the abuse of smoking tobacco and immoral excesses, to most of which it is probable he was previously unaccustomed.'[44] In 1864 Admiral W F Martin called for more to be done to provide recreation facilities for sailors and marines on shore as alternatives to the attractions of the public house and the brothel, since 'the men when on shore, having no rational pastimes, are almost forced into dissolute society at whose haunts alone is any trouble taken to amuse them. Places for recreation should be made by the government on a liberal scale.' Martin urged the building of barracks and sailor's homes, but there was little that could be done about the 'scandalous and barefaced immorality disgracing Portsmouth and other towns of the same class.'[45] In an attempt to stop the heavy drinking among men in the ports, Agnes Weston founded the Royal Naval Temperance Society in 1870 and, in an excess of missionary zeal, bravely went on board ships to persuade men to sign the pledge. On shore the first of Aggie Weston's Sailors' Rests was opened in 1875. Together with her friend Sophia Wintz, 'Mother Weston' had started her mission to seamen in 1873 by setting up a tea bar outside the dockyard gates at Plymouth, offering an alternative to the lure of the public house. In 1875 this became a hostel serving hot meals and providing accommodation at reasonable prices set so as to cover the actual costs rather than make a profit. The Sailor's Rest, intended as a home from home for her 'bluejackets', not only had cabins and a dining room, but also a hall that could be used for Bible classes, temperance meetings, and social activities. Following the loss of the frigate *Eurydice* in 1878, Weston went to Portsmouth to try to help the bereaved families of the 320 lost crew, and set up another Rest there.[46]

Not surprisingly, the British armed forces had long been a focus of concern about the spread of venereal disease, and in 1864 a Contagious Diseases Act, introducing what amounted to the state regulation of prostitution, was passed. It applied only to eleven port and garrison towns,[47] in which any woman now suspected of prostitution by a plain clothes member of a special Metropolitan police squad stationed within those areas could be arrested, examined by a doctor for disease without giving her consent and, if infected, forcibly admitted to a lock hospital for up to three months, or until she was considered 'cured'. If any woman refused to be examined or refused treatment, she could be imprisoned for a month if it was her first offence, and for up to two months if she re-offended against the Act.[48] The system was made permanent by a second Act in 1866, which extended the maximum period for which women could be detained to six months, then in 1869 a third Act extended it to cover eighteen military areas in all.[49] The assumption behind the Contagious Diseases Acts was that it was women who were the threat to the efficiency of the navy. In effect it ensured a supply of healthy and disease-free women to service the lusts of the naval rating, though that was never the intention. Florence Nightingale warned of the danger that 'any honest girl might be locked up all night by mistake by it', and the writer Harriet Martineau protested against a bill that 'promises to secure soldiers and sailors from the consequences of illicit pleasures'.[50]

The Admiralty was only interested in how effective the Contagious Diseases Acts were in safeguarding the health of its sailors. A committee set up in October 1864 under the chairmanship of F C Skey, a surgeon at St Bartholomew's Hospital, reported that the regulations were essential to prevent a daily loss of men hospitalised by venereal disease 'equal to the loss of . . . such a vessel as the Royal Oak'.[51] What the Acts failed to do was to 'seize upon and eradicate disease at its source', because of the difficulties of diagnosing the infection early enough. Many a sailor was drunk when he caught a venereal disease, failed to show any symptoms for twelve to fifteen days after intercourse, and then it was too late to trace the girl he had slept with, who might have infected other men in the meantime. What was necessary was the regular examination of all known prostitutes in all garrison towns and sea ports, as well as a ban on prostitutes living in beer shops and public houses, where they might prove too great a temptation to inebriated customers.[52] The Skey Committee was realistic enough to realise that regulation of prostitutions in the ports was not enough if nothing was done for 'preventing the men from carrying infection to the women.' However, the Admiralty was unwilling to countenance the medical examination of its sailors for signs of infection, and, in the absence of medical inspections, it remained the responsibility of the individual sailor to check for signs of disease when washing himself, and he could be punished for concealing it.[53] The provision of ablution blocks and personal towels by the Admiralty after 1867 was seen as encouraging sailors and marines to look after themselves by using soap and water on their genitalia as soon as possible after intercourse. The best means for a man to keep free of infection, though, was to avoid going with prostitutes entirely, and if the navy could improve the comfort of the ships and provide opportunities for healthy and manly exercise and other recreations for off-duty hours, then there was some hope of 'reducing indirectly the amount of venereal disease in both services, by lessening the temptation of the men to resort to beer shops and brothels'.[54] There was, however, realistically little that could be done to prevent bored and drunken sailors from seeking diversion in sex, and even less to deal with the men of the merchant navy who, 'it is well known, are frequently diseased and often remain for a long time without any kind of treatment.'[55] The legislation may even have encouraged some sailors to seek safe sex with those prostitutes calling themselves 'Queen's Women', who felt able to charge higher prices as state regulation was a guarantee to their clients that they were clean and free of disease.[56]

The seeming success of the Contagious Diseases Acts in the ports and garrison towns led to calls for their nationwide extension to counter the dangers besetting respectable middle-class young men who were considered especially vulnerable to being 'lured into debauchery'.[57] However, there was opposition to the Acts from religious groups concerned that they actually condoned the sins of prostitution, sanitary reformers who doubted that they did any good at all, feminists who deplored the discrimination that they only applied to women, and supporters of civil liberties who saw them as threats to the rights of the individual. Josephine Butler and the Ladies' National Association for the Suppression of the State Regulation of Vice led the attack on the Acts, by which 'the path of immorality is made more easy to our sons and to the whole youth of England'.[58] It was not until 1883 that the acts were repealed as part of a process of political horse-trading to keep William Gladstone's third administration in office.[59] By this time it was recognised that the Contagious Diseases Acts had not been so efficient in eliminating disease as their supporters had initially hoped. Without any effective form of treatment for venereal diseases, compulsory examination and hospital treatment could not cure the diseases. The Justices of the Peace in the ports lamented the 'disastrous effects' of the withdrawal of the Metropolitan Police who had enforced the Contagious Diseases Act, most notably 'the increase in prostitution, and especially of youthful prostitution, in the more reckless conduct of prostitutes in the streets, in the increase of disease and in its more virulent character'.[60]

Syphilitics had long made up a significant proportion of the patients being treated in the naval hospitals, which were increasingly coming under criticism for being expensive and having been 'founded and endowed on a scale more ample than any civil institution, and are consequently able to aspire to greater perfection in hospital management', which was 'in all respects admirably adapted to secure the comfort and well-being of their patients.' At Haslar, the construction of a 'zymotic department', in which sufferers from different infectious diseases could be treated in separate wards and airing grounds, isolated not only from the other parts of the hospital but from men with different infections, was something none of the great voluntary hospitals of London, run by charitable efforts, could equal. However, in peacetime the naval hospitals were greatly underused, yet remained staffed as if on a wartime footing, though an outbreak of fever or a ship full of tropical diseases brought from overseas stations could rapidly fill the underused beds. Haslar had 1,120 beds yet was rarely more than half full, and on one day in 1867 only had 322 patients. At Plymouth there was accommodation for 760 officers and men, but the average number of patients on any one day was just over 243. Such arrangements were 'far more costly than those of city hospitals', but were not considered a 'waste' because they represented 'the perfection of intelligent hospital construction and administration, but are unattainable in our London hospitals.' Nevertheless, a reduction in the medical staffing, secretarial staff, and servants, and even in the current rather generous ratio of one nurse to seven patients, was proposed in 1869 by a civil commission to investigate the working of the naval hospitals. However, one common economical measure already in force was condemned, the practice of discharging all the nurses of an empty ward 'however long they may have been in service', which was 'a serious obstacle to them in procuring and keeping efficient nurses'.[61] Another obstacle may have been the strict naval discipline, which saw Haslar 'treated more as if it was a man-of-war than as an institution for the amelioration of sickness, wounds and suffering', and where there was 'constant friction between the fighting and healing forces.'[62]

The low standard of nursing at sea compared with that in the naval hospitals was a matter of great concern. The loblolly boys of Nelson's navy and earlier had given way in 1833 to sick berth attendants, but these continued to be seamen or marines who had drifted into the work from vague humanitarian impulses or because they were useless for any other duties. In 1854 men had replaced the female nurses in the naval hospitals, despite a suggestion that the example of Eliza Mackenzie and her nurses at Therapia might be a model for female nursing throughout the service. The sick berth attendants were criticised in 1898 as men who had been 'failures elsewhere', and this was reflected in their pay rates, which at 1s 4d were 3d a day less than those received by an able bodied seaman. This lowness of pay ensured that 'the material from which the sick berth staff is recruited is inferior to that for other non-executive ratings', and the 'pay and prospects offered are not sufficient to induce a better class of man to come forward.'[63] Even men who had been recruited from dispensaries or chemists' shops proved to be 'quite without any preparatory knowledge or training to fit them for their duties in the Navy, while after entry they are entirely dependent on natural aptitude and training for any proficiency to which they may attain.'[64] This was despite reforms suggested in 1883, by a committee chaired by Sir Anthony Hoskins, that a trained sick berth staff should be recruited from boys educated at the Greenwich Hospital School, who had first served on a training ship and then studied nursing, anatomy, first aid, dispensing, and invalid cooking at Haslar Hospital.[65] These recommendations were a failure, and instead ratings were recruited from the Royal Marines, but there were not always suitable men available, which meant that men still had to be appointed who were 'unfitted for the discharge of the duties devolving upon them', and in many cases were 'men who had been rejected by other branches of the service.'[66]

However, the Hoskins Committee did recommend the appointment of women as nurses in the naval hospitals, since 'trained female nursing is of the highest value to the sick and wounded' and 'life would often be saved or prolonged by it'.[67] Such nurses could also be used to train the sick berth staff. On 1 April 1885 a naval nursing service was formed from 'a limited number of trained Sisters of the position of gentlewomen under the superintendence, in each Hospital, of a Head Sister.' They were to have trained for three years in a civil hospital with at least two hundred beds, and could count on the support of the sick berth attendants to whom they would give nursing instruction.[68] The 'youths who are to undergo a preliminary course of instruction before going to sea' may have had no objection to being under women nurses, but older male sick berth attendants resented them. William Charles Parkhurst, sick berth steward on the *President* with twenty-three years' service, did not think that the gentleness and kindliness of a woman nurse 'would do in the Navy', because 'when a man is very bad a female nurse may be a very good kind of person about him, but I do not think he could have better attention than he would have from the present sick bay staff when he is getting around.'[69] In March 1902 Queen Alexandra took on the presidency of the Naval Sisters' Service, which was thereafter entitled Queen Alexandra's Royal Naval Nursing Service,[70] and enjoyed the well-intentioned if never less than imperial interference, especially over the minute details of uniform, of a woman described by Lord Haldane, a later Secretary of State for War, as 'about the stupidest woman in England'.[71]

Improvements were similarly made to the arrangements for the training of naval doctors. The Hoskins Committee had recommended that a medical school be established at Haslar. Until 1871 it had not been considered either necessary or desirable to offer a newly-appointed surgeon any training for his new role, beyond any lectures on military and naval hygiene he might have attended while at medical school. Then in 1871 it was decided that newly-appointed naval doctors should attend a special course on naval medicine at the Army Medical School at Netley Hospital near Southampton. The instruction at Netley was not particularly useful for a naval surgeon, and also made him aware that the pay and conditions of army doctors were superior to his own. In 1881 Walter Reid, a staff surgeon at Haslar, began to give lectures on naval medicine which included bandaging and the management of fractures, surgery, ventilation, diet, meteorology, ship's hygiene, and post-mortem examination. The first students arrived even before the necessary microscopes and chemical reagents had been ordered. However, after the initial enthusiasm for the new courses, complacency set in, and the courses lagged behind the considerable progress being made in such areas as bacteriology, which was 'now one of the most important subjects of instruction at Netley', and the study of tropical diseases. By 1897 the courses on naval surgery were being given by an instructor based on his personal experiences in the Russo-Turkish War of 1878, and the camp hygiene lectures were only slightly more up to date, being based on personal experience from the Egyptian campaign of 1882.[72] Alexander Turnbull, Inspector General at Haslar, attempted to introduce a new, more up-to-date curriculum for the four-month introductory course in 1897, but made no headway with his proposals and was placed on the retired list for his pains. Despairing of effecting reform at Haslar, he suggested that newly-entered medical officers should be given introductory training at the Royal Naval College, which had been based in the Greenwich Hospital buildings since 1873, since this would bring them into contact with other branches of the navy. Instead, in 1899 the training course at Haslar was modernised to 'include special instruction in those diseases which occur on foreign stations on which Her Majesty's ships are, the diagnosis and treatment of which have recently made much progress.' Bacteriology, tropical diseases, the examination of blood for diagnostic purposes, serum therapy, and even the recently developed use of X-rays were all added to the curriculum.[73]

However, the position of the naval surgeon still remained unsatisfactory compared with the equivalent posts in the Army Medical Service. In 1908 there was still a shortfall in the number of surgeons, with only 504 out of 593 posts being filled. Not only were there more opportunities now available for newly-qualified doctors, but the extension of the medical school curriculum from four to five years had temporarily reduced the supply of suitable young men, 'while the conditions of life as a naval surgeon are not at present such as render that service attractive to a young medical student who looks forward to his future', and would be unwilling to put up with the discomforts of life at sea, the lack of promotion prospects, and the difficulties of keeping up with modern advances in medicine.[74] This pointed to the need not only for higher salaries, but also a 'teaching centre . . . in touch with the scientific world', and in 1911 a School of Medical Instruction and Research was to be established at Greenwich in contact with the Army Medical School, now moved to Millbank from Netley, and with the Dreadnought Seamen's Hospital and the London School of Tropical Diseases.[75]

The need to 'extend the benefits of medical science to the natives of the tropical colonies and protectorates and to diminish the risks to the lives of those Europeans who as government officers or private employees are called upon to serve in unhealthy climates' had been recognised by Joseph Chamberlain in 1898, when he called upon medical schools to give special lectures on tropical diseases, since over a fifth of their graduates would serve in the colonies or as army or naval doctors.[76] Tropical diseases had become a problem for the Royal Navy once naval vessels began to be stationed for long periods in such insalubrious waters as those off West Africa, the 'White Man's Grave'. It was difficult to differentiate between such diseases as malaria, yellow fever, dengue and jaundice, and it was widely believed that they were all caused by the unhealthy air of the tropics. Bad air was believed to have a depressing effect on the nervous system which in turn caused fever, vomiting and anaemia. Patrick Manson, who had first become interested in exotic diseases when serving as a customs officer in south-east China, and was one of the founders of the London School of Tropical Medicine attached to the Albert Dock Branch of the Dreadnought Hospital in 1899, became convinced that malaria was transmitted by the bite of the mosquito, a theory confirmed by the Indian medical service doctor Ronald Ross, and the Italian scientists Giovanni Grassi and Amico Bignami. Ross believed that the only way to eliminate malaria was to eradicate the mosquito. Other scientists thought that the only way of controlling the disease was to use quinine, a constituent of the tonic that went with the gin enjoyed in the naval officer's wardroom.[77] It was not until the development and use of DDT spraying in the 1940s that there was real hope of tackling the problems of mosquito-borne disease.[78]

It was collaboration between the naval, army and civilian medical services, using the new and rapidly developing science of bacteriology, which was to overcome the effects of a debilitating illness that struck the fleet in the Mediterranean throughout the nineteenth century. Known variously as Malta fever, Gibraltar fever, and Mediterranean fever, this illness, characterised by intermittent feverishness, anaemia, and rheumatic pains, was most common in summer and autumn. The bacterium causing the disease was identified by the army doctor David

Bruce as *Brucella melitensis* in 1886, but the way in which the infection was passed on to humans remained a mystery.[79] In Malta it was thought to have been caused by miasma from sewerage in the Grand Harbour, and appalling social hygiene.[80] The Mediterranean Fever Commission under the chairmanship of David Bruce was set up in 1904, under the aegis of the Royal Society and the Governor of Malta, and made up mainly of army and navy doctors. It was a military doctor, Captain Crawford Kennedy, who, escorted by a police officer, got the most interesting task of investigating the possibilities of catching Malta fever in the well-frequented brothels of Malta, where 'one would think that it would be possible to contract any disease in existence', in case there was a connection between venereal disease and Malta fever, since many of the patients in the naval hospital at Bighi seemed to be suffering from both infections.[81] However, it was the Maltese civilian doctor and archaeologist Themistocles Zammit who correctly identified the cause as the milk of the Maltese goat in 1905.[82] A naval surgeon E A Shaw, who had previously helped the pathologist Almroth Wright to develop a diagnostic test for the disease at the Army Medical School at Netley, had made a similar observation, but he failed to follow it through.[83] The role of goats was confirmed by the work of another naval surgeon, Frank Clayton, who demonstrated a clear connection between the drinking of goats' milk by staff and patients at Bighi, and the high incidence of Malta fever among them.[84] The British forces in Malta were at once forbidden to drink unpasteurised goats' milk, and Malta fever, now better known as brucellosis, ceased to be a problem for the Royal Navy.[85]

Scurvy remained a problem for the polar explorers whose exploits thrilled the world in the early years of the twentieth century. The Norwegian Fridtjof Nansen believed that preserved meat and lime juice could actually cause scurvy, whereas fresh meat was good. Alexander Turnbull was impressed that Nansen's expedition of 1893–5 was free of scurvy, which he attributed to a 'proper antiscorbutic diet by the scrupulous care with which the provisions of the *Fram* were selected and prepared, by sterilising in some cases.'[86] Almroth Wright, professor of pathology at the Army Medical School at Netley, advanced the theory that scurvy was the result of acid intoxication of the blood, which could be worsened by the use of lime juice or other citrus fruits, and that only fresh vegetables could prevent scurvy.[87] Edward Atkinson, the surgeon on Robert Scott's Antarctic expedition of 1912, accepted Wright's ideas, and carried out litmus tests on the blood of members of sledging parties to try to identify those who were susceptible to scurvy. Scott considered that 'scurvy seems very far away from us at this time, yet . . . one feels that no trouble can be too great or no precaution too small to be adopted to keep it at bay.'[88] Lime juice was ignored, but supplies of tinned tomatoes, rich in vitamin C, prevented scurvy from becoming an even bigger problem than it was on the sledging parties. However, what did doom Scott and his men was lack of food, frostbite, and exposure.[89] Ernest Shackleton's Antarctic expedition of 1914–17 was even better provisioned with tinned foodstuffs, dried milk, and lime juice capsules, although most of these supplies were lost when the *Endurance* was crushed by pack ice in the Weddell Sea, 'but we could at least count on getting enough seal and penguin meat.'[90]

Scott's last expedition to the South Pole may have been a disaster, but it cemented the image of the gallant naval officer who 'can endure hardship, help one another and meet death with as great a fortitude as ever in the past.'[91] Lawrence Edward Oates was an army officer, not a naval officer, whose delicate health should have excluded him from the expedition had he not purchased his place for £1,000, but he still proved himself a 'brave soul' worthy of the tradition of the officers of the senior service when, conscious that his severe frostbite was holding everyone up, left his comrades with the words, 'I am just going outside and may be some time.'[92] Edward Wilson, who had been surgeon and naturalist on both of Scott's Antarctic expeditions of 1901–4 and 1910–12, had shown a 'self-sacrificing devotion' in his care of Oates, in what was depicted as the true tradition of the naval surgeon and naturalist.[93] The other naval surgeon on the expedition, Edward Atkinson, survived at the base camp, and took command of the expedition. It was a display of heroism all round, which was to set the tone for the coming world war. Atkinson, indeed, was to prove himself a hero of the Great War in the best *Boy's Own* mode. When his ship the *Glatton* blew up in Dover Harbour in 1918, blinded and with his leg scarred by shrapnel, he crawled around the ship treating the wounded.[94]

# CHAPTER TEN

# Stormy Waters

THE ROYAL NAVY had expected to be at the centre of any war against Germany, not to be sidelined. The Imperial German navy had attempted to challenge Britain's long-standing naval superiority in the arms race of the early twentieth century, but when war broke out in August 1914 Britain was still the world's premier naval power. Despite the competition to build more dreadnoughts, the latest in fast, heavily-armoured battleships, than its arch rival, the German navy was outnumbered by the British fleet. In Britain it was expected that this naval supremacy would ensure a swift victory. Instead, the First World War was to be a land conflict fought in the mud and mire of the Flanders trenches. The German ships remained in harbour, denying the British the great naval victories they had expected as a reprise of the glories of the age of Nelson. The inconclusive battle of Jutland of 1916, action at Coronel off the coast of Chile, and naval engagements in the Falklands in the first year of the war were to be the closest to the anticipated set-piece battles. Yet the Royal Navy was still to play a crucial role in the defeat of Imperial Germany by transporting the armed forces to France, maintaining a naval blockade on Germany, and defending the trade lines of the Empire through convoys. Over the course of the next century, Britain was to lose its naval superiority and see the retreat of its Empire, despite the vital part that the navy was to play in ensuring that Britain did not starve, and that it had the resources it needed to continue the fight for survival and democracy in the Second World War. As ever in wartime, naval medicine had its familiar part to play in the advances to victory, and in ensuring the health of the fleet, as well as the necessary task of patching up the war wounded. Long periods of tedium, with little for the medical officer to do, were punctuated by brief but horrific action, during which 'down below we had no idea how the fight was really going'.[1]

The naval medical services began the war in an undermanned condition, just as they had been throughout the Crimean War. This shortage of navy doctors was now met by recruiting senior medical students to the new grade of surgeon probationer. This was touted as giving them a period of practical experience aboard a ship or in a naval hospital that might be considered the equivalent of the clinical clerkships and dresserships of a normal medical school course. Invariably, though, the range of experience was more limited than they would have experienced at home.[2] It did give the student the opportunity to serve his country immediately, rather than waiting to join up once he had qualified as a doctor, and allowed him to directly use his medical studies for the benefit of 'his profession, his Empire and Humanity', rather than serve as an ordinary seaman, squandering his training in those medical and surgical skills that were to be needed in wartime.[3] The surgeon probationer was looked down upon by some regular officers who dismissed him as a 'medicinal midshipman'. For many of these young medical students, service on a hospital ship, which could offer experience of 'some jolly good cases', was preferable to the 'dreary days on patrol.'[4]

Hospital ships were mainly used for transport rather than treatment during the war and had only a small number of doctors on board. Most of the surgery took place in France and Belgium with patients then being brought back home for further treatment and rehabilitation. Many hospital ships were fitted up on private yachts offered for the war effort, or on vessels requisitioned from the merchant navy.[5] They enjoyed international protection under the Geneva Convention, though that did not prevent them from being sunk by enemy action.[6] Moreover in the Dardanelles hospital ships were fitted up and staffed so that the wounded from Gallipoli could be operated upon and looked after by qualified doctors and nurses.[7] Alfred Hope Gosse, serving as physician and anaesthetist on the Hospital Yacht *Liberty*, considered the hospital ship to be 'essential in that it brings all the aids of modern surgery to the side of the battleship.'[8] The importance of transferring the sick and wounded to a hospital ship as soon as possible after action had been realised in 1909, since conditions on the battleships and cruisers would be intolerable, when 'all efforts of nature would have to be carried out in buckets or receptacles of that sort, steam would be up in the ships, the temperature hot, the ventilation bad and the air would become foetid in a few hours.'[9]

Fleet Surgeon Teans, on the *Euryalus* serving in the Dardanelles, saw the role of a ship's surgeon with regard to casualties as being 'to make them all fit to be transferred to the Naval Hospital Ship *Sudan*' as soon as he could, when casualties from Gallipoli were brought to his ship by a Royal Army Medical Corps orderly who was keen to return to the beaches since 'there must be a great lot of lads want something doing for them on shore, sir. I'd best be there, sir.' The boat bearing the casualties was 'six or seven inches deep in blood . . . and packed closely with mangled dead and dying.' One of the first casualties brought onboard was 'a man of magnificent physique, paralysed below the waist without any signs of injury', who had lain in the sea for an hour and still did not accept that he had been hit. One naval officer died as he was laid down on the deck, another man cried out for a drink, but since his face and lower jaw muscles were 'hanging down his neck' there was no way of slaking his thirst, and another young seaman with abdominal wounds 'shrieked like a wounded hare.' In such conditions the naval surgeons, in some cases, 'civilian doctors in uniform', found it difficult to cope, when even experienced naval medical officers were not used to the conditions of battle.[10]

At the battle of Jutland in May 1916, 'all the tiresome awaiting of action had been there but usage had probably dimmed the sense of actuality' for the men on *Warspite,* but when the combat started 'the whole action seemed like an exaggerated battle practice and men were busy with their work and possibly a little curious as to what was happening outside their vision', even as 'the enemy hits could be felt like hammer strikes against the ship's sides'. Stretcher parties brought the men down to the dressing station, the chaplains took charge of first aid on the battery deck, officers had had training in bandaging and the application of tourniquets from a surgeon who had 'experience in lecturing to railwaymen' on first aid, and once men reached the operating table they were stripped and thoroughly examined for any additional injuries, since often 'only one occupies his whole attention and then he is apt to think he has no other.'[11] When stretcher cases had to be transferred from one ship to another, there was a danger of accidents. When one young sailor was being transferred by stretcher from *Warrior* to *Engadine* at Jutland, he slipped off the stretcher and fell between the two ships. He was rescued, but 'unfortunately the poor lad, a handsome lad too he was, no more than eighteen, died of his wounds.'[12] Surgery on many of the ships was 'of the crudest description, time being the most necessary factor.'[13] Coffee and brandy were given to men picked up from ships that had been sunk, some of them 'trembling, moaning and staring vacantly before them, quite oblivious to their surroundings.'[14] However, for the company of the ships such as *Southampton*, picking up the survivors of *Indefatigable* and *Queen Mary* which they had seen sunk, 'the mental effect was interesting . . . no fear was perceptible, only rage and hatred of the foe.'[15] Most men hit by shells were killed outright and the majority of the casualties were 'burns and some of these very bad', the worst cases being 'men who had little clothing upon them, and one man's facial burns were minimised by the fact that he wore his respirator.'[16]

Burns victims from Jutland were sent to the Queen's Military Hospital at Sidcup where the ear, nose and throat surgeon Harold Gillies was doing pioneering work in plastic surgery. One of his patients was an able seaman, W Vickarage, aged twenty, who had suffered severe cordite burns to his face, neck, and hands on board HMS *Malaya* at Jutland, and was unable to close his mouth. He was not admitted to the Queen's Military Hospital until August 1917, some fourteen months after the action, and his nose and hands had to be rebuilt. He was the first patient to be treated with a 'tube pedicule', when Gillies sutured two flaps of skin from his chest together into a tube, which enhanced the blood flow to the reconstructed nose, chosen from an album of photographs of handsome young men. The results were not as aesthetically pleasing as Gillies hoped. Even when he was finally discharged in September 1920, this young sailor remained horribly disfigured by scar tissue.[17]

Shore leave and boundless self-confidence offered a release from the fear of disfigurement and the strains of life at sea. Pilots in the newly-founded Royal Naval Air Service on HMS *Furious* were praised for their youthful high spirits and *joie de vivre*; 'being in their early twenties, in fact very little more than boys in habits and manners, full of merriment and energy', they did not 'allow their minds to think too much of the dangerous side of their calling.'[18] Other young officers were just as active in seeking pleasure from the immediate moment. Robert Goldrich at the age of twenty had been fast-tracked in 1917 from a young midshipman to First Lieutenant in charge of the sloop *Poppy*, but had only seen action for one day at the battle of Jutland. On his twenty-first birthday he noted that 'the health is good. The spirits are good and the powers of seduction are at a maximum', a week before he went on leave while his sloop was undergoing maintenance following a collision at sea, an opportunity for him to prove to himself the truth of his birthday self-assessment. On his first day of leave in London he went to see the popular musical *Maid of the Mountains* with his father and uncle, but afterwards gave them the slip and 'spent the night with a rather revolting wench'; his father 'tumbled that I had been on the batter.' The next day he went to see the rest of his family in Brighton, where he met a 'finely built girl', for whom he 'did a good turn on the beach'. The day after that he 'got hooked by an old cow of 40 or 400, or maybe more', but was not to make his usual conquest, which he put down to 'attacking the eternal problem too sober.' Further brief encounters with 'very worthy bedfellows' punctuated his leave, as well as the evenings on which he 'got rather canned before the bar closed but had a fair to middling evening.'[19] Ordinary sailors just paid for a whore and got drunk.

An attempt was made to deal with the threat to discipline and efficiency from widespread drunkenness. Opening hours of public houses were reduced in port and dock areas, there were local limits on the hours in which women could be served drink, sales of alcohol were forbidden to anyone under eighteen, treating and credit in pubs were banned, and public houses near crucial munitions plants at Enfield Lock, Carlisle, and Gretna Green, and the naval bases at Inverness and Cromarty were nationalised.[20] The problem of inebriation was seen as closely linked with that of prostitution. In Cardiff the military authorities tried and failed to impose a night-time curfew on women. In February 1916, the army and navy were given the power to ban convicted prostitutes and brothel-keepers from areas in which troops were stationed, a regulation which saw thirty-seven people expelled from Folkestone in one month.[21] In April 1917 these restrictions were extended to anyone convicted of offences against public order or decency, who could now be removed from any area in which troops were stationed or munitions manufactured.[22]

Such local action was not enough to stop the problem, and on 22 March 1918 Regulation 40D under the Defence of the Realm Act came into force, decreeing that 'no woman who is suffering from venereal disease in a communicable form shall have sexual intercourse with any member of His Majesty's forces, or solicit or invite any member of His Majesty's forces to have sexual intercourse with her'.[23] The penalty was six months' imprisonment, or a swingeing fine of £100. There was an immediate outcry against a measure that, because it was specifically aimed at women, could be seen as 'making vice safe for men', although the War Office and Home Office preferred to see it as a regulation 'to keep the realm safe by stamping out centres of infection which injure the fighting capacity of the nation'.[24] As catching a venereal disease was classed under military law as a self-inflicted injury, it could be argued that sailors and soldiers were already liable for punishment and did not need to be brought under Regulation 40D. However, a naval chief petty officer pointed out that women were not the only ones spreading disease, and that 'sodomy in the navy is by no means as rare a practice as is believed. The guilty persons are usually long service petty officers who terrorise new and fair boys into submission.'[25]

Nothing was done to stamp out this particular abuse, as the regulation only applied to civilians and did not even allow for the possibility of civilian homosexual men passing on the infection. Such a clause would have been unnecessary, since homosexuality was illegal and could have been prosecuted under existing laws.

In the Royal Navy, the practice of issuing 'dreadnought packets', containing calomel for syphilis, potassium permanganate for gonorrhoea, and cotton wool swabs for applying them to the penis, to sailors going ashore was believed to encourage 'the ignorant class' to 'assume that sexual indulgence is a necessity and plunge in to it dragging other hesitant youths with them.'[26] As a result, a useful protection against syphilis and gonorrhoea was ignored. The German navy was more pragmatic in its approach to sexually transmissible infections, and had offered skilled disinfection by a medical orderly to its sailors since the turn of the century. Much more popular with the men themselves was the introduction of vending machines dispensing prophylactic packets, but Kaiser Wilhelm II had banned these contraptions in 1912 after they had been denounced as 'an official invitation to shamelessness'. Since only the sale of prophylactics was officially banned, the machines were removed and instead the disinfectants were distributed free of charge on request by medical orderlies. After the outbreak of war the German navy opened ablution centres in such major ports as Kiel and Wilhelmshaven, and by 1917 the vending machines had reappeared. The United States navy first issued calomel in 1908, but the practice had been stopped in 1915 after protests from moral purity groups, only to be re-introduced in wartime.[27] Eventually, the British too were forced to set up ablution chambers, known as 'Blue Lamp Depots', on account of the blue lights they used to advertise their location at night; in these a man who had had sex could have his penis irrigated with the chemical protargol, and calomel ointment rubbed on his genitals in a procedure that was unpleasant, painful, undignified, and not particularly effective. The issue of condoms in the first place would have saved a lot of future problems.[28]

Hereditary syphilis was a particular problem in the major ports, where prostitution and venereal diseases were widespread. In Plymouth a considerable number of children were being sent to a clinic supposedly because of their backwardness, but in reality because they suffered from hereditary syphilis. This clinic for the treatment of venereal diseases was undercover, because many parents would have refused to send their children had syphilis been mentioned, but mental retardation had none of the same taboos attached to it. Many of these children, classified as 'slow learners', were found to improve considerably, and 'become quite nice children', if they were treated with mercury. Dr G D Kettlewell, the medical officer in charge of the clinic, believed that 'if we could get hold of these children early enough, there would be fewer stunted crippled children and adults walking around Plymouth, and there are a large number.'[29] The fear was that feeble-minded young women were the most likely people to be tempted into prostitution, and if they also had congenital syphilis they would perpetuate a vicious circle by passing the condition on to the next generation. In Portsmouth it was observed that 'the number of suspects varies according to the social status of the school', with more cases in schools in the slum areas than in the better residential areas inhabited by the families of the non-commissioned petty officers.[30] It was feared that this concentration of children with congenital syphilis in Portsmouth and Plymouth might be reflected across the country, but further investigation showed that, whilst prevalent in the naval ports, the problem was not as great throughout the country as a whole and did not demand special measures to deal with it.[31]

Greater efforts, however, were needed to deal with the recruitment of medical officers to serve at sea. In 1930 it was lamented that 'the shortage of suitable candidates for the Naval Medical Service is at present without exaggeration a very serious menace to the efficiency of the Navy.' The problem was that pay and conditions continued to be poor, and 'the income available to the young medical man in civil practice is undoubtedly much higher in proportion to the naval medical officer.'[32] An advertising campaign was aimed at medical schools, with visits to them by serving officers and even by the Medical Director General Arthur Gaskell himself, as well as articles in medical school magazines. When war did come in 1939, conscription made recruitment easier, though some doctors sent to sea after completing their medical studies found the monotony irksome.

A frustrated sense of idle waiting remained a common feature of the life of the Second World War naval surgeon, summed up in the popular wartime morale-booster *In Which We Serve* by the elegantly languid ship's surgeon played by James Donald, when he remarks on 'years of expensive medical training resulting in complete atrophy: the doctor wishes he was dead.'[33] In most ships, the doctor's duties were centred on him acting as wine steward in the wardroom, messing, substituting as a cipher officer, and censoring mail, except when treating battle casualties or minor ailments, when the priority was to return the sailor to duty.[34] Yet even the non-medical duties could have a value since 'the doctor ... can make himself very useful and busy in his capacity of being an officer, yet not bound by the same rigid code of his executive colleagues ... responsible for doing all he can for their mental as well as their physical health'.[35] Moreover, the battleships did at least have large, well-appointed sick bays with isolation wards, operating theatres, X-ray apparatus and dispensaries which would have been the envy of less well-equipped hospitals at home.[36] One young surgeon, Peter McRae, described the life as being 'as good as it can when one hasn't a job to do.'[37] It was one in which 'the staple food, nourishment, business, hobby and relaxation of all the officers is gin.'[38] McRae was to see action when his destroyer *Mahratta* was hit by a torpedo while escorting a convoy to Russia in 1944. Finding himself on an overcrowded raft with seventeen other men, he is said to have jumped back into the sea with the words, 'I seem to be in the way here'.[39]

There was a fear that when there was no action the sick berth attendants could become as bored as some of the surgeons, and 'it is too easy for the ordinary SBA in these ships to become slovenly in appearance, careless and merely a passenger.' This happened all too often, whereas the sick berth attendant 'should always be the cleanest man on board, have a pride in his work as well as self-respect, and the officers and men should respect him.'[40] All too often a new recruit was 'allocated to the Sick Berth Branch merely because he has a physical defect (eg defective vision) which renders him unfit for other employment.'[41] When this happened 'inefficient nursing is due to the insufficient training of probationers who are conscripts and have no interest in the work, and who are largely old and of low educational standards.'[42] Some of the men sent for training as sick berth attendants were 'so illiterate that they have to be returned to the depot the day after they arrive.' Some of the examination papers of those who made it through training were not only poorly written, but contained serious misconceptions. One man described the lungs as 'two large organs which are on top of the hart [sic].' Another advised treating a patient rendered insensible by a blow on the head with a warm drink, fresh air, and 'slap his hands and face until he comes round'. Other men believed that syphilis was caused by 'touching something which is infected, spoons, forks and other things', and that the patient should be told 'to wash his hands before passing urine' to avoid infection.[43] It was not only at sea that the nursing was bad. There were also problems at the large Royal Navy hospitals at Haslar, Plymouth, and Chatham, and at the smaller wartime naval hospitals set up in evacuation areas less likely to be attacked as intensively as the naval bases.[44] At Chatham ignorant staff had attempted to lower a man with a hernia into a bath with a blanket when instructed to give a blanket bath, and had not noticed when another patient stopped breathing.[45]

In general, though, the navy prided itself on its superior recruits and the good psychiatric health of its men, which 'may be attributed to the good material which was until recently self-selected by expressing a Naval preference at recruitment.'[46] The image of the sailor remained a wholesome and resourceful one. He was the hero of many a wartime film such as *In Which We Serve* and *We Dive at Dawn*. In *Went the Day Well?*, it is a sailor on leave, played by Frank Lawton – in real life the husband of the navy's sweetheart and director of entertainments, Evelyn Laye – who saves an English village from a German invasion, giving leadership to villagers and land girls.[47] However, the good quality of naval recruits was not true of the entire war. When the manning crisis became acute in 1942, the Admiralty was compelled to accept for the first time 'Medical Grade II' recruits. In order to get these men to the necessary physical level of fitness for service at sea, remedial training was given at the Mullers Orphanage in Bristol for 'recruits from every walk of life, the well educated, intelligent, the dullard, the professional man, the small trader, the underdeveloped child of 18 years weighing 200 lbs, the policeman with flat feet, the banker with kyposis.'[48] Here they received physical training, a good diet, and were forced to adopt a good posture.

Morale was seen as being as important as good physique, but was not always easy to maintain. On *Repulse* in 1940 the surgeon reported:

> There is an atmosphere of cheerfulness in the ship, but I do know that everyone feels tired and strained owing to the lack of leave, monotony of surroundings, constant watch keeping and the ever present anxiety for families and relatives, most of whom live in districts frequently attacked by enemy aircraft . . . The burden lies less heavily on the younger members who have fewer res-ponsibilities and greater powers of recuperation.[49]

The companies of those ships involved in the Dunkirk evacuation of 1940 were put under severe 'mental strain combined with a lack of sleep and proper meals' but, because there was a vital task to be achieved, the men of a ship such as *Icarus* 'bore the strain well and only three cases of mental disturbance were encountered.'[50] Morale was understandably low among survivors of sinkings when they were picked up, mainly because they had nothing to do, and were 'not used to being passengers', which made them critical of the crew of the rescue ship.[51] If one seaman showed signs of mental unbalance this could affect the rest of the company. John Harries, a 21-year-old able bodied seaman on *Belfast* in 1944 was 'continually frightened and nervous', and as his state of mind deteriorated, 'tended to lose his self-respect by revealing his fears to his companions'. Although his was not 'a particularly serious case of anxiety neurosis ... he was undermining the remainder of his watch, and as the ship was in a continual state of action stations off the Normandy coast, it was not practicable to treat him onboard.'[52] Generally, the mental strain at sea was considered to be greater than in the Great War, especially when possibilities for relaxation were limited.[53] Where it was possible to organise cricket and hockey when in port, and water polo, swimming, and sunbathing at sea, 'it was most pleasing to walk around at Sunday Divisions and observe a well set-up and healthy-looking collection of officers and men.'[54] As the war went on this was rarely possible.

Rum, buggery and floggings were traditionally seen as characteristics of life at sea, but once ashore the seaman sought a remedy for his 'night starvation' in the pleasures of the flesh, especially when 'alcohol increases desire and impairs judgement, so that a man becomes easy prey on the streets.'[55] Homosexuality was dealt with severely by court martial. Robert Herriman, the surgeon on *Berwick*, had the task of examining two men being court-martialled for sodomy, and found 'spermatozoa in specimens from the anal canal and shirt of the passive agent.'[56] However, sailors who went with women and became infected with a venereal disease could also get into trouble if they concealed their condition, most often caught from 'the amateur, the prostitute is much less commonly responsible.'[57] Regulation 33B under the Defence Regulation Act of November 1943 made it compulsory for doctors treating any patient with syphilis or gonorrhoea to notify the medical officer of health for the county or county borough, together with details of any sexual contacts from whom the sufferer may have contracted the disease or to whom it may have been passed. If the patient twice refused treatment or would not name his sexual contacts, the medical officer of health could enforce compulsory treatment.[58] Many doctors deplored the new element of compulsion, albeit only once persuasion had failed, even if it was 'to bring under medical care those infected persons who have shown themselves unresponsive to education, work or to methods of treatment and who, owing to this refusal to undertake treatment, remain a constant source of danger to the health of the community and a drain on the man-power and woman-power of the nation in its war effort'.[59]

The Green Cross Chambers, disinfection chambers ashore, where a man could be treated with douches of potassium permanganate and perchloride of mercury, and have his genitals rubbed with a calomel cream after intercourse, were so uninviting as to be hardly ever used.[60] Aboard ship the facilities for self-disinfection were also poor. On HMS *Hood* there was no room for a prophylactic ablution cabinet in the main heads, and the men were reluctant to use the one attached to the sick bay for prophylactic irrigation because they did not wish to be observed by the medical officer, so it was decided to build one next to the night heads on the battery deck, where it 'should be useful, as it is easy of access to all men coming off from shore.'[61]

A great breakthrough in the treatment of venereal diseases, rendering disinfection facilities obsolete, came with the use of penicillin to check their course, and it was predicted that 'in future gonorrhoea could cause far less trouble and disability in the Royal Navy than the common cold.'[62] Penicillin had been discovered by Alexander Fleming in 1928, but was not brought into clinical use until the 1940s as a result of the work of a team of scientists at the University of Oxford.[63] Its value for the treatment of syphilis was established by John Mahoney, director of the United States Marine Hospital and Venereal Disease Research Laboratory at Staten Island, New York, in June 1943. After positive results with using it on syphilitic rabbits, he tried it out on a young sailor only recently infected with syphilis who volunteered to take part in the experiment, and within four months of receiving his first injection of penicillin, the young man was found to be completely free from infection and could be declared cured.[64] The United States Public Health Service studied the effects of penicillin on patients in the Coast Guard, but rejected any massive use on merchant seamen, 'due to the fact that the study has been largely experimental and in order to evaluate the results the selected cases must be among patients who can be followed'.[65] The sailor was considered a good human guinea pig for medical experiments, but could sometimes be too much of a wanderer for his progress to be followed closely for medical trials and studies.

The importance of penicillin for the Royal Navy was great enough for it to attempt in 1943 to produce its own at the Royal Navy Medical School which had been evacuated to Clevedon in Somerset. Surgeon Commander C A Green argued that since penicillin was not yet available from any commercial sources, and that even when it was obtainable, it would be expensive, it would give the Navy an advantage if it could 'increase production and offer it for therapeutic purposes'.[66] Howard Florey, whose team of scientists had brought penicillin in to use, was dismissive of the idea, since he believed 'the time is now past for the material to be manufactured on a laboratory scale', even though his own laboratory at Oxford was doing just that.[67] Green, however, persevered and visited Oxford to see what was being done there to produce penicillin. Production at Clevedon was got underway using that officer's staple, the gin bottle, for growing the penicillin in.[68]

The Royal Navy not only took advantage of penicillin, but also of other developments in medicine, such as blood transfusion, immunisation, the use of anti-malarial drugs and insecticides, and mass radiography in its efforts to maintain wartime fighting efficiency.[69] Preventative medicine still remained at the core of this endeavour, whilst emergency surgery onboard ship often remained as chaotic and demanding as ever. In the midst of battle, 'the crump of bombs, the rattle of splinters against the ship's side and the noise of our own guns, were not conducive to the steady hand' on the operating table.[70] The official advice was that 'during action conditions in the operating theatre are such that no serious surgical work can be attempted.'[71] Sometimes there was no choice but to do so. Jack Coulter recalled

> The whole operating theatre swaying, shuddering and tilting as the ship zigzags in her course; instruments, doctors and even the patient sliding about; the haze of smoke everywhere; the lights suddenly going out; above all the deafening wall of noise . . . noise which is so intense that you get punch drunk with it, and then that inward fear, which every normal sailor feels, that at any moment the ship may be hit and start to sink.[72]

When his ship HMS *Cossack* was torpedoed in 1941, Surgeon-Lieutenant Walter Scott was picked up after an hour and a half in the water by a corvette, the *Carnation*, which did not carry a doctor, so he 'took charge of the wounded survivors' and, though having lost his instruments, he 'treated them for shock with hot cocoa, warmth and saline compresses to the burnt areas, while awaiting a syringe to be sent from another ship.' In reporting on his work, he apologised for the state of his report as 'I much regret the oil on the enclosed form, but my bottle of hair oil was broken during the journey home.'[73]

Generally, during action the doctor confined himself to the debridement of wounds, suturing, and life support using blood and plasma. Dale L Groom, an American naval doctor who had recently qualified from the University of Chicago, later reflected on his role on D-Day, and mused that 'I have often been asked how much of my medical education I got to use, and my answer to that is damned little. I didn't have much equipment. I was just doing glorified first aid.'[74] HMS *Belfast* had a fairly well equipped operating theatre and sick berth, but it was only used for emergencies because of the vibration and movement of the ship. During the Normandy landings, casualties from the beaches and other ships were 'rapidly evacuated to the sick bay by first aid parties.' They were given blood transfusions using the latest in transfusion equipment, which 'was found extremely useful.' During its time off the Normandy coast in June and July 1944, *Belfast* remained for twenty days in 'a sustained degree of readiness for action, [men] sleeping in their clothes at or near their action stations, but most nights, little sleep was obtained as sporadic air raids occurred when the ships fired barrages.' All watertight doors and hatches, and all ports were closed for protection against gun blast, restricting ventilation. Many of the men developed boils from the lack of fresh vegetables, and disliked the dehydrated cabbage and potato they were given instead.[75] As the weather improved men had to be warned of the dangers of sunbathing, 'as many ratings were exposing themselves for too long, naked, on deck during quiet periods'.[76]

The heat was even more of a problem in the tropics, where 'the state of ventilation and temperature within the living and working compartments is highly unsatisfactory.' On these ships the crew existed in a continual and unremitting state of discomfort, 'which may be aggravated by the occasion of going on watch, to be relieved somewhat only by resting on the weather deck in the shade of awnings.'[77] The opposite extreme of cold was the lot of men on the Arctic convoys to Russia. As protection against the cold and wet, the Kapok was developed, a wool-padded overall worn under oilskins. However, the Kapok was bulky, and impeded the free movement of men through the passageways. It also made it difficult for stretcher-bearers to 'put a man who is dressed in Arctic clothing into a Neil Robinson stretcher . . . In one case it was impossible.'[78] There was also confusion about the function of the Kapok, and 'some officers believe it is sufficiently buoyant to replace the life-jacket, others insist on their crews wearing life-jackets in addition.'[79]

Conditions were yet more severe and extreme on board submarines, which had been a practical naval arm since the First World War. Well into the 1960s the smaller submarines had no more medical treatment than the training in first aid received by a coxswain in a few hours at

Haslar.[80] Illnesses were diagnosed using a 'paper doctor', a medical textbook in which 'you started off with how he looked, and you had to turn to such and such a page, and eventually you hoped to come to what was wrong.'[81] On HMS/M *Thule* the coxswain 'wasn't a doctor, but he was as good as a doctor', who used a hacksaw 'out of the engine room and sawed the leg off above the knee; and it was just like being in a butcher's shop.'[82] Living conditions were primitive, drinking water was in short supply, and there was even less for hygiene, vegetables soon went rotten, and men froze in the Arctic and North Atlantic, but boiled in hotter climes. It was very little different from the cramped conditions on German U-boats during the First World War, with the head merely separated off from the living space by a curtain. Men 'awoke in the morning with considerable mucous in our heads and frequently with so-called oil-head' from condensation from the steel hull plates. When Johannes Spiess was appointed watch officer on U–9 in 1912, the officer whom he was replacing 'recommended the use of opium before all cruises lasting over twelve hours.'[83] On submarines in the tropics in the Second World War 'the hot atmosphere and sea temperatures' aggravated 'most of the hardships which are attendant upon submarine service generally.' Although dehumidifiers were used three times a day for half an hour a time, the crew of one submarine complained on their return from a three-week patrol of prickly heat, slight constipation, and the lack of ventilation; the cook 'showed a combination of pustular acne and septic prickly heat.' In general, morale was high and 'the chaps are very much on their toes' and more alert after a successful trip, when they were looking forward to rest in port and leave on the upcountry estates of tea planters.[84]

At the end of the war, the navy was involved in the repatriation of prisoners of war and civilian internees.[85] The fall of Singapore and Malaysia had symbolised the beginning of the end of the British Empire in the Far East, and the post-war years were to see a change in the role of the Royal Navy as the retreat from Empire gathered pace. Through the strains of these years of change in the world role of the United Kingdom, one constant remained, in that 'the Royal Navy has the training for war as its almost entire object', and in this the role of the naval doctor remained vital:

Although he may be also a specialist in other subjects such as surgery, radiology or ophthalmology, he is essentially a naval doctor and should be able to deal with the numerous problems of naval hygiene so that he is able to maintain the fighting efficiency of the Navy under conditions which vary in different classes of ships serving in extremes of climate.[86]

In peacetime his duties were centred on maintaining health at sea rather than repairing war injuries.

Living conditions at sea improved in the new ships built after 1945. Until then the ratings' messes would have been all too familiar to the Jack Tar of Nelson's navy. Officers may have been allocated cabins, but the ratings had no choice other than to sling their hammocks wherever they could. In the mess areas hammocks were officially hung 21 inches (52 centimetres) apart, but on many a crowded wartime ship it was common for men from different watches to share hammocks, or even sleep on the deck beneath one of the mess tables. In the 1950s bunks replaced hammocks, as new ships were built and older ones refitted and modernised, but the quarters for naval ratings and marines remained cramped with very little storage space – though not as confined as on submarines. In the twenty-first century Type 45 destroyers, junior ratings enjoy the luxury of six-berth cabins and access to recreation spaces, gyms and cafeterias. In the 1950s the provision of laundries was seen as a great advance. Hitherto the crew of a ship had been expected to wash their own clothes in buckets and basins, often using salt water. Manned by locally recruited Chinese laundrymen in ships in the Far East, these laundries were equipped with washing machines, dryers, and steam presses. Washrooms and showers, however basic, were an improvement on the heads of earlier days. Maintaining a smart appearance was made easier for the ratings as it had ever been for the officers.[87]

Perhaps the greatest improvement of all was in the area of diet. Until the 1950s, Broadside Messing, another legacy from the past, was the norm, in which each mess member took his turn as duty cook responsible for collecting rations from the purser, preparing a meal, taking it to the galley for it to be cooked, collecting and serving the meal, and washing up. Such a system, however much it may have sustained the solidarity of the mess and continued a long tradition, often resulted in a poorly-cooked, unbalanced diet. From the late 1920s onwards, galley cooks had taken over the preparation of the food in bigger galleys, and the role of the mess cook had been reduced to merely collecting the cooked food from the galley and serving it to his messmates. During the Second World War, General Messing was introduced on ships which had been transferred to the Royal Navy from the United States under the lend-lease arrangements. Such ships had canteens, known as Ship's Company Dining Halls, in which the men could eat, rather than at their mess tables, and food was served cafeteria-style. Meals on such American-built ships as the escort carrier *Tracker* were prepared by cooks in well-equipped galleys containing such luxuries as mechanical potato-peelers, ice cream makers, and soda fountains. Bakers produced fresh bread each day, and specially-trained Royal Marine butchers provided fresh meat. Refrigeration and freezing also improved the range of food available.[88] Since 1921 the Navy Army and Air Force Institute's Naval Canteen Service had also provided little luxuries in terms of food, in addition to selling duty free tobacco, confectionery known as 'nutty', toothpaste, and shoe polish. A percentage of the profits generated from the NAAFI on board ship went towards a canteen fund for the benefit of the whole crew.[89] The NAAFI did not sell wine or spirits, but from 1960 onwards sold two cans of beer a day to the men. There was concern, even after the abolition of the rum ration, that 'there might be problems of loss of efficiency effects on skills arising from the use of alcohol', but there was a blanket refusal to admit that alcoholism might ever be a problem in the Royal Navy.[90]

Living and working conditions on submarines remained cramped and uncomfortable, although better than in earlier submarines. HM Submarine *Andrew* had been built in the late 1940s and later modernised, but by 1966, when a report was made on its operation in tropical waters, living standards on board were old-fashioned, and deteriorating through the age of the submarine. Despite the confined environment, smoking was not restricted, and the 'consumption of tobacco was considerable', resulting in high concentrations of carbon monoxide, though it was found that 'admittedly the presence of tobacco smoke in the atmosphere could be unpleasant especially to non-smokers there was no evidence that harmful concentrations were attained on this patrol'. Improvements to air conditioning were recommended. Water, as on all submarines, was in short supply on patrol. Men had to rinse the worst dirt off themselves in a communal bucket, before using wash basins for a more thorough wash. Unlike in earlier submarines, where the heads were emptied by blowing their contents into the sea (when there was always a danger for a submariner of 'getting his own back' when sea pressure was more than blowing pressure), the heads now drained into a sewage tank which was blown periodically into the sea, usually at night when the resulting bubbles would be less visible. Living spaces were cramped, and working spaces varied from 'satisfactory' to 'potentially dangerous'. In the tropics prickly heat was a problem. Diet was considered 'excellent'; the 'meals were appealing and varied and the cooking was nothing short of miraculous considering the appalling conditions under which the two cooks worked.'[91] The problems of keeping men fit under sea, and later on nuclear submarines, demanded more specialist training for doctors charged with such responsibilities.

In the post-war years, all branches of medicine became increasingly specialised. Naval medicine now demanded an expansion of research and training facilities to keep up with developments in the discipline on land. The Institute of Naval Medicine was opened at Alverstoke, near Gosport in 1969, as the direct successor to the Royal Naval Medical School, and was now headed by a Surgeon Rear Admiral in the role of Dean of Nautical Medicine.[92] As well as offering research and postgraduate training in naval occupational medicine, the Institute also provided operational support to the fleet. This support included radiological and environmental safety surveillance, radio-chemical analysis, mobile mass miniature radiography, the control of toxicological and biochemical hazards, and a general investigation of environmental effects on the health of the ship's crew. Projects were undertaken relating to the physiological dangers of diving, nuclear radiation, the confined conditions in submarines, and survival in extreme conditions. Research was also conducted into more general medical problems affecting a high proportion of sailors, including renal and gastroenterological problems.[93] Ships' companies had long offered an opportunity for medical research in controlled conditions as Sir Henry Dale, Director of the Medical Research Council, had acknowledged in 1938, when he urged a trial of an influenza vaccine on boys at the Royal Navy Training Establishment at Shotley near Portsmouth, since 'whether the result was positive or negative . . . it would have a scientific value as having been obtained in such a uniform and controlled community.'[94] Whilst much of this research had wider implications for medicine than just the Royal Navy, it was inevitably very much related to the service needs of an increasingly technologically advanced navy. For a trial into how adequate survival rations for emergency use actually were, eleven men were housed in a hyperbaric chamber, simulating conditions in a disabled submarine for up to seven days at 4°C. Another investigation was made into whether prior hyperventilation would reduce the risk of decompression illness during escape from a submarine, and increase the depth from which escapes can be made. One of its studies into the best ways of cooling men after strenuous activity came up with the answer that the most effective action was simply to plunge the forearms into cool water.[95]

Training of medical staff, medical ratings, and nurses continued to be centred on the naval hospitals, but sick berth attendants, like doctors, were becoming increasingly specialised, with many men in the 1950s training as radiographers, laboratory technicians, pharmacy dispensers, mental health nurses, or physiotherapists. In November 1965, the Sick Berth Attendants were formed into the Medical Branch of the Royal Navy, and divided into medical assistants and technicians. Their roles were closer to those of their equivalents in the National Health Service, but there remained something distinctive about the naval Medical Assistant who, according to Gregory Clark writing in 1984 at the centenary of the formation of the Sick Berth Branch, was 'a unique sort of person. He is given positions of responsibility early in his career and, as a leading rating, can be in sole charge of his own department at sea ... Outside the Ministry of Defence it would be illegal to teach him the diagnostic and therapeutic skills he requires to perform his naval task.'[96] Certainly, demarcation of duties had no place in a medical emergency onboard ship. At sea, just like the medically qualified officers, they were widely referred to as 'Doc'. With their smart double-breasted jackets and caps, they were proud of both their calling and their natty appearance, though sometimes this led to hubris. In the early 1970s, as a newly-qualified medical assistant, K A Brown could not resist showing off to some tourists, especially a group of pretty girls, as he passed them on a boat taking him from Haslar to Portsmouth Harbour, and heaved his kit bag at the jetty only for it to fall into the sea, then, as he retrieved it, he knocked his suitcase into the water, with the result that 'it was a very humbled and red faced young M.A. that had to walk with them towards the station, dirty green sea water dripping from suitcase and kit bag', and rueing that 'the excursion into Portsmouth Harbour had cost me dearly – all my spare uniforms and my civvies were ruined.'[97] However, the days of an all-male navy, and of segregated male and female nursing services were numbered. On 1 April 1983 all new entrants to the nursing service, whether men or women, now joined Queen Alexandra's Royal Naval Nursing Service. It was the precursor to women serving at sea alongside their male colleagues after 1993.[98]

The Falklands Campaign of 1982, in contrast to the modernising trends in the navy of the time, was something of a throwback for the United Kingdom to the colonial wars of the nineteenth century. The greatest military challenge that it posed, one with repercussions for the provision of medical services, was of maintaining a sea and air supply line stretching for 8,000 miles, in order to liberate the distant Falkland Islands in the South Atlantic after their seizure by Argentine forces. Some of the shipboard surgery practised in war conditions also seemed to hark back to earlier wars. In peacetime, a ship would normally take a seriously-ill sailor to the nearest port for treatment, but in wartime with radio silence this was not an option. A stoker on the frigate *Ambuscade* had been injured in a fight in Gibraltar, and septicaemia had set in with the danger that the man might lose the use of his hand or arm. His condition deteriorated and his life was feared for, but the medical officer was inexperienced, and had to operate by following step by step his medical manuals with the help of the Executive Officer, Lieutenant Commander John Lippiett, whose role was to 'engage the patient in conversation throughout the operation to keep his eyes (and mine) from straying to the gory mess as his hand was cut apart, and also had to turn the pages of the medical manual that the MO was consulting as the operation progressed', something that both Lippiett and the patient found 'rather disconcerting.'[99]

The luxury cruise liner *Canberra* was pressed into service, alongside regular vessels of the Royal Navy, such as the aircraft carriers *Hermes* and *Invincible,* to carry troops, and sick bays were set up on board these ships. The SS *Uganda,* another cruise liner specialising in educational cruises for schoolchildren, was requisitioned specifically as a hospital ship. During the Second World War, luxury liners had been requisitioned as troop carriers and hospital ships for the duration of the conflict. The last naval hospital ship in the fleet, the *Maine,* had been decommissioned in 1952, when the Royal Yacht *Britannia* was planned as a floating palace that could be converted into a hospital ship if necessary. It had on board a small doctor's surgery, sick bay, dispensary, and operating theatre, but only for the crew of 'yachties' and marines, as the Queen and royal family came under the care of the medical officers of the Royal Household. The state apartments were designed for conversion into hospital wards. When the *Britannia* was needed as a hospital ship in 1982, it was considered unsuitable for service in the South Atlantic, and instead of the luxurious apartments of the monarch, it was the humbler quarters of schoolchildren that were hurriedly converted, when the *Uganda* became a hospital ship. A helicopter landing pad was installed. The spacious dormitories became wards, recreation spaces were adapted to accommodate up to a thousand casualties, the school tuck shop became a pharmacy, a hairdressing salon housed radiography facilities, and a cocktail bar for adult passengers became a laboratory. It was all carried out in sixty-five hours at Gibraltar.[100]

The first casualties were evacuated by helicopter to the *Uganda* from the stricken HMS *Sheffield* on 4 May 1982. When the *Sheffield* was first hit by an Exocet missile, G A Meager, the petty officer medical assistant, found the 'doctor slightly dazed but OK, the sick berth door was inside the bay, a pillow was embedded in the formica behind the doctor's chair and the operating table was slightly buckled.' He was further shocked at the sight of an engineering mechanic, 'who came into the Bay, looking like a gollywog, his hair had been badly scorched and his face, arms and hands severely burned.' Many other burns cases presented themselves. Chaos ensued. One man had his leg amputated by getting it trapped in a steel door, yet was still unable to get free. Smoke inhalation, shock and exhaustion affected many other men, who 'were alright when they were fighting the fire, but as soon as they were relieved they collapsed and were useless for a while until they regained their senses.' Even Meager, the medical assistant, at one point 'cracked up and I went completely to pieces, feeling bloody useless.' As the ship burned, he reflected that 'it's an incredible feeling to see nearly everything you own going up in smoke, the only things you've got left are the clothes you stand up in, it is a very strange feeling.'[101] The need for a fully-equipped hospital ship was further underlined, and certainly more than justified, after the bombing of the landing ships *Sir Galahad* and *Sir Tristram* at Bluff Cove on 8 June 1982. The attack killed fifty-six Welsh Guards and over one hundred others were severely wounded or burned. They were evacuated swiftly to the hospital ship for immediate treatment. For the most severely burned, such as Guardsman Simon Weston, whose burnt face and courage became emblematic of the casualties of the Falklands War, plastic surgery awaited them at home. Many men were treated for post-traumatic stress disorder.[102] However, the days of dedicated hospital ships were numbered. On its return to Portsmouth, after having treated 730 inpatients, including 150 Argentine prisoners, and having performed 504 operations, *Uganda*, perhaps the last of the hospital ships, bore a banner boasting that 'We came, we saw, we treated.'[103]

Medicine in the twenty-first century Royal Navy remains concerned with ensuring operational effectiveness in war and peace, through maintaining the health and physical fitness of the sailor. In order to do this, medical officers and medical assistants are assigned to surface and submarine flotillas, the Fleet Air Arm, and the Royal Marines. Only the larger ships and submarines carry medical officers permanently. On smaller ships basic primary care is the responsibility of medical assistants, trained to give simple first aid and day-to-day medical care, often without direct supervision from a doctor. The medical assistants also train members of the ship's company to form first aid parties capable of recovering injured men and giving them first aid in battle. Medical assistants working with the Royal Marines are given the opportunity for commando training, which entitles them to wear the much coveted Green Beret, since they need the same level of fitness as the Commandos to whom they may be called upon to give first aid in action. Royal Marine Units, aircraft carriers, and some larger ships also have dental officers providing mobile dental services to groups of ships. Higher levels of surgical and medical treatment are available on aircraft carriers. A Primary Casualty Reception Ship, with four fully-equipped operating theatres, is kept ready on RFA *Argus* to deal with a major emergency, and can be staffed by specialist orthopaedic and general surgical teams, intensive care and high dependency nurses, pathologists, radiographers, and technical support.[104]

Yet at the same time as naval medicine has become ever more specialised and diverse, there has been a new emphasis on collabora-tion and co-ordination between the medical services of the Army, Navy and Royal Air Force. This tri-service co-operation was given added impetus by the recommendations of the Defence Medical Services Inquiry Committee in 1973, which led to the establishment of a joint Directorate of Medical Policy and Plans, as well as tri-service training schools for physiotherapists, radiographers, dental hygienists, and laboratory technicians. In 1985 co-ordination of the medical services of all three armed services became the responsibility of the Defence Medical Services Department under a single Director-General. This was not only an economical measure, but also had the advantage of co-ordinating military and naval medicine at a time when co-operation and interdependence between the services in general was becoming much greater in modern warfare. For separate services, each with their own pride in long-cherished traditions, it was not so easy to see their independence eroded. All were united in mourning the closure of the specialist military and naval hospitals.

The naval hospitals had changed in character since the end of the Second World War. Following the foundation of the National Health Service in 1948, these hospitals were increasingly opened to civilian patients, while there was also provision for service patients in civilian hospitals. There had never been a tradition of the navy arranging medical treatment for the families of its men at home, although it had often been found necessary to provide care for their dependants overseas. In the inter-war years many men stationed with the Mediterranean Fleet had taken their wives and families to Malta with them, a practice which was considered desirable, since 'undoubtedly it prevents much unhappiness; two year's separation has long been regarded as the maximum which is desirable', but which meant the need for a dispensary for the wives and children of naval ratings living there.[105] At Singapore it was found necessary to provide a medical facility for the families of Asian dockyard workers, since 'in any community, and especially in an Asiatic community, the women and children are the main vectors of infection for the whole herd', and to control the spread of infection it was essential that the naval medical officers at the naval base should be able to examine and treat them and everyone else 'living on Admiralty property.'[106] The end of National Service meant that in peacetime the well-equipped naval hospitals were no longer fully used by service patients in areas where there was a shortage of beds for civilians, whilst there were distinct advantages in admitting civilian patients which opened up a wider range of clinical experience to naval doctors and nurses.

Overseas naval hospitals were closed as the British colonial presence was run down. The naval hospital in Hong Kong closed in 1956, when naval patients began to be treated at the British Military Hospital in Kowloon, Bighi in Malta closed in 1970, and on 3 March 2008 the last of the great overseas naval hospitals, the Royal Naval Hospital Gibraltar, closed after 104 years of service in its latest incarnation. However, by the mid 1980s the future of all service hospitals was being questioned at a time of defence cuts. The end of the Cold War, signalled by the fall of the Berlin Wall in 1989, saw cuts in manpower in the Army, Navy and Air Force, resulting in even fewer service patients and a proposal in 1993 that only three service hospitals, Haslar, Aldershot and Wroughton, should remain, one for each of the services, followed almost immediately in 1994 by a revised plan for Haslar Royal Naval Hospital to become the only service hospital catering for patients from all three services. By 1998 it was decided that Haslar, too, should be closed, and service patients sent to a Centre of Defence Medicine at Birmingham. Henceforward, service patients would be treated in civilian hospitals.[107] The Royal Naval Hospital at Plymouth closed on 31 March 1995. Twelve years later the Royal Hospital Haslar was decommissioned on 30 March 2007. Its commanding officer, J K Campbell, in his speech at the closure ceremony, said that 'we no longer see the survivors of a distant battle brought home after a long sea journey, which was the model that the Royal Hospital Haslar was built to serve. They now fly home swiftly and need immediate high level care from a legion of top specialists ... We can no longer respond to those demands here.'[108] However, there was doubt as to whether the treatment of service casualties from the wars in Iraq and Afghanistan in civilian hospitals was any more adequate a response. Service patients felt abandoned by their country to National Health Service waiting lists, civilians with little understanding of what they had been through as fellow patients, and the loss of the emotional support they could have expected from their comrades, and from naval and military doctors and nurses.[109]

Maritime medicine in the twenty-first century is changing quickly, with old ways and ideas being swept aside by the mass communications revolution. In an age when ordinary seamen have their laptops and email accounts not only for recreation, but for communication when in range of signals, the doctor at sea, with access to the sophisticated communications systems of his ship, is never driven on to his own resources when faced with the medical emergencies that still, and always will, occur at sea. It is always possible to seek advice, patients can usually be got to shore medical facilities fairly quickly, and conditions at sea are much improved, and ship hygiene easier to police. Medicine at sea has kept pace with the rapid pace of modern social change, just as it always has done and always will.

# *Notes*

## Chapter One: Deadly Cargoes

1. William Shakespeare, *Richard II*, 2:1, 43–7.
2. F P Wilson, *The Plague in Shakespeare's England* (1927), p. 111.
3. Now Theodosia.
4. S A Epstein, *Genoa and the Genoese* (2001), pp. 212–13.
5. G De Mussis, *Historia de Morbo, Archiv fur die Gesammte Medizin,* 2 (1842), 26–59.
6. Chronicler of Este, quoted in P Ziegler, *The Black Death* (2003), p. 4.
7. Ibid.
8. K F Kiple, *The Cambridge Historical Dictionary of Disease* (2003), p. 50.
9. A G Carmichael, *Plague and Poor* (1986), pp. 5–6.
10. M W Flinn, 'Plague in Europe and the Mediterranean Countries', *Journal of European Economic History,* 8/1 (1979), 134–8.
11. S K Cohn, *The Black Death Transformed* (2002), pp. 78–80.
12. R Horrox, *The Black Death* (1994), pp. 24–5, 40, 42, 74, 81, 84.
13. Ibid., p. 70, quoting the chronicle of William Dene of Rochester, 1348.
14. M Prestwich, *Plantagenet England* (2005), pp. 538–53.
15. G Chaucer, *The Canterbury Tales*, Prologue, verse 18.
16. N Cohen, *The Pursuit of the Millennium* (1962), pp. 127–47.
17. S Watts, *Epidemics and History* (1997), p. 10.
18. N G Siraisi, *Medieval and Early Renaissance Medicine* (1990), pp. 84–5, 97–107.
19. A G Carmichael, *Plague and Poor* (1986), pp. 98–9, 108–10.
20. Present day Latvia and Estonia.
21. R Reidna, *Tallinna Mustpeade Vennaskonna Maarja Altar: The Altar of Holy Mary of the Tallinn Brotherhood of the Blackheads* (1995), pp. 10–12.
22. M Harrison, *Disease and the Modern World* (2004), p. 26.
23. D Chambers and B Pullan (ed.), *Venice: A Documentary History, 1450–1630* (2001), pp. 118–9.
24. A G Carmichael, 'Plague Legislation in the Italian Renaissance', *Bulletin of the History of Medicine,* 57 (1983), 519–25.
25. H Teonge, *The Diary of Henry Teonge, Chaplain on board HM Ships Assistance, Bristol and Royal Oak, 1675–1679* (1825), p. 57.
26. A Hervey, *Augustus Hervey's Journal* (2002), p. 187.
27. G Sandys, *Travels* (1673), p.178
28. C Savona-Ventura, *Knight Hospitaller Medicine in Malta* (2004), pp. 46–9.
29. J Yonge, *Journal* (1963), p. 70.
30. P Cassar, 'Slitting of Letters for Disinfection in the eighteenth century in Malta', *British Medical Journal* (1967), 105–6.
31. J Yonge, *Journal* (1963), p. 44.
32. E A Carson, 'The Customs Quarantine Service', *Mariner's Mirror,* 64 (1978), 63–9.

33. G Hampson (ed.), *Portsmouth Customs Letter Books 1748–1750* (1994), pp. xxviii-xxix.

34. Ibid., p. 65.

35. Ibid., p. 185.

36. G R Crone (ed.), *The Voyages of Cadamosto and Other Documents on Western Africa in the Second Half of the Fifteenth Century* (1937), p. 2.

37. L H Roddis, *A Short History of Nautical Medicine* (1941), pp. 15–17; R H Fritze, *New Worlds* (2002), pp. 66–73.

38. E LeRoy Ladurie, *Mind and Method of the Historian* (1981), p. 28.

39. A W Crosby, *The Columbian Exchange* (1972), p. 49.

40. B De Las Casas, *A Short Account of the Destruction of the Indies* (1991), p. 15.

41. F Guerra, 'The Earliest American Epidemic: The Influenza of 1493', *Social Science History*, 12 (1988), 305–25.

42. B Díaz del Castillo, *The Conquest of New Spain* (1963), p. 216.

43. J H Elliot, 'The Overthrow of Moctezuma and his Empire', C McEwan and L López Luján, *Moctezuma: Aztec Ruler* (2009), pp. 230–3.

44. Thirteenth month of Aztec calendar beginning in October.

45. B de Sahagún, *Florentine Codex: General History of the Things of New Spain* (1955), p. 81.

46. B Díaz del Castillo, *The Conquest of New Spain* (1963), p. 309.

47. H Thomas, *Rivers of Gold* (2004), p. 552.

48. W H McNeill, *Plagues and Peoples* (1977), p. 207.

49. J N Leonard, *Ancient America* (1967), p. 164.

50. Cited in M Oldstone, *Viruses, Plagues and History* (1998), p. 32.

51. S Watts, *Epidemics and History* (1997), p. 92.

52. I and J Glynn, *The Life and Death of Smallpox* (2004), p. 34.

53. Quoted in S Watts, *Epidemics and History* (1997), p. 93.

54. A Benedetti, *Anatomice sive Historia Corporis Humani*, Venice, 1497, quoted in C Quétel, *History of Syphilis* (1990), p. 10. See also A Benedetti, *Diario de Bello Carolino*, Padua, 1496.

55. R Diaz de Isla, 'Tractado contra el Mal Serpentino: que vulgamente en España es llamado Bubas' in I Bloch, *Der Ursprung der Syphilis* (1901–2), vol. 1, pp. 306–7.

56. See C Columbus, *The Four Voyages of Christopher Columbus* (1969), pp. 139, 156.

57. A W Crosby, *The Columbian Exchange* (1972).

58. F Guerra, 'Aztec Medicine', *Medical History*, 10/4 (1966), 320.

59. C Kidwell, *Pietro Bembo: Lover, Linguist, Cardinal* (2004).

60. G Fracastoro, *Syphilis* (1984), pp. 86–100.

61. Ibid., p. 102.

62. Ibid., p. 104.

63. K Brown, *The Pox* (2006), p. 21.

64. C Roberts and M Cox, *Health and Disease in Britain* (2003), pp 272–4. In the 1994 excavation of a medieval friary in Hull, palaeopathological evidence seemed to suggest that 60 per cent of the skeletons earlier than the late fifteenth century in the cemetery showed bone changes in the leg compatible with syphilis, a high incidence of disease, but which it has been suggested may be associated more with nutritional or febrile diseases confined within a small and poor community rather than arising from syphilitic infection; see R S Morton and S Raschid, 'The Syphilis Enigma: the Riddle Solved?', *Sexually Transmitted Infections*, 77 (2001), 322–4.

65. H Miller, *Secrets of the Dead* (2000), pp. 183–4.

66. E H Hudson, *Non-venereal Syphilis* (1958), C J Hackett, 'On the Origin of the Human Treponematosis', *Bulletin of the World Health Organisation* 29 (1963), 7–41; H H Scott, 'The Influence of the Slave Trade in the Spread of Tropical Diseases', *Transcripts of Royal Society of Tropical Medicine and Hygiene,* 38 (1943), 169.

67. K Manchester, *The Archaeology of Disease* (1982), p. 49; S Zivanovic, *Ancient Disease: the Elements of Palaeopathology* (1982), pp. 232–4.

68. T Sydenham, 'History and Cure of the French Pox' in *Works* (1729), p. 248.

69. R S Morton, *Venereal Diseases* (1974), p. 556.

70. Ibid., pp. 24–5.

71. K Brown, *The Pox* (2006), pp. 14–15.

72. G Torella, *Dialogus de Dolore cum Tractatu de Ulceribus in Pudendagra Evenire Solitis* (1500), sig. D4ᵛ.

73. D MacCulloch, *Reformation* (2003), p. 632.

74. J D Comrie, *History of Scottish Medicine* (1932), vol. 1, p. 200.

75. J Yonge, *Journal* (1963), pp. 48–9.

76. D MacCulloch, *Reformation* (2003), p. 631.

77. M Sanudo, *Venice, Cítá Excelentissima: Selections from the Renaissance Diaries of Marin Sanudo* (2008), p. 329.

78. J Arrizabalaga, J Henderson and R French, *The Great Pox* (1997), pp. 172–6.

**Chapter Two: Surgeon's Mate**

1. J Yonge, *Journal* (1963), pp. 41–2.

2. Ibid., p. 41.

3. *Iliad,* 2:834–5.

4. Ibid., 11:606–7.

5. Ibid., 4:222–52.

6. 'D[is] M[anibus] Iuliae Veneriae M[arcus] Satarius Longin[us] Medic[us] Dupl[icarius] Triremi Cupid[ine] Et Iuliae Veneria Liber[ta] Her[edes] Ben[e] M[erente] Fec[erunt]', R S Allison, *Sea Diseases* (1943), p. 3.

7. V Nutton, *Ancient Medicine* (2004), p.181.

8. R Jackson, *Doctors and Diseases in the Roman Empire* (1988), p. 129.

9. V Nutton, 'The doctors of the Roman Navy', *Epigraphica,* 32 (1970), 66–71.

10. J Keevil, *Medicine and the Navy* (1957), vol. 1, p. 20.

11. A Jal, *Archéologie Navale* (1840), p. 337.

12. J Muscat and A Cuschieri, *Naval Activities of the Knights of St John 1530–1798* (2002), pp. 76–8.

13. E Krause, *The Adventures of Count George Albert of Erbach* (1890), p. 53.

14. P Cassar, 'A Medical Service for Slaves in Malta during the rule of the Order of St John of Jerusalem, *Medical History,* 12 (1968), 270–7.

15. H Thomas, *Rivers of Gold* (2004), p. 111.

16. Ibid., pp. 145, 154.

17. R Hakluyt, *Principal Navigations* (1903–5), vol. 8, p. 183.

18. Ibid., p. 250.

19. T Twiss (ed.), The *Black Book of the Admiralty* (1871–6), vol. 1, pp. 94–7.

20. S Doran (ed.), *Henry VIII, Man and Monarch* (2009), p. 248.

21. J Castle, J Kirkup, B Derham, J Montagu, R Wood and J Hather, ' Septicaemia, Scurvy and the Spanish Pox: Provision for Sickness and Injury at Sea' in J Gardiner (ed.), *Before the Mast: Life and Death Aboard the Mary Rose* (2005), pp. 189–225.

22. C S Knighton and D Loades (ed.), *Letters from the Mary Rose* (2002), p. 63–4.

23. J Gardiner (ed.), *Before the Mast: Life and Death Aboard the Mary Rose* (2005), pp. 515–44.

24. D Childs, *The Warship Mary Rose* (2007), pp. 86, 90–4.

25. J Gardiner (ed.), *Before the Mast: Life and Death Aboard the Mary Rose* (2005), pp. 153–4.

26. N A M Rodger, *Freedom of the Sea* (1997), p. 320; J Smith, *The Seaman's Grammar* (1654), p. 36.

27. Ibid., p. 161.

28. J Watt, 'Surgeons of the *Mary Rose*', *Mariner's Mirror* 69/1 (1983), 3–19.

29. J Castle, J Kirkup, B Derham, J Montagu, R Wood and J Hather, 'Septicaemia, Scurvy and the Spanish Pox: Provision for Sickness and Injury at Sea' in J Gardiner (ed.), *Before the Mast: Life and Death Aboard the Mary Rose* (2005), p. 171.

30. M Pelling, 'Appearance and Reality: Barber Surgeons, the Body and Venereal Disease in Early Modern London' in A I Beieir and R Finlay (ed.), *The Making of the Modern Metropolis: London 1500–1700* (1986), pp. 82–112.

31. S Young, *Annals of the Barber-Surgeons of London* (1890), p. 258.

32. Ibid., p. 321.

33. R Hakluyt, *Principal Navigations* (1903–5), vol. 2, pp. 195–200.

34. J K Laughton (ed.), *Naval Miscellany* (1902), p. 57.

35. R Hakluyt, *Principal Navigations* (1903–5), vol. 10, pp. 98–9.

36. Ibid., p. 130.

37. R Hakluyt, *Voyages and Discoveries* (1972), p. 172.

38. Ibid., p. 186.

39. R Hakluyt, *Principal Navigations* (1903–5), vol. 3, p. 542.

40. Ibid., vol. 10, p. 109.

41. Ibid., p. 120.

42. Ibid., p. 134.

43. Ibid., vol. 11, p. 293.

44. R Hakluyt, *Voyages and Discoveries* (1972), pp. 327–8.

45. J R Dasent (ed.), *Acts of the Privy Council of England 1542–1604* (1890–1907), vol. 16, p. 5.

46. R L Pollitt, 'Bureaucracy and the Armada: the Administrator's Battle', *Mariner's Mirror*, 60 (1974), 125.

47. J K Laughton (ed.), *State Papers relating to the Defeat of the Spanish Armada, 1588* (1894), vol. 1, pp. 65–6.

48. Ibid., vol. 2, pp. 290–3.

49. Ibid., pp. 289–95.

50. Ibid., vol. 1, p. 258.

51. J Keevil, *Medicine and the Navy* (1957), vol. 1, pp. 129–37.

52. R Hakluyt, *Principal Navigations* (1903–5), vol. 2, p. 97.

53. J K Laughton (ed.), *State Papers relating to the Defeat of the Spanish Armada, 1588* (1894), vol. 2, pp. 96–7.

54. Ibid., p. 159.

55. R B Wernham (ed.), *The Expedition of Sir John Norris and Sir Francis Drake to Spain and Portugal, 1589* (1988), pp. 194–5.

56. Cited in N A M Rodger, *Freedom of the Sea* (1997), p. 408.

57. Letter from Sir John Coke to the Duke of Buckingham, 25 August 1625; S R Gardiner

(ed.), *Documents illustrating the Impeachment of the Duke of Buckingham in 1626* (1889), p. 15.

58. N P Bard (ed.), 'The Earl of Warwick's Voyage of 1627' in N A M Rodger (ed.), *Naval Miscellany V* (1984), p. 52.

59. J Bruce (ed.), *Calendar of State Papers Domestic, Charles I, 1627–28* (1858), p. 478.

60. Ibid., p. 507.

61. R Hakluyt, *Principal Navigations* (1903–5), vol. 7, pp. 41–81.

62. S Purchas, *Hakluytus Posthumus* (1905–7), vol. 17, p. 78.

63. Ibid., p. 90.

64. Ibid., p. 188.

65. J Keevil, *Medicine and the Navy* (1957), vol. 1, p. 170.

66. Ibid., p. 196.

67. W Monson, The Naval Tracts of Sir William Monson (1902–14), vol. 4, pp. 63–4.

68. L A Kvarning and B Ohrelius, *The Vasa: Royal Ship* (1998), pp. 110–12.

69. There is now some doubt as to whether what was identified as a surgeon's chest in the 1960s was indeed one. Personal information from Marika Hedin, Director of *Vasa* Warship Museum, 2009.

70. L A Kvarning and B Ohrelius, *The Vasa: Royal Ship* (1998), pp. 120, 126.

71. Ibid., p. 130.

72. I Bruijn, *Ship's Surgeons of the Dutch East India Company: Commerce and the Progress of Medicine in the Eighteenth Century* (2009), pp. 59–60.

73. J Yonge, *Journal* (1963), p. 98.

74. Ibid., p. 96.

75. S Purchas, *Hakluytus Posthumus* (1905–7), vol. 2, p. 545.

76. Ibid., vol. 3, pp. 51–60.

77. Ibid., vol. 10, p. 515.

78. J Woodall, *The Surgions Mate* (1978), p. xiv.

79. A G Debus, 'John Woodall, Paracelsian surgeon', *Ambix*, 10 (1962), 108–18.

80. J Woodall, *The Surgions Mate* (1978), p. 2.

81. Ibid., pp. 2–5.

82. Ibid., p. 3.

83. Ibid., pp. 160–76.

84. Ibid., p. 3.

85. E G Atkinson (ed.), *Acts of the Privy Council 1613–1628* (1940), pp. 70–1.

86. J Woodall, *The Surgions Mate* (1978), p. xv.

87. J Yonge, *Journal* (1963), pp. 56, 58.

88. Ibid., p. 59.

89. Ibid., p. 160.

90. J Smith, *The Seaman's Grammar.*

## Chapter Three: Sick and Hurt

1. TNA, SP 25/32/54–9, State Papers, 7 September 1652.

2. TNA, SP 18/46/44, State Papers, January 1652.

3. Ibid.

4. TNA, SP 25/71/19, State Papers, 29 September 1653.

5. J Keevil, *Medicine and the Navy* (1957), vol. 1, p. 6.

6. L H Roddis, *A Short History of Nautical Medicine* (1941), p. 10.

7. R Reidna, *Tallinna Mustpeade Vennaskonna Maarja Altar: The Altar of Holy Mary of*

the Tallinn Brotherhood of the Blackheads (1995), p. 10–12.

8. J Keevil, Medicine and the Navy (1958), vol. 1, pp. 10–11.

9. The Chatham Chest is now displayed at the Chatham Dockyard Museum on loan from the National Maritime Museum.

10. NMM, MS 53/008, Decree of the Commissioners of Charitable Uses, 1617.

11. BL, Eg MS 2975, f. 47.

12. J Keevil, Medicine and the Navy (1957), vol. 1, p. 194.

13. NMM, MS 9633, P Ward and E Hayward, Naval Accounts for 1637–43.

14. J Keevil, Medicine and the Navy (1958), vol. 2, p. 9.

15. Ibid., pp.3–4.

16. TNA, SP 16/139/2, regulations for Savoy Hospital and Ely House, 1644.

17. K Brown, The Pox (2006), p. 20.

18. TNA, SP 18/34/26, letter from Daniel Whistler to the Council of State, 16 March 1653.

19. TNA, SP 18/34/46, letter from Daniel Whistler to Sir Harry Vane, 21 March 1653.

20. TNA, SP 18/38/35, letter from Peter Pett to Admiralty, 10 July 1653.

21. TNA, SP 18/39/75, report of Daniel Whistler, 25 August 1653.

22. Ibid.

23. Mercurius Pragmaticus, 13–20 February 1649, sig. 2v.

24. TNA, SP 18/38/5, letter from Elizabeth Alkin, 2 July 1653.

25. J Keevil, Medicine and the Navy (1958), vol. 2, p. 56.

26. Ibid., pp. 37–9.

27. N A M Rodger, The Command of the Ocean (2004), p. 215.

28. E Barlow, Journal (1934), vol. 1, pp. 213–14.

29. TNA, ADM 106/289, f. 99, note by Captain H Priestman at Sheerness, 30 October 1673.

30. TNA, ADM 1/3554/140, letter from Navy Board, 1685.

31. J D Davies, Pepys's Navy (2008), p. 166.

32. TNA, ADM 106/3539, petition of Robert Moore, 1685.

33. Ibid., petition to Principal Officers and Commissioners of HM Navy from surgeons, 1685.

34. Ibid., petition of John Conny, 20 August 1686.

35. Ibid., petition of Joan Ramsay, 1687.

36. TNA, PC 6/1, Privy Council, 2 February 1665.

37. TNA, ADM 106/295, letter from Sir John Berryman at Long Reach to the Commissioners, 16 January 1674.

38. TNA, ADM 106/3539, certificate given to John Moyle by the men on the James Galley, 14 August 1680.

39. J Moyle, Chirurgus Marinus or The Sea Chirurgion: Being Instructions to Junior Chirurgie Practitioners who design to serve at Sea (1693).

40. J Yonge, Journal (1963), pp. 213–14.

41. J Keevil, Medicine and the Navy (1958), vol. 2, pp. 131–47.

42. J Yonge, Journal (1963), p. 146.

43. S Pepys, The Shorter Pepys (1985), pp. 163, 560.

44. S Pepys, Pepys's Later Diaries (2004), pp. 124–5.

45. E Barlow, Journal (1934), vol. 1, p. 54.

46. Ibid., p. 127.

47. Ibid., p. 68.

48. TNA, ADM 1/3551, letter from Robert Robinson, 1681.

49. S Pepys, *Samuel Pepys's Naval Minutes* (1925), p. 250.
50. H Teonge, *The Diary of Henry Teonge, Chaplain on board HM Ships Assistance, Bristol and Royal Oak, 1675–1679* (1825), p. 31.
51. J D Davies, *Pepys's Navy* (2008), p. 154.
52. J Yonge, *Journal* (1963), p. 33.
53. J Moyle, *Chirurgus Marinus* (1693), p. 46.
54. Ibid., pp. 145–8.
55. Ibid., pp. 11–17.2
56. Ibid., pp. 48–9.
57. R Wiseman, *A Treatise of Wounds* (1672), p. 91.
58. E Barlow, *Journal* (1934), vol. 1, p. 119.
59. S Pepys, *The Shorter Pepys* (1985), pp. 494–5.
60. C R Markham (ed.), *Life of Captain Stephen Martin, 1666–1740* (1895), pp. 8–9.
61. J White, *De recta Sanguinis Missione, or New and Exact Observations of Fevers in which Letting of Blood is shew'd to be the True and solid Basis of their Cure* (1712), p. 3.
62. J D Davies, *Pepys's Navy* (2008), p. 165.
63. J Keevil, *Medicine and the Navy* (1958), vol. 2, p. 87.
64. TNA, SP 29/134/80, State Papers, 12 October 1665.
65. J Keevil, *Medicine and the Navy* (1958), vol. 2, p. 90.
66. TNA, PC 6/1, Privy Council, 11 November 1663.
67. TNA, SP 29/140, report of Thomas Alllin to Navy Commissioners, 25 December 1665.
68. J Evelyn, *Diary* (1955), vol. 3, p. 418.
69. TNA, SP 29/154/37, Commander Middleton, 22 August 1666.
70. S Pepys, *The Shorter Pepys* (1985), p. 494.
71. Ibid., p. 547.
72. Ibid., p. 565.
73. Ibid., p. 535.
74. Ibid., p. 211.
75. Ibid., p. 239.
76. Ibid., p. 383.
77. Ibid., p. 579.
78. TNA, SP 29/133/63, John Evelyn, 30 September 1665.
79. J Evelyn, *Diary* (1955), vol. 3, p. 407.
80. Ibid., pp. 447–8.
81. Ibid., p. 431.
82. TNA, ADM 3/5, Admiralty minutes, 31 October 1690.
83. Ibid.
84. TNA, ADM 3/5, Admiralty minutes, 9 January 1691.
85. TNA, ADM 3/6, Admiralty minutes, 10 July 1691.
86. H Richardson (ed.), *English Hospitals 1660–1948* (1998), p. 77.
87. J Keevil, *Medicine and the Navy* (1958), vol. 2, p. 195.
88. B Tunstall (ed.), *The Byng Papers* (1930), pp. 79–80.
89. TNA, SP 29/116/78, letter from James Pearse to Samuel Pepys, 29 March 1665.
90. TNA, SP 29/323/122, list of equipment for hospital ship by James Pearse, March 1672.
91. TNA, SP 29/324/16, report of Hugh Ryder, 27 April 1672.
92. TNA, SP 29/307/134, Prince Rupert, 6 May 1672.
93. J J S Shaw, 'The Hospital Ship 1608–1740', *Mariner's Mirror*, 22 (1939), 306–27.
94. C Lloyd and J L S Coulter, *Medicine and the Navy* (1961), p. 110.

95. C Stevenson, *Medicine and Magnificence* (2000), p. 174.

96. N Hawksmoor, *Remarks on the founding and carrying on the building of the Royal Hospital at Greenwich* (1728), p. 9.

97. Ibid., p. 13.

98. Later the regulation coat was blue.

99. TNA, ADM 67/3, regulations of Greenwich Hospital, August 1704.

100. C Lloyd and J L S Coulter, *Medicine and the Navy* (1963), vol. 4, pp. 263-4.

## Chapter Four: Plague of the Sea

1. G Williams (ed.), *Documents relating to Anson's Voyage round the World, 1740–1744* (1967), p. 77.

2. R Walter, *A Voyage around the World by George Anson* (1838), p. 102.

3. C Lloyd (ed.), *The Health of Seamen* (1965), p. 9.

4. L de Camões, *The Lusiads* (1997), p. 114.

5. Cited in J Keevil, *Medicine and the Navy* (1957), vol. 1, p. 99.

6. S Purchas, *Hakluytus Posthumus* (1905–7), vol. 2, p. 396.

7. J Woodall, *The Surgions Mate* (1978), p. 185.

8. Ibid., p. 180.

9. Ibid., p. 179.

10. R Mead, *A Discourse on Scurvy* (1749), p. 111.

11. TNA, ADM 106/1027/187, letter from P Fowke, 11 April 1746.

12. TNA, ADM 106/1031/27, letter from T Lloyd, 5 April 1746.

13. TNA, ADM 354/132/41, James Cleveland, 19 February 1746.

14. NMM, ADM/E/43, Admiralty to Sick and Hurt Board, 1781–1783, 15 August 1782, ADM/E/12, Admiralty to Sick and Hurt Board, 1746–1750, 15 October, 11 December, 1747, 24 May, 27 December, 1748.

15. TNA, ADM 354/113/143, letter from W Cockburn, 1 November 1740.

16. NMM, ADM/F/17, letter from surgeon on HMS *Intrepid* to Sick and Hurt Board, 4 January 1758.

17. NMM, ADM/G/785, Abstracts of Admiralty orders to Victualling Board, 1770–1774, 25 November 1771; ADM/E/41, Admiralty to Sick and Hurt Board, January 1770-December 1774, 20 January 1772.

18. J Lind, *A Treatise of the Scurvy* (1753), p. 203.

19. Ibid., p. 137.

20. Ibid., pp. 137–8.

21. Ibid., pp. 145–8.

22. K Carpenter, *The History of Scurvy and Vitamin C* (1966), p. 53. See also D I Harvie, *Limeys* (2002).

23. G Blane, *Observations on the Diseases of Seamen* (1789) in C Lloyd (ed.), *The Health of Seamen* (1965), p. 160.

24. TNA, ADM 354/149/241, John Cleveland, 15 February 1755.

25. J Lind, *An Essay on the most Effectual Means of Preserving the Health of Seamen* (1779) in C Lloyd (ed.), *The Health of Seamen* (1965), p. 28.

26. Ibid., p. 27.

27. G Blane, *Observations on the Diseases Incident to Seamen* (1785), p. 251.

28. Ibid., p. 172.

29. Ibid., p. 178.

30. TNA, ADM 354/182/198, petition of Captain Murray, 1 September 1769.

31. TNA, ADM 101/81/5, surgeon's log, James Scott, *Ajax*, 27 July 1799–31 January 1800.

32. J Lind, *Treatise on Scurvy* (3rd edition, 1772) in C Lloyd (ed.), *The Health of Seamen* (1965), p. 24.

33. TNA, ADM 101/82/3, surgeon's journal, *Albion*, 1799–1800.

34. TNA, ADM 101/85/4A/1, surgeon's journal, Thomas Tappen, *Arab*, 27 March 1799 – 27 March 1800.

35. TNA, ADM 101/96/1, surgeon's journal, Peter Henry, *Daedalus*, 1 January–4 December 1802.

36. N A M Rodger, *Command of the Navy* (204), p. 308. Rodger is dismissive of such exaggerated figures.

37. J Lind, *An Essay on the most Effectual Means of Preserving the Health of Seamen* (1779) in C Lloyd (ed.), *The Health of Seamen* (1965), p. 121.

38. G Blane, *Observations on the Diseases of Seamen* (1789) in C Lloyd (ed.), *The Health of Seamen* (1965), p. 229.

39. NMM, ADM/Y/G/51, estimates, 16 April 1741.

40. TNA, ADM 2, Sick and Hurt Board petition, 26 October 1741.

41. TNA, ADM 98/2, Petition of Lord Sandwich, 15 September 1744.

42. NMM, ADM/F/6, Sick and Hurt Board, 27 June 1746.

43. Cited in A L Revell, *Haslar the Royal Hospital* (2000), p. 14.

44. TNA, ADM 98/2, letter from Admiralty to Sick and Hurt Board, 18 June 1745.

45. H Richardson, *English Hospitals 1660–1948* (1998), p. 79.

46. A L Revell, *Haslar the Royal Hospital* (2000), p. 25.

47. J Howard, *The State of the Prisons in England and Wales* (1784), p. 389.

48. J Tenon, *Journal d'observations sur les principaux hôpitaux d'Angleterre* (1992), p. 150.

49. NMM, ADM/F/6, letter from R Forbes, 9 August 1745.

50. A L Revell, *Haslar the Royal Hospital* (2000), p. 21.

51. TNA, ADM 98/7, pp. 374–5, Sick and Hurt Board, 7 February 1759.

52. TNA, ADM 98/6, p. 150, Sick and Hurt Board, 19 January 1757.

53. C Lloyd and J L S Coulter, *Medicine and the Navy*, vol. 3 (1961), p. 253.

54. TNA, ADM 1/3533, Marine instructions for taking care of sick and wounded seamen, 12 January 1782.

55. J Tenon, *Journal d'observations sur les principaux hôpitaux d'Angleterre* (1992), pp. 183–4.

56. Regulations drawn up by James Lind, 1777, in C Lloyd and J L S Coulter, *Medicine and the Navy*, vol. 3 (1961), pp. 219–26.

57. J Tenon, *Journal d'observations sur les principaux hôpitaux d'Angleterre* (1992), pp. 154–5.

58. T Trotter, *Medicina Nautica* (1803), vol. 3, p. 18.

59. TNA, ADM 1/3534, letter from Stephen Love Hammick, 4 September 1805.

60. C Lloyd and J L S Coulter, *Medicine and the Navy*, vol. 3 (1961), pp. 227–8.

61. TNA, ADM 98/13, report of Admiral Barrington to Sick and Hurt Board, 25 July 1780.

62. TNA, ADM 1/3533, Remarks made upon an examination of the Royal Hospital at Haslar, 28 March–4 April 1792.

63. E Birbeck, A Ryder and P Ward, *The Royal Haslar Hospital* (2009), p. 65.

64. TNA ADM 1/3534, statement of May Bill, 27 February 1805.

65. Ibid., statement of Sarah Perrott, 27 February 1805.

66. A L Revell, *Haslar the Royal Hospital* (2000), pp. 36–7.

67. TNA, ADM 105/28, remarks on lunatic cases at Hoxton, 13 November 1812.

68. C Lloyd and J L S Coulter, *Medicine and the Navy*, vol. 3 (1961), p. 266.
69. Ibid., p. 276.
70. C Lloyd and J L S Coulter, *Medicine and the Navy*, vol. 4 (1963), pp. 218–19.
71. NMM, ADM/E/8b, Admiralty to Sick and Hurt Board, 1741, 2 January, 23 January; ADM/F/3, Sick and Hurt Board to Admiralty, October 1742–April 1744, 31 January 1743
72. C Lloyd and J L S Coulter, *Medicine and the Navy*, vol. 3 (1961), pp. 11–12.
73. L Brockliss and C Jones, *The Medical World of Early Modern France* (1997), pp. 689–700.
74. TNA, ADM 106/2896, p. 55, register of officers appointed to ships, 10 March 1739/40.
75. T Smollett, *Roderick Random* (1979), p. 86.
76. Ibid., p. 149.
77. Ibid., p. 157.
78. Ibid., p. 191.
79. Ibid., p. 183.
80. NMM, ADM/354/140/94, Thomas Corbett, 9 January 1748.
81. W N Boog Watson, 'Two British Naval Surgeons in the French Wars', *Medical History*, 13 (1969), 215.
82. TNA, ADM 106/1027/106, letter from W Dymer to Mr Waugh, 14 October 1746.
83. TNA, ADM 106/1027/101, letter from Apothecaries' Hall, 22 October 1746.
84. J Cook, *The Journals* (1999), p. 38.
85. J Banks, *Journal* (1896), p. 71.
86. J Cook, *The Journals* (1999), pp. 189–90.
87. J Cook, *The Voyages of Captain Cook* (1999), p. 228.
88. Ibid., p. 227.
89. Ibid., p. 468.
90. C Lloyd and J L S Coulter, *Medicine and the Navy*, vol. 3 (1961), p. 319.
91. W Bligh, *Mutiny on the Bounty* (2006), pp. 54–5.

## Chapter Five: England's Expectations

1. NMM, BHC2894 (Greenwich Hospital Collection), Arthur William Devis, 'The Death of Nelson', 1805–7.
2. M Lincoln (ed.), *Nelson and Napoleon* (2005), p.226.
3. NMM, UNI0024 (Greenwich Hospital Collection), Nelson's undress coat worn at Trafalgar, 1805.
4. L Brockliss, M J Cardwell and M Moss, *Nelson's Surgeon* (2005), p. 120.
5. Beatty's case and instruments used in 1805 at the Battle of Trafalgar are held by the Royal College of Physicians and Surgeons of Glasgow.
6. W Beatty, *Authentic Narrative of the Death of Lord Nelson* (1807), p. 38.
7. Ibid., p. 39.
8. Ibid., p. 84.
9. Wellcome Library, MS 5141, report on the wounding, death and post-mortem examination of Viscount Nelson, 15 December 1805.
10. L Brockliss, M J Cardwell and M Moss, *Nelson's Surgeon* (2005), pp. 195–6.
11. C Lloyd and J L S Coulter, *Medicine and the Navy* (1961), vol. 3, p. 139.
12. T Coleman, *The Nelson Touch* (2002), p. 34.
13. A M E Hills, 'Nelson's Illnesses', *Journal of the Royal Naval Medical Service*, 86 (2000), 72–80.

14. L P Le Quesne, 'Nelson and his Surgeons', *Journal of the Royal Naval Medical Service*, 86 (2000), 85–8.
15. H Nelson, *Nelson's Letters to his Wife* (1959), p. 119.
16. W Beatty, *Authentic Narrative of the Death of Lord Nelson* (1807), p. 70.
17. Ibid., p. 374.
18. TNA, ADM 101/123, surgeon's journal, *Theseus*, James Farquhar, 25 July 1797.
19. C Lloyd and J L S Coulter, *Medicine and the Navy* (1961), p. 144.
20. TNA, ADM 101/124/1, surgeon's journal, *Vanguard*, 1 September 1798.
21. NMM, BHC 2903, Portrait of Nelson wounded at the Nile, possibly by Guy Head, 1798.
22. NMM, PAD 5574, William Heath, Cockpit of HMS *Vanguard*, 1 August 1798.
23. TNA, ADM 101/85, surgeon's journal, *Ardent,* Robert Young, 11 October 1797.
24. W Robinson, *Jack Nastyface* (2002), p. 113.
25. Ibid., p. 50.
26. TNA, ADM 101/118/1, surgeon's journal, *Russell,* George Magrath, 1797.
27. W Robinson, *Jack Nastyface* (2002), pp. 115–6.
28. S Leech, *Thirty Years from Home* (1844), p.142.
29. Ibid., p. 144.
30. TNA, ADM 101/125/1, surgeon's journal, *Victory,* William Beatty, 21 October 1805.
31. TNA, ADM 101/72, surgeon's journal, *Pickle,* Simon Gage Britton, 24 October 1805.
32. TNA, ADM 101/125/1, surgeon's journal, *Victory,* William Beatty, January 1806.
33. L Brockliss, M J Cardwell and M Moss, *Nelson's Surgeon* (2005), p. 98.
34. TNA, ADM 101/125/1, surgeon's journal, *Victory,* William Beatty, 21 April 1805.
35. H G Thursfield (ed.), *Five Naval Journals* (1951), pp. 28–9.
36. TNA, ADM 101/85, surgeon's journal, *Ardent,* Robert Young, 11 October 1797.
37. TNA, ADM 101/125/1, surgeon's journal, *Victory,* William Beatty, January 1806.
38. W Beatty, *Authentic Narrative of the Death of Lord Nelson* (1807), p. 20.
39. Wellcome Library, MS 3680, report of John Snipe, 19 September 1803.
40. H Nelson, *Dispatches and Letters* (1844–6), vol. 7, p. 215.
41. TNA, ADM 1/407, letter from Snipe to Nelson, 7 December 1803.
42. G Blane, *On the Comparative Health of the Navy* (1789) in C Lloyd (ed.), *The Health of Seamen* (1965), pp. 182–3.
43. TNA, ADM 1/411, report of Leonard Gillespie, 14 August 1805.
44. Wellcome Library, MS 3680, letter from Snipe to Nelson, 9 September 1803.
45. G Blane, *On the Comparative Health of the Navy* (1789) in C Lloyd (ed.), *The Health of Seamen* (1965), pp. 164–5.
46. T Trotter, *Medicina Nautica* (1797), vol.1, p.48.
47. H Nelson, *Dispatches and Letters* (1844–6), vol. 6, p. 154.
48. Ibid., vol. 6, p. 276.
49. Ibid., vol. 6, p. 74.
50. T Trotter, *Medicina Nautica* (1804) in C Lloyd (ed.), *The Health of Seamen* (1965), pp. 270–1.
51. R and L Adkins, *Jack Tar* (2008), pp. 75–7.
52. T Trotter, *Medicina Nautica* (1804) in C Lloyd (ed.), *The Health of Seamen* (1965), p. 271.
53. G Blane, *On the Comparative Health of the Navy* (1789) in C Lloyd (ed.), *The Health of Seamen* (1965), pp. 162–3.
54. Ibid., p. 164.

55. TNA, ADM 1/232, order from Admiral Vernon, 21 August 1740.
56. G Blane, *On the Comparative Health of the Navy* (1789) in C Lloyd (ed.), *The Health of Seamen* (1965), p. 191.
57. TNA, ADM 101/125/1, surgeon's journal, *Victory,* William Beatty, 29 December 1804–January 1806.
58. W C Russell, *Life of Admiral Lord Collingwood* (1895), p. 125.
59. L Brockliss, M J Cardwell and M Moss, *Nelson's Surgeon* (2005), p. 111.
60. TNA, ADM 101/118/1, surgeon's journal, *Russell,* George Magrath, 1797.
61. Ibid., 1798.
62. TNA, ADM 101/10/4, surgeon's journal, *Racehorse,* Lionel Gillespie, 1797.
63. T Trotter, *Medicina Nautica* (1804) in C Lloyd (ed.), *The Health of Seamen* (1965), p. 229.
64. Ibid., pp. 312–3.
65. Ibid., pp. 310–13.
66. NMM, ADM/F/31, Sick and Hurt Board, 13 September 1800.
67. I and J Glynn, *The Life and Death of Smallpox* (2004), p. 121.
68. NNM, ADM/F/31, Sick and Hurt Board, 13 September 1800.
69. I and J Glynn, *The Life and Death of Smallpox* (2004), p. 123.
70. H Nelson, *Dispatches and Letters* (1844–6), vol. 7, p. 19.
71. TNA, ADM 98/17, letter from Sick and Hurt Board, 27 May 1795.
72. Wellcome Library, MS 3680, report of L Gillespie, 24 February 1805.
73. Wellcome Library, MS 3681, letter from Sick and Hurt Board to Nelson, 29 May 1805.
74. BL, Add MS 34992, letter from W Beatty to Nelson, 15 April 1805.
75. Wellcome Library, MS 3680, letter from J Snipe to Nelson, 7 November 1803.
76. Wellcome Library, MS 3677, account of wine and spirits supplied to surgeon of *Spencer,* October 1804.
77. TNA, ADM 1/407, letter from Nelson to W Pemberton, 21 December 1803.
78. Wellcome Library, MS 3681, contracts for victualling naval hospitals at Gibraltar and Malta, 1803.
79. Ibid., letter from J Gray to Nelson, 22 February 1804.
80. Ibid., letter from Nelson to Sick and Hurt Board, 7 August 1804.
81. TNA, ADM 1/407, letter from Nelson to J Snipe, 25 November 1803.
82. Ibid., letter from J Snipe to Nelson, 9 December 1803.
83. C Lloyd and J L S Coulter, *Medicine and the Navy* (1961), vol. 4, p. 247.
84. TNA, ADM 1/407, letter from J Snipe to Nelson, 9 December 1803.
85. Ibid., letter from Nelson to Dr Baird, 30 May 1804.
86. H Nelson, *Dispatches and Letters* (1844–6), vol. 6, p. 41.
87. C Savona-Ventura, *Contemporary Medicine in Malta* (2005), pp. 216–21.
88. Observation of the author from visits to Haslar in November 2009 and Bighi in January 2010.
89. H Nelson, *Dispatches and Letters* (1844–6), vol. 5, p. 438.
90. TNA, ADM 1/411, report of L Gillespie, 14 August 1805.
91. H G Thursfield (ed.), *Five Naval Journals* (1951), p. 88.
92. C Lloyd and J L S Coulter, *Medicine and the Navy* (1961), vol. 3, p. 163.
93. British Optical Association Museum, London, LDBOA1999.167, portrait of Peter Rainier by Arthur Devis, c. 1805.
94. TNA, ADM 101/81/1, surgeon's journal, *Aetna,* James Campbell, 8 July 1808.
95. M J Caldwell, 'Royal Naval Surgeons, 1793–1815: A Collective Biography' in D B

Haycock and S Archer (ed.), *Health and Medicine at Sea* (2009), pp. 38–62.

96.  H G Thursfield (ed.), *Five Naval Journals* (1951), p. 49.

97.  NMM, ADM/F/36, Sick and Hurt Board, 8 December 1804.

98.  J Austen, *Mansfield Park* (1953), p. 314.

99.  M J Caldwell, 'Royal Naval Surgeons, 1793–1815: A Collective Biography' in D B Haycock and S Archer (ed.), *Health and Medicine at Sea* (2009), p. 61.

100.  T Trotter, *Medicina Nautica* (1804) in C Lloyd (ed.), *The Health of Seamen* (1965), pp. 257–8.

101.  TNA, ADM 101/106/1, surgeon's journal, *Leviathan*, William Shoveller, 1805.

102.  W Robinson, *Jack Nastyface* (2002), pp. 61, 78.

103.  G Blane, *Observations on the Diseases Incident to Seamen* (1785), pp. 109–10.

104.  L Brockliss, M J Cardwell and M Moss, *Nelson's Surgeon* (2005), p. 126.

105.  H Nelson, *Dispatches and Letters* (1844–6), vol. 5, p. 43.

## Chapter Six: Middle Passage

1.  T Trotter, *Medicina Nautica* (1797), vol. 1, pp. 9, 322.

2.  S Lambert (ed.), *House of Commons Sessional Papers of the Eighteenth Century* (1975), vol. 73, p. 85.

3.  T Trotter, *Medicina Nautica* (1797) in C Lloyd (ed.), *The Health of Seamen* (1965), p. 284.

4.  S Lambert (ed.), *House of Commons Sessional Papers of the Eighteenth Century* (1975), vol. 73, p. 101.

5.  Ibid., pp. 81–101 for Trotter's testimony and pp. 109–21 for the testimony of Clement Noble, captain of the *Brooks*.

6.  Ibid., p. 110.

7.  Ibid., p. 112.

8.  Ibid., p. 119.

9.  Ibid., p. 120.

10.  Ibid., p. 117.

11.  Ibid., pp. 88–9.

12.  R Woodman, *Neptune's Trident* (2008), pp. 171–80.

13.  M Park, *The Travels of Mungo Park* (1907), p. 249.

14.  H Thomas, *The Slave Trade* (2006), pp. 393–4.

15.  E Donnan (ed.), *Documents Illustrative of the Slave Trade to America* (1930), vol. 1, p. 399.

16.  O Equiano, *The Interesting Narrative of the Life of Olaudah Equiano* (1794), pp. 46–7.

17.  Ibid., p. 48.

18.  Ibid., p. 51.

19.  Ibid., p. 52.

20.  E Donnan (ed.), *Documents Illustrative of the Slave Trade to America* (1931), vol. 2, p. 573.

21.  Ibid., vol. 1, p. 272.

22.  H Thomas, *The Slave Trade* (2006), pp. 507–9.

23.  S Lambert (ed.), *House of Commons Sessional Papers of the Eighteenth Century* (1975), vol. 68, p. 19.

24.  Ibid., vol. 73, p. 87.

25.  Ibid., vol. 82, p. 33.

26. A Falconbridge, *An Account of the Slave Trade on the Coast of Africa* (1788), p. 32.

27. S Lambert (ed.), *House of Commons Sessional Papers of the Eighteenth Century* (1975), vol. 72, p. 303.

28. R H Steckel and R A Jensen, 'New Evidence on the Causes of Slave and Crew Mortality in the Atlantic Slave Trade', *Journal of Economic History*, 46 (1986), 57–77.

29. L Stewart, 'The Edge of Utility: Slaves and Smallpox in the Early Eighteenth Century', *Medical History*, 29 (1985), 54–70.

30. E Donnan (ed.), *Documents Illustrative of the Slave Trade to America* (1932), vol. 3, p. 555.

31. C Lloyd and J L S Coulter, *Medicine and the Navy* (1963), vol. 4, p. 172.

32. M Rediker, *The Slave Ship* (2007), p. 239.

33. R B Sheridan, *Doctors and Slaves* (1985), pp. 292–320.

34. H Thomas, *The Slave Trade* (2006), p. 437.

35. J Irving, *Slave Captain* (1995), pp. 94–5.

36. Ibid., pp. 112–13.

37. S Lambert (ed.), *House of Commons Sessional Papers of the Eighteenth Century* (1975), vol. 73, p. 136.

38. A Falconbridge, *An Account of the Slave Trade on the Coast of Africa* (1788), p. 30.

39. M Rediker, *The Slave Ship* (2007), pp. 245–6.

40. O Equiano, *The Interesting Narrative of the Life of Olaudah Equiano* (1794), p. 49.

41. T Clarkson, *History of the Rise, Progress and Accomplishment of the Abolition of the African Slave Trade* (1808), vol. 1, p. 316.

42. Ibid., p. 318.

43. T Clarkson, *An Essay on the Impolicy of the Slave Trade* (1788), p. iii.

44. S Lambert (ed.), *House of Commons Sessional Papers of the Eighteenth Century* (1975), vol. 72, pp. 183–4.

45. Ibid., vol. 82, p. 30.

46. T Clarkson, *The Substance of the Evidence of Sundry Persons on the Slave Trade* (1789), p. 41.

47. S Lambert (ed.), *House of Commons Sessional Papers of the Eighteenth Century* (1975), vol. 82, p. 199.

48. J Lind, *An Essay on Diseases Incidental to Europeans in Hot Climates* (1808), p. 8.

49. T Trotter, *A View of the Nervous Temperament* (1807), pp. 143–4.

50. J Hunter, *Observations on the Diseases of the Army in Jamaica and on the Best Means of Preserving the Health of Europeans in that Climate* (1788), p. 24.

51. J Lind, *An Essay on Diseases Incidental to Europeans in Hot Climates* (1808), p. 136.

52. D Alden and J C Miller, 'Out of Africa: The Slave Trade and the Transmission of Smallpox to Brazil, 1560–1831' in R I Rotberg, *Health and Disease in Human History* (2000), pp. 204–30.

53. J Wilson, *Outline of Naval Surgery* (1846), p. 92.

54. R M Anderson and R M May, *Infectious Diseases in Humans* (1991), pp. 374–418.

55. J Boyle, *A Practical Medico-Historical Account of the Western Coast of Africa* (1831), p. 196.

56. W B Baikie, *Narrative of an Exploring Voyage up the Niger* (1856), p. 453.

57. J D Goodyear, 'The Sugar Connection: A New Perspective on the History of Yellow Fever in West Africa', *Bulletin of the History of Medicine*, 52 (1978), 5–21.

58. TNA, ADM 101/122, *Termagant*, surgeon's journal, 1856.

59. A Bryson, *Report on the Climate and Principal Diseases of the African Station* (1847),

p. 161.

60. Ibid., p. 20.
61. ADM 51/4094, *Eden*, ship's log, 1829.
62. Ibid.
63. Cited in C Lloyd and J L S Coulter, *Medicine and the Navy* (1963), vol. 4, p. 170.
64. A Bryson, *Report on the Climate and Principal Diseases of the African Station* (1847), p. 256.
65. J Cook, *The Journals* (1999), p. 277.

**Chapter Seven: Huddled Masses**
1. O Handlin, *The Uprooted* (2002), p. 47.
2. M A Jones, *American Immigration* (1992), pp. 152–6.
3. D R McNeil, 'Medical Care Aboard Australian-bound Convict Ships 1786–1840', *Bulletin of Medical History*, 26 (1952), 117–40.
4. John White, principal surgeon to the first convict fleet, cited in C Bateson, *The Convict Ships* (1959), p. 87.
5. Ibid., p. 153.
6. E Ford, *Life and Work of William* Redfern (1953), pp. 24–33.
7. C Bateson, *The Convict Ships* (1959), p. 188.
8. Ibid., p. 205.
9. TNA, ADM 101/31/3, journal of Convict Ship *Guildford*, surgeon James Mitchell, 9 March 1822–24 July 1822.
10. TNA, ADM 101/31/4, journal of Convict Ship *Guildford*, surgeon Charles Linton, 7 March 1827–15 August 1827.
11. TNA, ADM 101/41/1, journal of Convict Ship *Lady East*, surgeon William McDowell, 16 September 1824–4 May 1825.
12. N Fogg, *The Voyages of the Great Britain* (2004), pp. 97–8.
13. TNA, ADM 101/77/7, journal of Hired Ship *James Pattison*, surgeon-superintendent G Roberts, 25 October 1839–11 February 1840.
14. TNA, ADM 101/76/1, journal of Emigrant Ship *Adam Lodge*, surgeon Alexander Stewart, 9 October 1839–18 February 1840.
15. TNA, ADM 101/78/1, journal of Emigrant Ship *Maitland*, surgeon John Smith, 21 June–5 November 1838.
16. R Haines, *Life and Death in the Age of Sail* (2006), pp. 29–30.
17. Ibid., pp. 86–7.
18. Ibid., p. 110.
19. TNA, HO 45/1467, letter from Frederick Elliot and Alexander Wood, Colonial Land and Emigration Office, to James Stephen, 5 February 1846.
20. TNA, HO 45/1920 report on typhus fever in emigrant ships, 28 April 1847.
21. R Haines, R Shlomowitz and L Brennan, 'Maritime Mortality Revisited', *International Journal of Maritime History*, 8 (1996), 113–24.
22. *Report from the Select Committee on the Passengers' Act*, 1851, PP 1851, XIX (632), p. xviii.
23. Ibid., Q2889, evidence of Sir George Stephen.
24. R Whyte, *The Ocean Plague* (1848), p. 16.
25. Ibid., pp. xxix-xxx.
26. W Hancock, *An Emigrant's Five Years in the Free States of America* (1860), pp. 9–10.
27. Dr Joseph Morin, quarantine station inspector, quoted in *Report on the Affairs of*

*British North America from the Earl of Durham,* PP 1839, XVII (3), Appendix A, pp. 86–7.

28. M A Jones, *Destination America* (1976), p. 41.

29. *A Report on Emigrant Ships by the Sanitary Commission of the Lancet* (1873), p. 26.

30. TNA, MT 9/340, Extract from Minute of Mr Chamberlain on 'Horrors of an Emigrant Ship', 1888.

31. Teodorico Rosati, Medical Inspector of Emigrant Ships, 1908, cited in A Nicosia and L Prencipe (ed.), *Museo Nazionale Emigrazione Italiana* (2009), p. 415.

32. TNA, MT 9/340, 'Report of the Lancet Special Sanitary Committee on the British Emigrant Service', 24 November 1888, p. 1041.

33. *Report with regard to the Accommodation and Treatment of Emigrants,* PP 1881, LXXXII (2995), pp. 3–5.

34. Baking soda.

35. TNA, CO 384/88, letter from William Mure to Frederick W Hart, 29 March 1851.

36. *A Copy of a Letter addressed to the Land and Emigration Commission,* PP 1851, XL (198), pp. 2–7.

37. TNA, CO 384/88, letter from William Mure to Lord Palmerstone, 4 February 1850.

38. Teodorico Rosati, Medical Inspector of Emigrant Ships, 1908, cited in A Nicosia and L Prencipe (ed.), *Museo Nazionale Emigrazione Italiana* (2009), pp. 414–5.

39. W Bell, *Hints to Emigrants* (1824), p.26.

40. R Whyte, *The Ocean Plague* (1848), p. 60.

41. *Report by Dr F H Blaxall on the Sanitary Aspects of Emigration and Immigration from and into the United Kingdom,* 1883, C3778, p. 160.

42. Ibid., p. 149.

43. TNA, MT 9/340, 'Report of the Lancet Special Sanitary Committee on the British Emigrant Service', 24 November 1888, p. 1041.

44. Cited in T Motta and A Dentoni (ed.), *L'America* (2008), p. 17.

45. *Papers relative to Emigration,* PP 1847–8, XLVII (932), p. 5.

46. R Whyte, *The Ocean Plague* (1848), p. 15.

47. W Smith, *An Emigrant's Narrative, or A Voice from the Steerage* (1850), p. 17.

48. TNA, CO 318/220, letter from J W Murdoch, Emigration Office, to Herman Merrivale, 22 July 1858.

49. Ibid., letter from J W Murdoch to H Merrivale, 11 August 1858.

50. K F Kiple, *The Cambridge Historical Dictionary of Disease* (2003), pp. 76–7.

51. M A Jones, *Destination America* (1976), p. 38.

52. J Simon, *Eighth Report to the Privy Council* (1865) in Privy Council, *Reports of the Medical Officer of the Privy Council and Local Government Board* (1875), p. 55.

53. TNA, MT 9/436, sanitary regulations, 1892; W M Frazer, *History of English Public Health 1834–1939* (1950), pp. 212–4.

54. J Higham, *Strangers in the Land* (1988), pp. 52, 100.

55. J Jensen, 'Before the Surgeon General: Marine Hospitals in Mid-Nineteenth Century America, *Public Health Reports,* 112 (1997), 525–7.

56. J Parascandola, 'Doctors at the Gate: PHS at Ellis Island', *Public Health Reports,* 113 (1998), 83–4.

57. G B Scalabrini, cited in A Nicosia and L Prencipe (ed.), *Museo Nazionale Emigrazione Italiana* (2009), p. 418.

58. S Graham, *With Poor Immigrants to America* (1914), pp. 41–2.

59. H Markel, 'The Eyes have It: Trachoma, the Perception of Disease, the United States

Public Health Service and the American Jewish Immigration Experience, 1897–1924', *Bulletin of Medical History*, 74 (2000), 525–60.

60. A M Kraut, *Silent Travellers* (1994), pp. 383–4.

61. M A Jones, *Destination America* (1976), pp. 45–46.

62. H H Groppe and U Wöst, *Via Hamburg to the World* (2007), p. 39.

63. TNA, MT 9/309, Merchant Shipping Act, 1854, section 230.

64. TNA, MT 9/309, Passenger Act, 1855, sections 41–44.

65. TNA, MT 9/309, Merchant Shipping Act, 1867, section 4.

66. TNA, MT 9/103, medical scale for emigrant ships, January 1875; MT 9/221, 'scale of medical comforts per 100 passengers', 1883.

67. TNA, MT 9/340, 'Report of the Lancet Special Sanitary Committee on the British Emigrant Service', 24 November 1888, p. 1039.

68. TNA, MT 9/103, letter from Mississippi and Dominion Steam Ship Company, 22 March 1875.

69. TNA, MT 9/340, 'Report of the Lancet Special Sanitary Committee on the British Emigrant Service', 24 November 1888, p. 1039.

70. TNA, MT 9/322, letter from representatives of Royal Colleges of Physicians and Surgeons and Board of Trade, November 1888.

71. TNA, MT 9/309, Dr Tanner, MP for Mid-Cork, quoted in *The Times,* 13 May 1889.

72. MT 9/122, *Lancet* (13 November 1875), 707.

73. Ibid., 708.

74. TNA, MT 9/86, qualifications of surgeons on emigrant ships, 1874.

75. MT 9/612, 'Health of Seamen', 1899.

76. TNA, MT 9/309, Dr Tanner, MP for Mid-Cork, quoted in *The Times,* 13 May 1889.

77. TNA, MT 9/316, 'Hospitals on board Ships', 1888.

78. *Report by Dr F H Blaxall on the Sanitary Aspects of Emigration and Immigration from and into the United Kingdom*, 1883, C3778, p. 160.

79. TNA, MT 9/333, letter from Union Line, 15 June 1888.

80. J Simon, *Public Health Reports* (1887), vol. 2, p. 101.

81. J Druett, *Rough Medicine* (2001), p. 158–60.

82. J Wilson, *Memories of a Labour Leader* (1910), pp. 125–6.

83. T S Wells, *The Scale of Medicines with which Merchant Vessels are to be Furnished* (1851), p. 17.

84. W M Frazer, *History of English Public Health 1834–1939* (1950), pp. 145, 456–7.

85. T S Wells, *The Scale of Medicines with which Merchant Vessels are to be Furnished* (1851), p. 17.

86. W M Frazer, *History of English Public Health 1834–1939* (1950), p. 457.

87. A Cowper, *A Backward Glance on Merseyside* (1948), pp. 67–8.

88. G Jameson Carr, 'Health Problems in the Merchant Navy', *British Journal of Industrial Medicine* (1945), 65–73.

89. Cited in R Woodman, *Masters under God* (2009), p. 349.

90. TNA, ADM 101/335, HMS *Ben-my-Chree*, H R Barnes Hull, surgeon, 15 March–31 December 1915.

91. G C Cook, 'Medical Disease in the Merchant Navies of the World in the Days of Sail: the Seamen's Hospital Society's Experience', *Mariner's Mirror* 91 (2005), 46–51.

92. G C Cook, *Disease in the Merchant Navy: A History of the Seamen's Hospital Society* (2007), p. 630.

93. C Savona-Ventura, *Contemporary Medicine in Malta* (2005), pp. 230–5.

94. J Wilson, *Memories of a Labour Leader* (1910), pp. 129–30.
95. R Kverndal, *Seamen's Missions: their Origin and Early Growth* (1986), pp. 330–9.
96. J Conrad, *Notes, Life and Letters* (1924) p. 262.
97. G H and R Bennett, *Survivors* (1999), pp. 203–4.
98. TNA, ADM 199/2138, statement of Captain H M McLean, 1941.

**Chapter Eight: Sea Airs**
1. 'Sea Voyages', *British Medical Journal*, 2 (July 1889), 167.
2. 'Books', *British Medical Journal*, 2 (September 1889), 666.
3. 'Sea Voyages', *British Medical Journal*, 2 (July 1889), 167.
4. J K Jerome, *Three Men in a Boat* (1993), p. 9.
5. A Hill, letter, *British Medical Journal*, 1 (1896), 882.
6. J K Walton, *The English Seaside Resort: A Social History* (1983).
7. S Fox, *The Ocean Railway* (2004), p. 4.
8. Ibid., pp. 70–1.
9. C Dickens, *American Notes* (1908), p. 12.
10. Ibid., p. 2.
11. Ibid., p.18.
12. Queen Victoria, *Journal,* 22 April 1845: A Ball and D Wright, *SS Great Britain* (1981), p. 22.
13. *Brooklyn Eagle,* 12 August 1845.
14. *New York Evening Post,* 11 August 1845.
15. J E Alexander (ed.), *The Albatross: A Voyage from Victoria to England* (1863), p. 23.
16. M Crompton, *A Journal of a Honeymoon on the SS Great Britain* (1992), p. 19.
17. Ibid., p. 16.
18. S Fox, *The Ocean Railway* (2004), p. 339.
19. *Oxford English Dictionary.*
20. L Beesley, *The Loss of the SS Titanic* (1912), p. 14.
21. J B Geller, *Titanic: Women and Children First* (1998), p. 51.
22. Ibid.
23. L Beesley, *The Loss of the SS Titanic* (1912), p. 15.
24. J P Eaton and C A Haas, *Titanic: Triumph and Tragedy* (1994), pp. 179–80.
25. *Nova Scotia Evening Mail,* 31 April 1912.
26. D A Butler, *Unsinkable* (1998), p. 201.
27. J Kent Layton, *Lusitania: An Illustrated Biography of the Ship of Splendor* (2007), p. xxiii.
28. B S Frey, D A Savage and B Torgler, 'Interaction of Natural Survival Instincts and Internalized Social Norms: Exploring the Titanic and Lusitania Disasters', *Proceedings of the National Academy of Sciences of the United States of America* (2010), 1091–6490.
29. A W Bourne, *A Doctor's Creed* (1963), p. 36.
30. Notice of Death, *British Medical Journal* (November 1924), 188.
31. S A Tidey, 'Treatment of Seasickness', *St Mary's Hospital Gazette*, 34/5 (1928), 55.
32. J K Jerome, *Three Men in a Boat* (1993), p. 11.
33. E Waugh, *Brideshead Revisited* (1962), p. 240.
34. S A Tidey, 'The Ship's Surgeon', *St Mary's Hospital Gazette*, 34/3 (1928), 35.
35. M Crompton, *A Journal of a Honeymoon on the SS Great Britain* (1992), p. 23.
36. Ibid., p. 17.

37. SS *Great Britain* Museum, BRSGB 1997.003, letter to family of William Wheatley, 24 April 1866.
38. Ibid., BRSGB 1997.014, diary of female passenger, 14 October 1865.
39. D and S Howarth, *The Story of P&O* (1986), p. 59.
40. Anon, 'Notes from a Pilgrim Ship', *St Mary's Hospital Gazette*, 17/9 (1911), 133.
41. Ibid., 134.
42. 'Argonaut', 'From the Diary of a Ship's Doctor', *St Mary's Hospital Gazette*, 16/3 (1910), 39–40.
43. Anon, 'Some Sensations of a Ship's Surgeon', *St Mary's Hospital Gazette*, 18/10 (1912), 163.
44. 'Argonaut', 'From the Diary of a Ship's Doctor', *St Mary's Hospital Gazette*, 16/3 (1910), 40.
45. Ibid., 41.
46. Ibid., 40.
47. E C Hardwicke, 'Some Reminiscences of a Ship's Surgeon', *St Mary's Hospital Gazette*, 18/9 (1912), 145.
48. J Graves, *Waterline* (2004), pp. 247–8.
49. Ibid., p. 167.
50. D and S Howarth, *The Story of P&O* (1986), p. 133.
51. J Graves, *Waterline* (2004), p. 144.
52. L H Roddis, *A Short History of Maritime Medicine* (1941), pp. 306–21.
53. 'GP', 'Ship's Surgeon', *St Mary's Hospital Gazette*, 41/10 (1935), 209–10.
54. R J Blackham, 'Sea-Sickness', *British Medical Journal*, 1 (1939), 163.
55. Ibid.
56. D and S Howarth, *The Story of P&O* (1986), p. 196.
57. J Graves, *Waterline* (2004), p. 248.
58. John W Carter, 'Shipboard Medicine on Package Cruises', *British Medical Journal*, 1 (1972), 553.
59. Ibid., 554.
60. Personal information, Dr Evi Kalodiki.
61. J Graves, *Waterline* (2004), pp. 92–4.
62. R Goldstein, *Desperate Hours* (2001), pp. 70–1.
63. *Newsweek*, 48/13 (1956), 55.
64. R Goldstein, *Desperate Hours* (2001), p. 170.
65. Ibid., p. 125.
66. Author's observations at a medical open day for the recruitment of doctors and nurses held on *Queen Mary II* at Southampton on 24 July 2009. I wish to thank Sally Bell for arranging for me to attend this event.
67. 'Working as a Ship's Doctor', *British Medical Journal*, 2 (1998), 316.
68. J K Makert, 'Adventures in Nursing Aboard a Cruise Ship', *Nursing Forum*, 37/2 (2002), 36.
69. P&O Brochure, 2010.

**Chapter Nine: Bright and Breezy**
1. 'Sons of the Sea' by Felix McGlennon, 1897.
2. 'All the Nice Girls Love a Sailor' by A J Mills, 1909.
3. TNA, ADM 1/3532, report of J Liddell, 30 April 1839.
4. Ibid.

5. Royal Marines Museum, Eastney Barracks, Portsmouth, recruiting posters.
6. A Miller, *Dressed to Kill* (2007), p. 84.
7. Information from Lorenzo Glavici, communications manager, Brioni SpO; E Musgrave, *Sharp Suits* (2009), pp. 79–80.
8. A Scrimgeour, *Scrimgeour's Small Scribbling Diary 1914–1916* (2008), p. 250.
9. A Miller, *Dressed to Kill* (2007), pp. 88–90.
10. C Lloyd and J L S Coulter, *Medicine and the Navy* (1963), vol. 4, p. 96.
11. T E Lawrence, *Seven Pillars of Wisdom* (1962), p. 202.
12. C Lloyd and J L S Coulter, *Medicine and the Navy* (1963), vol. 4, p. 101.
13. TNA, ADM 101/91, surgeon's journal, *Blossom,* 1824.
14. J Lenihan, *The Crumbs of Creation* (1988), pp. 99–100.
15. R E Johnson, *Sir John Richardson* (1976), pp. 43–4.
16. TNA, ADM, surgeon's journal, *Modeste,* T Spencer Wells, 1852.
17. D B Reid, *Illustration of the Theory and Practice of Ventilation* (1844), p. 358.
18. G Milroy, *The Health of the Royal Navy* (1862), p. 46.
19. C Lloyd and J L S Coulter, *Medicine and the Navy* (1963), vol. 4, pp. 88–9.
20. TNA, ADM 106/3093, regulations for medical officers, 1825.
21. TNA, ADM 105/27, report on use of chloride of lime in East India Company's Ship *Windsor,* 25 May 1828.
22. TNA, ADM 304/13, circular on deodorants, 31 August 1867.
23. H D Langley, *A History of Medicine in the Early US Navy* (1995), p. 357.
24. G Milroy, *The Health of the Royal Navy* (1862) p. 61.
25. Editorials, *The Lancet,* 2 (1838), 21, 193.
26. TNA, ADM 1/3532, letter from W Burnett, 9 August 1841.
27. J Shepherd, *The Crimean Doctors* (1991), vol. 1, p. 49.
28. J A Shepherd, *Spencer Wells* (1965), p. 21.
29. TNA, ADM 102/850, medical journal, Hospital Ship *Belleisle,* R Beith, first report, 8 June–30 June 1854.
30. Ibid., report, 26 May–30 June 1855.
31. Ibid., report, 1 July–30 September 1854.
32. E H Cree, *The Cree Journals* (1981), p. 246.
33. TNA, WO 32/7580, proceedings of Sanitary Committee dispatched to the seat of war in the East, 1855.
34. TNA, WO 33/1, regulations on board ships for the conveyance of the sick and wounded, March 1855.
35. J Rees, 'Report on the Recent Outbreak of Cholera in HMS *Britannia*,' *Medical Times and Gazette,* 2 (1854), 609–10.
36. TNA, ADM 101/120/5, medical and surgical journal, *Sphinx,* H Sabben, 1854–5.
37. TNA, ADM 101/86/2, medical journal, *Arethusa,* Charles Deane Steel, 17 September 1855.
38. TNA, ADM 101/120/5, medical and surgical journal, Sphinx, H Sabben, 17 September 1855.
39. TNA, WO 32/7580, proceedings of Sanitary Committee dispatched to the seat of war in the East, 1855.
40. TNA, ADM 102/901, Therapia Hospital muster book, 1855.
41. J Shepherd, *The Crimean Doctors* (1991), vol. 2, p. 553.
42. S G Osborne, *Scutari and its Hospitals* (1855), pp. 49–50.
43. TNA, ADM 102/849, register of important cases at Royal Naval Hospital, Therapia,

1853–6.

44. TNA, ADM 1/3532, report of J Liddell, 30 April 1839.

45. TNA, WO 23/6210 Skey Commission, 1864.

46. A Weston, *My Life among the Bluejackets* (1909).

47. Portsmouth, Plymouth, Woolwich, Chatham, Sheerness, Aldershot, Colchester, Shorncliffe, Curragh, Cork, and Queenstown.

48. *An Act for the Prevention of Contagious Diseases at Certain Naval and Military Stations*, 29 July 1864, 27 & 28 Vic. c.85.

49. *An Act to amend the Contagious Diseases Act 1866*, 11 August 1869, 32 & 33 Vic. c.96; the additional towns were Dover, Gravesend, Maidstone, Windsor, Dartmouth, Southampton, Winchester.

50. *Daily News,* 2 July 1864.

51. TNA, WO 33/17A, 'Report of Committee to Enquire into the Treatment and Prevention of Venereal Diseases in the Army and Navy', 1864, p. 141.

52. Ibid., pp. 143–7.

53. Ibid., p. 149.

54. Ibid., p. 151.

55. TNA, WO 23/6210, Skey Commission, 1864.

56. *Report of the Royal Commission upon the Administration and Operation of the Contagious Diseases Act*, C 408, 19, 1871, recommendations, 48.

57. Thomas Wakley quoted in T Fisher, *Prostitution and the Victorians* (1997), p. 71.

58. *Daily News,* 31 December 1869.

59. K Brown, *The Pox* (2006), pp. 63–75.

60. TNA, HO 45/9511/17273A, memorial from JPs of Devonport, Aldershot, Greenwich, Winchester, Portsmouth, Maidstone, Windsor, Canterbury and Gravesend, June 1884.

61. TNA, ADM 304/13, report of civil commission into the naval hospitals, 20 July 1869.

62. J B Richardson, *A Visit to Haslar 1916* (2004), p. 7.

63. TNA, ADM 116/516, report of committee on sick berth nursing staff, 1898.

64. TNA/ADM 116/220, report on the organisation and training of sick berth staff and the nursing staff of the Royal Hospital Haslar, 1883.

65. TNA, ADM 116/1101, report of committee on naval medical services, 1909.

66. TNA, ADM 116/516, second report on training of medical officers, 1899.

67. TNA/ADM 116/220, report on the organisation and training of sick berth staff and the nursing staff of the Royal Hospital Haslar, 1883.

68. TNA, ADM 116/516, regulations for nursing sisters in RN Hospitals, 1899.

69. TNA/ADM 116/220, report on the organisation and training of sick berth staff and the nursing staff of the Royal Hospital Haslar, 1883.

70. TNA, ADM 116/1101, report of committee on naval medical services, 1909.

71. F Prochaska, *Royal Bounty* (1995), p. 126.

72. TNA, ADM 116/516, observations by Alexander Turnbull on the course of instructions for surgeons on entry, Royal Hospital Haslar, 1897.

73. Ibid., report of committee on the training of medical officers, 1899.

74. TNA, ADM 116/1101, report of committee on the Naval Medical Service, 1909.

75. Ibid., Circular letter, July 1911.

76. TNA, ADM 116/516, letter from Joseph Chamberlain to President of General Council of Medical Education and Registration, February 1898.

77. R Ross, *Studies on Malaria* (1928), pp. 1–40.

78. K Brown, *Fighting Fit* (2008), p. 125.

79. D Bruce, 'Observations on Malta Fever', *British Medical Journal* (1889), 1101–4.

80. M L Hughes, *Mediterranean, Malta or Undulant Fever* (1897), p. 54.

81. *Reports of the Commission for the Investigation of Malta Fever* (1905), p. 174.

82. T Zammit, 'A Preliminary Note of the Susceptibility of Goats to Malta Fever', *Proceedings of the Royal Society*, 76B (1905), 377–8.

83. *Reports of the Commission for the Investigation of Malta Fever* (1906), pp. 1–12, 37–41.

84. Ibid., (1907), pp. 65–70.

85. TNA, CO 885/9/11, CO 885/18/7, CO 885/19/14, correspondence on Malta Fever, 1905–6, 1906–7, 1908.

86. A Turnbull, 'Discussion on the Prevention of Scurvy', *British Medical Journal*, 2 (1902), 1023.

87. A E Wright, 'On the Pathology and Therapeutics of Scurvy', *Lancet* (1900), 565–7.

88. R F Scott, *Journals* (2006), p. 270.

89. Ibid., p. 41.

90. E Shackleton, *The Heart of the Antarctic and South* (2007), p. 475.

91. R F Scott, *Journals* (2006), p. 422.

92. Ibid., p. 410.

93. Ibid., p. 406.

94. Ibid., p. 506.

## Chapter Ten: Stormy Waters

1. T B Dixon, *The Enemy Fought Splendidly* (1983), p.30.

2. TNA, WO 293/3, Military Training for Medical Students, 10 December 1915.

3. Editorial, *St Mary's Hospital Gazette*, 20/9 (1914), 131.

4. Letter, *St Mary's Hospital Gazette*, 21/6 (1915), 90–91.

5. TNA, MT 23/404, Hospital Ships, 1915.

6. TNA, FO 83/2148, Hospital Ships Conference, The Hague, 1904–5.

7. A D Fripp, 'Experiences of a Civilian among the Naval Medical Service in War', *Guy's Hospital Reports*, 70/3 (1922), 229–55.

8. A Hope Gosse, 'The Liberty Hospital Yacht', *St Mary's Hospital Gazette*, 20/7 (1914), 116–17.

9. TNA, ADM 116/1245, evidence before Departmental Committee on the Naval Medical Service, 29 June 1909.

10. TNA, ADM 101/349, surgeon's journal, *Euryalus*, T T Teans, 25 April 1915.

11. TNA, ADM 101/399, medical officer's journal, *Warspite*, W W Kerr, 31 May 1916.

12. M Arthur (ed.), *Lost Voices of the Royal Navy* (2005), p. 56.

13. TNA, ADM 101/396, surgeon's journal, *Southampton*, Arthur R Schofield, 31 May 1916.

14. TNA, ADM 10/335, surgeon's journal, *Ben-my-Chree*, H R Barnes Hull, 31 May 1916.

15. TNA, ADM 101/396, surgeon's journal, *Southampton*, Arthur R Schofield, 31 May 1916.

16. TNA, ADM 101/399, medical officer's journal, *Warspite*, W W Kerr, 31 May 1916.

17. Gillies Archive, Queen Mary's Hospital, Sidcup, file 2324, Able Seaman W Vicarage, RN, 2 August 1917–8 September 1920.

18. TNA, ADM 261/12, report on Fleet Air Arm, 1946, citing senior medical officer of *Furious*, 1917.

19. S Palmer and S Wallis (ed.), *A War in Words* (2003), pp. 250–2.

20. Report of Central Board of Control, Cd. 8243, 1916.

21. TNA, HO 45/10802/307990/7, Defence of the Realm Act, 13A, 1916.

22. TNA, HO 45/ 10802/307990/15E, Defence of the Realm Act, 35C, 1917.

23. TNA, HO 45/10893/359931, Order in Council, 22 March 1918.

24. TNA, WO 32/4745, War Office Memorandum, 28 August 1918.

25. TNA, HO 45/10893/359931, letter from chief petty officer on active service, 2 November 1918.

26. Ibid.

27. K Brown, *The Pox* (2006), pp. 128–9.

28. TNA, WO 32/11404, B B Cubitt to Officers Commanding at Home, 18 March 1916.

29. TNA, MH 55/196, letter from Dr G D Kettlewell, 15 August 1923.

30. Ibid., report on VD in children at Portsmouth, 27 June 1924.

31. Ibid., report on inquiry into congenital syphilis, 1924.

32. TNA, ADM 116/3277, note by Arthur Gaskell on shortage of naval medical officers, 15 March 1930.

33. *In Which We Serve* (Two Cities, 1942), dir. Noel Coward (DVD, Carlton Visual Entertainment 37115 01663, 2003).

34. Letter from 'Nelson Expects', *St Mary's Hospital Gazette*, 49/3 (1943), 53–4.

35. R P M Miles, 'OHMS', ibid., 49/8 (1943), 143.

36. Letter from 'Surgeon Lieutenant, RNVR', ibid., 46/2 (1940), 36.

37. St Mary's Hospital Archives, DP 5/16, letter from F M McRae to A H Buck, 18 August 1943.

38. Ibid., DP 5/16, letter from McRae to Buck, 13 February 1943.

39. *The Times*, 19 October 1945.

40. TNA, ADM 261/6, memo by J Robertson on corvettes of Flower Class, 25 March 1942.

41. TNA, ADM 1/16764, memo from Medical Officer in Charge of Royal Naval Hospital Haslar, 5 October 1943.

42. Ibid., memo from Medical Officer in Charge of Royal Naval Hospital Plymouth, 20 October 1943.

43. Ibid., memo from Surgeon Rear Admiral, RN Hospital Chatham on 'Depreciation in the Standard of Nursing Efficiency', 20 September 1943.

44. TNA, ADM 261/7, mobilization in war, 1939.

45. Ibid., memo from Surgeon Rear Admiral, RN Hospital Chatham on 'Depreciation in the Standard of Nursing Efficiency', 20 September 1943.

46. TNA, ADM 116/5559, Ministerial Committee on the Work of Psychologists and Psychiatrists in the Services, 31 January 1945.

47. *Went the Day Well?* (Ealing Studios, 1942), dir. Albert Cavalcanti (DVD, Optimum Home Entertainment B000I5XNJ2, 2006).

48. TNA, ADM 261/6, report on scheme of training in HMS *Bristol*, 18 May–28 December 1943.

49. TNA, ADM 101/570, surgeon's journal, *Repulse*, J R Brennan, September 1940.

50. TNA, ADM 101/565, surgeon's journal, *Icarus*, Richard P Coldrey, June, 1940.

51. TNA, ADM 261/1, medical officer's journal, Rescue Ship *Zaafaran*, G McBain, 1942.

52. TNA, ADM 101/6528, medical officer's journal, *Belfast*, J H Nicolson, July–September 1944.

53. TNA, ADM 101/570, surgeon's journal, *Repulse*, J R Brennan, September 1940.

54. TNA, ADM 101/565, medical journal, *Hood*, K A Ingleby Mackenzie, August 1940.

55. TNA, ADM 261/4, guidelines for lectures on VD, 25 May 1944.

56. TNA, ADM 101/6528, medical journal, *Berwick,* Robert Vickery Herriman, 1944.
57. TNA, ADM 261/4, guidelines for lectures on VD, 25 May 1944.
58. TNA, MH 55/1341, Statutory Rules and Orders, amendment by Order in Council of Defence (General) Regulations Act of 1939, 5 November 1942.
59. Ibid., Ministry of Health circular, 8 January 1943.
60. TNA, WO 204/6725, notes on prophylactic treatment, 1944.
61. TNA, ADM 101/565, medical officer's journal, *Hood,* K A Ingleby Mackenzie, 1940.
62. TNA, ADM 261/4, guidelines for lectures on VD, 25 May 1944.
63. K Brown, *Penicillin Man* (2004).
64. J F Mahoney, R C Arnold and A Harris, 'Penicillin Treatment of Early Syphilis: A Preliminary Report', *Venereal Diseases Information,* 24 (1943), 355–7.
65. National Archives, College Park, Maryland, Records Group 90, Public Health Service, general classified records, group 9, box 531, file 0425, memorandum from W S Bean to R C Williams, 13 July 1944.
66. TNA, ADM 1/15311, memo from C A Green, 17 March 1942.
67. Ibid., letter from H W Florey to Admiral Griffiths, 28 April 1943.
68. Ibid., letter from C A Green to Admiral Dudley, 17 May 1943.
69. K Brown, *Fighting Fit* (2008), pp. 110–38.
70. ADM 101/570, surgeon's journal, *Resolution,* A W Gunn, 4 May 1940.
71. B Lavery (ed.), *The Royal Navy Officer's Pocket Book 1944* (2007), p. 65.
72. TNA, ADM 76/624, proposed BBC talk by J Coulter, April 1956.
73. TNA, ADM 261/1, report from W McC Scott, 12 November 1941.
74. J K Herman (ed.), *Battle Station Sick Bay* (1997), p. 203.
75. TNA, ADM 101/6528, medical officer's journal, *Belfast,* J H Nicolson, June 1944.
76. Ibid., July–September 1944
77. TNA, ADM 261/6, 'Living and Working Conditions among RN Personnel in the Tropics' by M Critchley and H E Hollins, 1945.
78. TNA, ADM 261/9, report on action damage on HMS *Norfolk,* 21 January 1944.
79. TNA, ADM 261/10, report of Royal Naval Personnel Research Committee visit to Coastal Forces, 13 January 1943.
80. Private information.
81. J Hood (ed.), *Submarine* (2007), p. 99.
82. Ibid., p. 35.
83. S Palmer and S Wallis (ed.), *A War in Words* (2003), p. 234.
84. TNA, ADM 261/6, 'Living and Working Conditions among RN Personnel in the Tropics' by M Critchley and H E Hollins, 1945.
85. TNA, WO 32/11697, report by R M Porter on role of British Pacific Fleet in repatriation of released allied prisoners of war and internees, 1945.
86. TNA, WO 183/485, committee on the organisation of the Medical Services, 24 January 1946.
87. C McKee, *Sober Men and True* (2002), pp. 73–144.
88. E Hampshire (ed.), *Brinestain and Biscuit* (2007), pp. 4–12.
89. NAAFI Public Relations Branch, *The Story of NAAFI* (1944).
90. TNA, FD 23/2176, letter from P Jeffrey Chapman to George C Drew, 20 June 1974.
91. TNA, ADM 105/95, 'Living and Working Conditions on HM Submarine *Andrew* Operating in Tropical Waters' by J D Walters, September 1966.
92. Visit by author, November 2009.
93. TNA, ADM 105/116, promotion brochure for Institute of Naval Medicine, 1985.

94. TNA, FD1/1115, letter from Henry Dale to P T Nichols, 16 September 1938.

95. www.royalnavy.mod.uk/training-and-people/rn-life/medical-branch/institute-of-naval-medicine/environmental-medicine-unit-emu/applied-physiology, accessed 12 April 2010.

96. G Clark, *Doc: 100 Year History of the Sick Berth Branch* (1984), p. 60.

97. Ibid., pp. 154–5.

98. Ibid., p. 60.

99. J Lippiett, *War and Peas* (2007), pp. 29–30.

100. G Clark, *Doc: 100 Year History of the Sick Berth Branch* (1984), pp. 70–1.

101. Ibid., pp. 158–67.

102. A R Marsh, 'A Short but Distant War: the Falklands Campaign', *Journal of the Royal Society of Medicine,* 76 (1983), 972–82.

103. D and S Howarth, *The Story of P&O* (1986), p. 198.

104. www.royalnavy.mod.uk/training-and-people/rn-life/medical-branch, accessed 12 April 2010.

105. TNA, ADM 116/6028, Proposed Dispensary for English Wives and Children of Naval Ratings living in Malta, 1 May 1925.

106. TNA, ADM 116/6399, note from N MacLeod on provision of a medical facility at Singapore Base, 6 February 1936.

107. A L Revell, *Haslar the Royal Hospital* (2000), pp. 41–6.

108. E Birbeck, A Ryder and P Ward, *The Royal Haslar Hospital* (2009), pp. 107–8.

109. *The Independent,* 16 May 2006, 8 October 2006, 13 January 2007.

# Bibliography

**Archive Sources**

*British Library, London*
BL, Eg. MS 2975, considerations on the present state of the navy by Sir Robert Cotton, 1608
BL, Add MS 34992, Viscount Nelson papers

*National Archives, Kew*
TNA, ADM, Admiralty
TNA, CO, Colonial Office
TNA, FD, Medical Research Council
TNA, FO, Foreign Office
TNA, HO, Home Office
TNA, MH, Ministry of Health
TNA, MT, Board of Trade
TNA, SP, State Papers
TNA, WO, War Office

*National Archives (USA), College Park, Maryland*
RG 90, Public Health Service

*National Maritime Museum, Greenwich*
NMM, ADM, Admiralty, Sick and Hurt Board
NMM, MS 53/008, Decree of the Commissioners of Charitable Use, 1617
NMM, MS 9633, P Ward and E Hayward, Naval Accounts for 1637–43

*Queen Mary's Hospital, Sidcup, Gillies Archive*
Case files of Harold Gillies, 1917–25

*St Mary's Hospital Archives, London*
DP 5, papers of F M McRae

*SS Great Britain Museum, Bristol*
BRSGB 1997.003, Letter to family of William Wheatley, 24 April 1866
BRSGB1997.014, Diary of woman passenger, 1865
BRSGB 1997.020, Diary of Allan Gilmour, 1852

*Wellcome Library, London*
MS 3667–81, Viscount Nelson papers

MS 5141, Report on the wounding, death and post-mortem examination of Viscount Nelson, 15 December 1805

*Parliamentary Papers*
Report on the Affairs of British North America from the Earl of Durham, PP 1839, XVII
Papers relative to Emigration, PP 1847–8, XLVII
A Copy of a Letter addressed to the Land and Emigration Commission, PP 1851, XL
Report from the Select Committee on the Passengers' Act, 1851, PP 1851, XIX
Report of the Royal Commission upon the Administration and Operation of the Contagious Diseases Act, C. 408, 19, 1871
Report with regard to the Accommodation and Treatment of Emigrants, PP 1881, LXXXII
Report by Dr F H Blaxall on the Sanitary Aspects of Emigration and Immigration from and into the United Kingdom, C.3778, 1883
Report of Central Board of Control, Cd. 8243, 1916

## Primary Printed Sources

Alexander, James E (ed.), *The Albatross: A Voyage from Victoria to England*, Stirling, Charles Rogers, 1863

Arthur, Max (ed.), *Lost Voices of the Royal Navy*, London, Hodder, 2007

Atkinson, E G (ed.), *Acts of the Privy Council 1613–1628*, London, HMSO, 1940

Austen, Jane, *Mansfield Park*, London, Collins, 1953

Baikie, W B, *Narrative of an Exploring Voyage up the Rivers Kwora and Binue commonly known as the Niger and Tsadda in 1854*, London, Murray, 1856

Banks, Joseph, *Journal of the Right Honourable Sir Joseph Banks during Captain Cook's first Voyage in HMS Endeavour*, London, MacMillan, 1896

Bard, N P (ed.), 'The Earl of Warwick's Voyage of 1627', in N A M Rodger (ed.), *Naval Miscellany V* (1984), pp. 15–93

Barlow, Edward, *Barlow's Journal of his Life at Sea in King's Ships, East and West Indiamen and other Merchantmen from 1659 to 1703*, ed. Basil Lubbock, London, Hurst and Blackett, 1934

Beatty, William, *Authentic Narrative of the Death of Lord Nelson*, London, Cadell, 1807

Beesley, Lawrence, *The Loss of the Titanic: Its Story and its Lessons*, New York, Houghton Miffin, 1912

Bell, William, *Hints to Emigrants*, Edinburgh, Waugh and Innes, 1824

Benedetti, Alessandro, *Diario de Bello Carolino*, Padua, M Cerdonis, 1496

———, *Anatomice sive Historia Corporis Humani*, Venice, J and G de Gregoriis, 1497

Blackham, Robert J, 'Sea-Sickness', *British Medical Journal*, 1 (1939), 163–7

Blane, Gilbert, *Observations on the Diseases Incident to Seamen*, London, Cooper, 1785

Bligh, William, *Mutiny on the Bounty*, Turin, White Star Publishers, 2006

Bloch, Iwan (ed.), *Der Ursprung der Syphilis*, Jena, G Fisher, 1901–11

Bourne, Aleck W, *A Doctor's Creed: the Memoirs of a Gynaecologist*, London, Victor Gollancz, 1963

Boyle, John, *A Practical Medico-Historical Account of the Western Coast of Africa*, London, Highley, 1831

Bruce, David, 'Observations on Malta Fever', *British Medical Journal* (1889), 1101–4

Bruce, John (ed.), *Calendar of State Papers Domestic, Charles I, 1627–28*, London, HMSO, 1858

# BIBLIOGRAPHY

Bryson, Alexander, *Report on the Climate and Principal Diseases of the African Station*, London, Clowes, 1847

Camões, Luis Vaz de, *The Lusíads*, tr. Landeg White, Oxford, Oxford University Press, 1997

Carter, John W, 'Shipboard Medicine on Package Cruises', *British Medical Journal*, 1 (1972), 553–6

Chambers, David and Pullan, Brian (ed.), *Venice: A Documentary History, 1450–1630*, Toronto, University of Toronto Press, 2001

Clarkson, Thomas, *An Essay on the Impolicy of the Slave Trade*, London, James Philips, 1788

————, *Substance of the Evidence of Sundry Persons on the Slave Trade Collected in the Course of a Tour Made in the Autumn of the Year 1788*, London, James Philips, 1789

————, *History of the Rise, Progress and Accomplishment of the Abolition of the African Slave Trade*, London, Hurst, Rees and Orme, 1808

Columbus, Christopher, *The Four Voyages of Christopher Columbus*, ed. and tr. J M Cohen, Harmondsworth, Penguin, 1969

Commission for the Investigation of Mediterranean Fever, *Reports of the Commission appointed by the Admiralty, the War Office, and the Civil Government of Malta, for the Investigation of Mediterranean Fever*, London, Royal Society, 1905–7

Compton, Mary, *A Journal of a Honeymoon Voyage on the SS Great Britain*, Bristol, SS Great Britain Trust, 1992

Conrad, Joseph, *Notes, Life and Letters*, New York, Doubleday, Page and Company, 1924

Cook, James, *The Journals*, ed. Philip Edwards, London, Penguin, 1999

————, *The Voyages of Captain Cook*, ed. Jonathan Barrow, Ware, Wordsworth Editions, 1999

Cowper, Agnes, *A Backward Glance on Merseyside*, Birkenhead, Willmer Brothers, 1948

Cree, Edward H, *The Cree Journals: The Voyages of Edward H Cree, Surgeon RN, as related in his Private Journals 1837–1856*, Exeter, Webb and Bower, 1981

Crone, G R (ed.), *The Voyages of Cadamosto and Other Documents on Western Africa in the Second Half of the Fifteenth Century*, London, Hakluyt Society, 1937

Dasent, J R (ed.), *Acts of the Privy Council of England 1542–1604*, London, HMSO, 1890–1907

De Las Casas, Bartolomé, *A Short Account of the Destruction of the Indies*, ed. and tr. Nigel Griffin, Harmondsworth, Penguin, 1991

Diaz de Isla, Ruiz, *Tractado Contra et Mal Serpentino*, Seville, D De Robertis, 1539

Díaz del Castillo, Bernal, *The Conquest of New Spain*, ed. and tr. J M Cohen, Harmondsworth, Penguin, 1963

Dickens, Charles, *American Notes and Pictures from Italy*, London, Dent, 1908

Dixon, Thomas Benjamin, *The Enemy Fought Splendidly: Being the 1914–1915 Diary of the Battle of the Falklands and its Aftermath by Surgeon T B Dixon of HMS Kent*, Poole, Blandford Press, 1983

Donnan, Elizabeth (ed.), *Documents Illustrative of the Slave Trade to the Americas*, Washington, Carnegie Institution, 1930–5

Equiano, Olaudah, *The Interesting Narrative of the Life of Olaudah Equiano or Gustavus Vassa the African*, London, Olaudah Equiano, 1794

Evelyn, John, *Diary*, ed. E S de Beer, Oxford, Oxford University Press, 1955

Falconbridge, Alexander, An *Account of the Slave Trade on the Coast of Africa*, London, J Phillips, 1788

Fracastoro, Girolamo, *Syphilis sive Morbus Gallicus*, ed. Geoffrey Eatough, Liverpool, Francis Cairns, 1984

Fripp, Alfred D, 'Experiences of a Civilian among the Naval Medical Service in War', *Guy's Hospital Reports,* 70/3 (1922), 229–55

Gardiner, S R (ed.), *Documents illustrating the Impeachment of the Duke of Buckingham in 1626,* London, Camden Society, 1889

Gosse, Alfred Hope, 'The Liberty Hospital Yacht,' *St Mary's Hospital Gazette,* 20/7 (1914), 116–17

Graham, Stephen, *With Poor Immigrants to America,* London, Nelson, 1914

Hakluyt, Richard, *The Principal Navigations, Voyages, Traffiques and Discoveries of the English Nation,* Glasgow, Hakluyt Society, 1903–5

————, *Voyages and Discoveries: The Principal Navigations, Voyages, Traffiques and Discoveries of the English Nation,* ed. Jack Beeching, Harmondsworth, Penguin, 1972

Hampshire, Edward (ed.), *Brinestain and Biscuit: Recipes and Rules for Royal Navy Cooks,* London, National Archives, 2007

Hampson, G, *Portsmouth Customs Letter Books 1748–1750,* Winchester, Hampshire County Council, 1994

Hancock, W, *An Emigrant's Five Years in the Free States of America,* 1860

Hardwicke, E C, 'Some Reminiscences of a Ship's Surgeon', *St Mary's Hospital Gazette,* 18/9 (1912), 144–5

Hawksmoor, Nicholas, *Remarks on the founding and carrying on the building of the Royal Hospital at Greenwich,* London, N Blandford, 1728

Herman, Jan K (ed.), *Battle Station Sick Bay: Navy Medicine in World War II,* Annapolis, Naval Institute Press, 1997

Hervey, Augustus, *Augustus Hervey's Journal: The Adventures Afloat and Ashore of a Naval Casanova,* ed. David Erskine, Rochester, Chatham Publishing, 2002

Hood, Jean (ed.), *Submarine: An Anthology of First-hand Accounts of the War under the Sea, 1939–1945,* London, Conway, 2007

Howard, John, *The State of the Prisons in England and Wales with Preliminary Observations and An Account of Some Foreign Prisons and Hospitals,* Warrington, W Eyres, 1784

Hughes, Matthew Louis, *Mediterranean, Malta or Undulant Fever,* London, MacMillan, 1897

Hunter, John, *Observations on the Diseases of the Army in Jamaica and on the Best Means of Preserving the Health of Europeans in that Climate,* London, G Nicol, 1788

Irving, James, *Slave Captain: the Career of James Irving in the Liverpool Slave Trade,* ed. Suzanne Schwarz, Liverpool, Liverpool University Press, 1995

Jameson Carr, G, 'Health Problems in the Merchant Navy', *British Journal of Industrial Medicine* (1945), 65–73

Jerome, J K, *Three Men in a Boat,* London, Wordsworth, 1993

Knighton, C S and Loades, David (ed.), *Letters from the Mary Rose,* Stroud, Sutton Publishing, 2002

Krause, Emil, *The Adventures of Count George Albert of Erbach,* tr. Princess Beatrice of Battenberg, London, J Murray, 1890

Lambert, Sheila (ed.), *House of Commons Sessional Papers of the Eighteenth Century,* Wilmington, Delaware, Scholarly Resources, 1975

Laughton, J K (ed.), *State Papers relating to the Defeat of the Spanish Armada, 1588,* London, Navy Records Society, 1894

Lavery, Brian (ed.), *The Royal Navy Officer's Pocket Book 1944,* London, Conway, 2007

Lawrence, Thomas Edward, *Seven Pillars of Wisdom,* Harmondsworth, Penguin, 1962

Leech, Samuel, *Thirty Years from Home, or a Voice from the Main Deck,* Boston, Tappan and Dennett, 1844

Lind, James, *A Treatise of the Scurvy*, Edinburgh, Kincaid and Donaldson, 1753

————, *An Essay on Diseases Incidental to Europeans in Hot Climates with the Method of Preventing their Consequences*, London, J and J Richardson, 1808

Lippiett, John, *War and Peas: Intimate Letters from the Falklands War 1982*, Bosham, Pistol Post Publications, 2007

Lloyd, Christopher, *The Health of Seamen: Selections from the Works of Dr James Lind, Sir Gilbert Blane and Dr Thomas Trotter*, London, Navy Records Society, 1965

Mahoney, J F, Arnold, R C and Harris, A, 'Penicillin Treatment of Early Syphilis: A Preliminary Report', *Venereal Diseases Information*, 24 (1943), 355–7

Makert, Janet K, 'Adventures in Nursing Aboard a Cruise Ship', *Nursing Forum*, 37/2 (2002), 33–6

Markham, C R (ed.), *Life of Captain Stephen Martin, 1666–1740*, London, Navy Records Society, 1895

Marsh, A R, 'A Short but Distant War: the Falklands Campaign', *Journal of the Royal Society of Medicine*, 76 (1983), 972–82

Mead, Richard, *A Discourse on Scurvy*, London, Brindley, 1749

Miles, R P M, 'OHMS', *St Mary's Hospital Gazette*, 49/8 (1943), 142–4

Milroy, Gavin, *The Health of the Royal Navy considered in a Letter Addressed to Sir John Packington*, London, Hardwicke, 1862

Monson, William, *The Naval Tracts of Sir William Monson*, ed. M Oppenheim, London, Navy Records Society, 1902–14

————, (ed.) Laughton, *Naval Miscellany*, London, Navy Records Society, 1902

Moyle, John, *Chirurgus Marinus or The Sea Chirurgion: Being Instructions to Junior Chirurgie Practitioners who design to serve at Sea*, London, E Tracy and H Bernard, 1693

Mussis, Gabriel de, 'Historia de Morbo', *Archiv fur die Gesammte Medizin*, 2 (1842), 26–59

NAAFI Public Relations Branch, *The Story of NAAFI*, London, HMSO, 1944

Nelson, Horatio, *The Dispatches and Letters of Lord Nelson*, ed. Nicholas Harris Nicolas, London, Colburn, 1844–6

————, *Nelson's Letters to his Wife*, ed. G P B Naish, London, Navy Records Society, 1959

Osborne, Sidney Godolphin, *Scutari and its Hospitals*, London, Dickinson, 1855

Palmer, Svetlana and Wallis, Sarah (ed.), *A War in Words*, London, Simon and Schuster, 2003

Park, Mungo, *The Travels of Mungo Park*, London, Everyman, 1907

Pepys, Samuel, *Samuel Pepys's Naval Minutes*, ed. J R Tanner, London, Navy Records Society, 1925

————, *The Shorter Pepys*, ed. Robert Latham, London, Bell and Hyman, 1985

————, *Pepys's Later Diaries*, ed. C S Knighton, Stroud, Sutton, 2004

Privy Council, *Reports of the Medical Officer of the Privy Council and Local Government Board, Issues 5–8*, London, HMSO, 1875

Purchas, Samuel, *Hakluytus Posthumus*, Glasgow, Hakluyt, Society, 1905–7

Rees, John, 'Report on the Recent Outbreak of Cholera in HMS *Britannia*', *Medical Times and Gazette*, 2 (1854), 609–10

Reid, D B, *Illustrations of the Theory and Practice of Ventilation*, London, Longman, 1844

Richardson, John B, *A Visit to Haslar 1916*, ed. Eric Birbeck, Gosport, Royal Hospital Haslar, 2004

Robinson, William, *Jack Nastyface: Memoirs of an English Seaman*, London, Chatham Publishing, 2002

Rodger, N A M (ed.), *Naval Miscellany V,* London, Navy Records Society, 1984

Ross, Ronald, *Studies on Malaria,* London, John Murray, 1928

Russell, William Clark, *The Life of Admiral Lord Collingwood,* London, Methuen, 1895

Sahagún, Bernardino, *Florentine Codex: General History of the Things of New Spain,* ed. and tr. Arthur J O Anderson and Charles E Dibble, Salt Lake City, University of Utah Press, 1955

Sandys, George, *Travels,* London, 1673

Sanitary Committee of *The Lancet, A Report on Emigrant Ships by the Sanitary Commission of The Lancet,* London, *The Lancet,* 1873

Sanudo, Marin, *Venice, Cítá Excelentissima: Selections from the Renaissance Diaries of Marin Sanudo,* ed. Patricia H Labalme and Laura Sanguineti White, tr. Linda L Carroll, Baltimore, Johns Hopkins Press, 2008

Scott, Robert Falcon, *Journals: Captain Scott's Last Expedition,* Oxford, Oxford University Press, 2006

Scrimgeour, Alexander, *Scrimgeour's Scribbling Diary 1914-1916: The Truly Astonishing Wartime Diary and Letters of an Edwardian Gentleman, Naval Officer, Boy and Son,* ed. Richard Hallam and Mark Beynon, London, Conway, 2008

Shackleton, Ernest, *The Heart of the Antarctic and South,* Ware, Wordsworth, 2007

Simon John, *Public Health Reports,* London, Sanitary Institute of Great Britain, 1887

Smith, John, *The Seaman's Grammar,* London, Jonas Mann and Benjamin Fisher, 1654

Smith, W, *An Emigrant's Narrative, or A Voice from the Steerage,* New York, William Smith, 1850

Smollett, Tobias, *The Adventures of Roderick Random,* Oxford, Oxford University Press, 1979

Sydenham, Thomas, *The Whole Works of that most excellent practical Physician Dr Thomas Sydenham,* 9th edition, tr. John Pechey, London, J Darby, 1729

Tenon, Jacques, *Journal d'observations sur les principaux hôpitaux d'Angleterre,* ed. Jacques Carré, Clermont-Ferrand, Université Blaise-Pascal, 1992

Teonge, Henry, *The Diary of Henry Teonge, Chaplain on board HM Ships Assistance, Bristol and Royal Oak, 1675-1679,* London, Charles Knight, 1825

Thursfield, H G, *Five Naval Journals,* London, Navy Records Society, 1951

Tidey, Stuart A, 'The Ship's Surgeon', St Mary's Hospital Gazette 34/3 (1928), 35-7

————, 'Treatment of Seasickness', St Mary's Hospital Gazette 34/5 (1928), 55-7

Torella, Gaspar, *Dialogus de Dolore cum Tractatu de Ulceribus in Pudendagra Evenire Solitis,* Rome, Giovanni Besicken and Martino D'Amsterdam, 1500

Trotter, Thomas, *Medicina Nautica,* London, Cadell, 1797-1803

————, *A View of the Nervous Temperament,* London, Longman, Hurst, Rees and Orme, 1807

Tunstall, Brian (ed.), *The Byng Papers,* London, Naval Records Society, 1930

Turnbull, Alexander, 'Discussion on the Prevention of Scurvy', *British Medical Journal,* 2 (1902), 1023

Twiss, Sir Travers, *The Black Book of the Admiralty,* London, HMSO, 1871-3

Walter, Richard, *A Voyage around the World by George Anson,* London, Hartley and Walker, 1838

Waugh, Evelyn, *Brideshead Revisited,* Harmondsworth, Penguin, 1962

Wells, Thomas Spencer, *The Scale of Medicines with which Merchant Vessels are to be Furnished with Observations on the Means of Preserving Health and Increasing the Comforts of Seamen,* London, Orr, 1851

Wernham, R B (ed.), *The Expedition of Sir John Norris and Sir Francis Drake to Spain and Portugal, 1589*, London, Navy Records Society, 1988

Weston, Agnes, *My Life with the Bluejackets*, London, Nisbet, 1909

White, James, *De recta Sanguinis Missione, or New and Exact Observations of Fevers in which Letting of Blood is shew'd to be the True and solid Basis of their Cure*, London, D Brown, 1712

Whyte, Robert, *The Ocean Plague: or a Voyage to Quebec in an Irish Emigrant Vessel*, Boston, Coolidge and Wiley, 1848

Williams, Glyndŵr (ed.), *Documents relating to Anson's Voyage round the World, 1740–1744*, London, Navy Records Society, 1967

Wilson, John, *Outline of Naval Surgery*, Edinburgh, Maclachlan and Stewart, 1846

Wilson, John, *Memories of a Labour Leader*, London, Fisher Unwin, 1910

Wiseman, Richard, *A Treatise of Wounds*, London, R Norton and J Maycock, 1693

Woodall, John, *The Surgions Mate: A Complete Facsimile of the Book Published in 1617*, Bath, Kingsmead, 1978

Wright, Almroth Edward, 'On the Pathology and Therapeutics of Scurvy', *The Lancet* (1900), 565–7

Yonge, James, *The Journal of James Yonge, Plymouth Surgeon 1647–1721*, ed. F N L Poynter, London, Longmans, 1963

Young, S (ed.), *Annals of the Barber-Surgeons of London*, London, Blades and East, 1890

Zammit, Themistocles, 'A Preliminary Note of the Susceptibility of Goats to Malta Fever', *Proceedings of the Royal Society*, 76 B (1905), 377–378

## Secondary Printed Works

Adkins, Roy and Lesley, *Jack Tar: Life in Nelson's Navy*, London, Little, Brown, 2008

Alden, Dauril and Miller, Joseph C, 'Out of Africa: The Slave Trade and the Transmission of Smallpox to Brazil, 1560–1831' in R I Rotberg, *Health and Disease in Human History* (2000), pp. 204–30

Allison, R S, *Sea Diseases: The Story of a Great Natural Experiment in Preventative Medicine in the Royal Navy*, London, John Bale, 1943

Anderson, Roy M and May, Robert M, *Infectious Diseases in Humans*, Oxford, Oxford University Press, 1991

Arrizabalaga, Jon, Henderson, John and French, Roger, *The Great Pox: the French Disease in Renaissance Europe*, New Haven, Yale University Press, 1997

Ball, Adrian and Wright, Diana, *SS Great Britain*, Newton Abbot, David and Charles, 1981

Bateson, C, *The Convict Ships, 1787–1868*, Glasgow, Brown, Son and Ferguson, 1959

Beieir, A I and Finlay, R (ed.), *The Making of the Modern Metropolis: London 1500–1700*, London, Longman, 1986

Bennett, G H and R, *Survivors: British Merchant Seamen in the Second World War*, London, Hambledon Press, 1999

Birbeck, Eric, Ryder, Ann and Ward, Philip, *The Royal Hospital Haslar: A Pictorial History*, Chichester, Phillimore, 2009

Boog Watson, William N, 'Two British Naval Surgeons in the French Wars, *Medical History*, 13 (1969), 213–25

Brockliss, Laurence and Jones, Colin, *The Medical World of Early Modern France*, Oxford, Clarendon Press, 1997

————, Cardwell, M John and Moss, Michael, *Nelson's Surgeon: William Beatty, Naval*

*Medicine and the Battle of Trafalgar,* Oxford, Oxford University Press, 2005

Brown, Kevin, *Penicillin Man: Alexander Fleming and the Antibiotic Revolution,* Stroud, Sutton, 2004

————, *The Pox: The Life and Death of a Very Social Disease,* Stroud, Sutton, 2006

————, *Fighting Fit: Health, Medicine and War in the Twentieth Century,* Stroud, History Press, 2008

Bruijn, Iris, *Ship's Surgeons of the Dutch East India Company: Commerce and the Progress of Medicine in the Eighteenth Century,* Amsterdam, Amsterdam University Press, 2009

Butler, Daniel Allen, *Unsinkable: the Full Story of RMS Titanic,* Mechanicsburg, Pennsylvania, Stackpole Books, 1998

Caldwell, M John, 'Royal Naval Surgeons, 1793–1815: A Collective Biography' in David Boyd Haycock and Sally Archer (ed.), *Health and Medicine at Sea* (2009), pp. 38–62.

Carmichael, Ann G, 'Plague Legislation in the Italian Renaissance', *Bulletin of the History of Medicine,* 57 (1983), 519–25

————, *Plague and Poor in Renaissance Florence,* Cambridge, Cambridge University Press, 1986

Carpenter, Kenneth, *The History of Scurvy and Vitamin C,* Cambridge University Press, 1966

Carson, E A, 'The Customs Quarantine Service', *Mariner's Mirror,* 64 (1978), 63–9

Cassar, Paul, 'Slitting of Letters for Disinfection in the eighteenth century in Malta', *British Medical Journal* (1967), 105–6

————, 'A Medical Service for Slaves in Malta during the rule of the Order of St John of Jerusalem', *Medical History,* 12 (1968), 270–7

Castle, Jo, Kirkup, John, Derham, Brendan, Montagu, Jeremy, Wood, Robin and Hather, John, 'Septicaemia, Scurvy and the Spanish Pox: Provision for Sickness and Injury at Sea' in Julie Gardiner (ed.), *Before the Mast: Life and Death Aboard the Mary Rose* (2005), pp. 171–225

Childs, David, *The Warship Mary Rose: The Life and Times of King Henry VIII's Flagship,* London, Chatham Press, 2007

Clark, Gregory, *Doc: 100 Year History of the Sick Berth Branch,* London, HMSO, 1984

Cohen, Norman, *The Pursuit of the Millennium,* New York, Secker and Warburg, 1962

Cohn, S K, *The Black Death Transformed: Disease and Culture in Early Renaissance Europe,* London, 2002

Coleman, Terry, *The Nelson Touch: The Life and Legend of Horatio Nelson,* Oxford, Oxford University Press, 2002

Comrie, J D, *History of Scottish Medicine,* London, Wellcome Historical Museum, 1932

Cook, Gordon C, 'Medical Disease in the Merchant Navies of the World in the Days of Sail: the Seamen's Hospital Society's Experience, *Mariner's Mirror* 91 (2005), 46–51

————, *Disease in the Merchant Navy: A History of the Seamen's Hospital Society,* Oxford, Radcliffe Publishing, 2007

Crosby, A W, *The Columbian Exchange: Biological and Cultural Consequences of 1492,* Westport, Connecticut, Greenwood Press, 1972

Davies, J D, *Pepys's Navy: Ships, Men and Warfare 1649–1689,* Barnsley, Seaforth Publishing, 2008

Debus, A G, 'John Woodall, Paracelsian Surgeon', *Ambix,* 10 (1962), 108–18

Doran, Susan (ed.), *Henry VIII: Man and Monarch,* London, British Library, 2009

Druett, Joan, *Rough Medicine: Surgeons at Sea in the Age of Sail,* New York, Routledge, 2001

Eaton, John P and Haas, Charles A, *Titanic: Triumph and Tragedy*, New York, Norton, 1994

Elliot, John H, 'The Overthrow of Moctezuma and his Empire', in Colin McEwan and Leonardo López Luján (ed.), *Moctezuma: Aztec Ruler*, London, British Museum Press, 2009, pp. 218–36

Epstein, Steven A, *Genoa and the Genoese 958–1528*, Chapel Hill, University of North Carolina Press, 2001

Fisher, Trevor, *Prostitution and the Victorians*, Stroud, Sutton, 1997

Flinn, M W, 'Plague in Europe and the Mediterranean Countries', *Journal of European Economic History*, 8/1 (1979), 134–8

Fogg, Nicholas, *The Voyages of the Great Britain: Life at Sea in the World's First Liner*, London, Chatham Publishing, 2004

Ford, E, *The Life and Work of William Redfern*, Sydney, Australian Medical Publishing Company, 1953

Fox, Stephen, *The Ocean Railway: Isambard Kingdom Brunel, Samuel Cunard and the Revolutionary World of the Great Atlantic Steamships*, London, Harper Perennial, 2004

Frazer, W M, *History of English Public Health 1834–1939*, London, Bailliere, Tindall and Cox, 1950

Frey, B S, Savage, D A and Torgler, B, 'Interaction of Natural Survival Instincts and Internalized Social Norms: Exploring the Titanic and Lusitania Disasters', *Proceedings of the National Academy of Sciences of the United States of America* (2010), 1091–6490

Fritze, Ronald, *New Worlds: The Voyages of Discovery 1400–1600*, Stroud, Sutton Publishing, 2002

Gardiner, Julie (ed.), *Before the Mast: Life and Death Aboard the Mary Rose*, Portsmouth, Mary Rose Trust, 2005

Geller, Judith B, *Titanic: Women and Children First*, Sparkford, Patrick Stephens, 1998

Glynn, Ian and Jenifer, *The Life and Death of Smallpox*, London, Profile Books, 2004

Goldstein, Richard, *Desperate Hours: The Epic Rescue of the Andrea Doria*, New York, John Wiley, 2001

Goodyear, James D, 'The Sugar Connection: A New Perspective on the History of Yellow Fever in West Africa', *Bulletin of the History of Medicine*, 52 (1978), 5–21

Graves, John, *Waterline: Images from the Golden Age of Cruising*, London, National Maritime Museum, 2004

Groppe, Hans Hermann and Wöst,Ursula, *Via Hamburg to the World: From the Emigrants Halls to BallinStadt*, Hamburg, Ellert and Richter, 2007

Guerra, Francisco, 'Aztec Medicine', *Medical History*, 10/4 (1966), 315–38

————, 'The Earliest American Epidemic: The Influenza of 1493', *Social Science History*, 12 (1988), 305–25

Hackett, C J, 'On the Origin of the Human Treponematosis', *Bulletin of the World Health Organisation* 29 (1963), 7–41

Haines, Robin, *Life and Death in the Age of Sail: The Passage to Australia*, London, National Maritime Museum, 2006

————, Shlomowitz, Ralph and Brennan, L, 'Maritime Mortality Revisited', *International Journal of Maritime History*, 8 (1996), 113–24

Handlin, Oscar, *The Uprooted: The Epic Story of the Great Migrations that made the American People*, Philadelphia, University of Pennsylvania Press, 2002

Harrison, Mark, *Disease and the Modern World, 1500 to the Present Day*, Cambridge, Polity Press, 2004

Harvie, David I, *Limeys: The Conquest of Scurvy,* Stroud, Sutton, 2002

Haycock, David Boyd and Archer, Sally (ed.), *Health and Medicine at Sea,* Woodbridge, Boydell Press, 2009

Higham, John, *Strangers in the Land: Patterns of American Nativism 1860–1925,* New Brunswick, Rutgers University Press, 1988

Hills, A M E, 'Nelson's Illnesses', *Journal of the Royal Naval Medical Service,* 86 (2000), 72–80

Horrox, R, *The Black Death,* Manchester, Manchester University Press, 1994

Howarth, David and Howarth, Stephen, *The Story of P&O,* London, Weidenfeld and Nicholson, 1986

Hudson, E H, *Non-venereal Syphilis,* Edinburgh, Livingstone, 1958

Jackson, Ralph, *Doctors and Diseases in the Roman Empire,* London, British Museum Press, 1988

Jal, A, *Archéologie Navale,* Paris, Arthus Bertrand, 1840

Jensen, John, 'Before the Surgeon General: Marine Hospitals in Mid-Nineteenth Century America', *Public Health Reports,* 112 (1997), 525–7

Johnson, Robert E, *Sir John Richardson: Arctic Explorer, Natural Historian, Naval Surgeon,* London, Taylor and Francis, 1976

Jones, Maldwyn A, *Destination America,* New York, Holt, Rinehart and Winston, 1976

————, *American Immigration,* Chicago, University of Chicago Press, 1992

Keevil, J J, Lloyd, C C and Coulter, J L S, *Medicine and the Navy 1200–1900,* Edinburgh and London, E and S Livingstone, 4 volumes, 1957–63

Kidwell, Carol, *Pietro Bembo: Lover, Linguist, Cardinal,* Montreal and Kingston, McGill-Queen's University Press, 2004

Kiple, Kenneth F, *The Cambridge Historical Dictionary of Disease,* Cambridge, Cambridge University Press, 2003

Kraut, Alan M, *Silent Travellers: Germs, Genes and the Immigrant Menace,* New York, Basic Books, 1994

Kvarning, Lars Åke and Bengt Ohrelius, *The Vasa: Royal Ship,* tr. Joan Tate, Stockholm, Atlantis, 1998

Kverndal, Roald, *Seamen's Missions: their Origin and Early Growth,* Pasadena, William Carey Library, 1986

Langley, Harold D, *A History of Medicine in the Early US Navy,* Baltimore, Johns Hopkins University Press, 1995

Layton, J Kent, *Lusitania: An Illustrated Biography of the Ship of Splendor,* Raleigh, Lulu.com, 2007

Lenihan, J, *The Crumbs of Creation,* Bristol, Adam Hilger, 1988

Leonard, Jonathan Norton, *Ancient America,* New York, Time, 1967

Le Quesne, L P, 'Nelson and his Surgeons', *Journal of the Royal Naval Medical Service,* 86 (2000), 85–8.

LeRoy Ladurie, Emmanuel, *Mind and Method of the Historian,* Brighton, Harvester, 1981

Lincoln, Margarette (ed.), *Nelson and Napoleon,* London, National Maritime Museum, 2005

MacCulloch, Diarmid, *Reformation: Europe's House Divided, 1490–1700,* Harmondsworth, Penguin, 2003

McEwan, Colin and López Luján (ed.), *Moctezuma: Aztec Ruler,* London, British Museum Press, 2009

McKee, Christopher, *Sober Men and True: Sailor Lives in the Royal Navy, 1900–1945,* Cambridge, Massachusetts, Harvard University Press, 2002

# BIBLIOGRAPHY

McNeil, D R, 'Medical Care Aboard Australian-bound Convict Ships 1786–1840', *Bulletin of Medical History*, 26 (1952), 117–40

McNeill, William H, *Plagues and Peoples*, Oxford, Blackwell, 1977

Manchester, Keith, *The Archaeology of Disease*, Bradford, Bradford University Press, 1982

Markel, Howard, 'The Eyes have It: Trachoma, the Perception of Disease, the United States Public Health Service and the American Jewish Immigration Experience, 1897–1924', *Bulletin of Medical History*, 74 (2000), 525–60

Miller, Amy, *Dressed to Kill: British Naval Uniform, Masculinity and Contemporary Fashions 1748–1857*, London, National Maritime Museum, 2007

Miller, Hugh, *Secrets of the Dead*, London, Macmillan, 2000

Morton, R S, *Venereal Diseases*, Harmondsworth, Penguin, 1974

———, and Rachid, S, 'The Syphilis Enigma: the Riddle Resolved?', *Sexually Transmitted Infections*, 77 (2001), 322–4

Motta, Titti and Dentoni, Anna (ed.), *L'America: Da Genova a Ellis Island, il Viaggio per Mare negli Anni dell' Emigrazione Italiani 1892–1914*, Genoa, Sagep Editori, 2008

Muscat, J and Cuschieri, A, *Naval Activities of the Knights of St John 1530–1798*, Valletta, Midsea Books, 2002

Musgrave, Eric, *Sharp Suits*, London, Pavilion, 2009

Nicosia, Alessandro and Prencipe, Lorenzo (ed.), *Museo Nazionale Emigrazione Italiana*, Rome, Gangemi Editori, 2009

Nutton, Vivian, 'The doctors of the Roman Navy', *Epigraphica*, 32 (1970), 66–71

———, *Ancient Medicine*, London and New York, Routledge, 2004

Oldstone, M, *Viruses, Plagues and History*, Oxford, Oxford University Press, 1998

Parascandola, John, 'Doctors at the Gate: PHS at Ellis Island', *Public Health Reports*, 113 (1998), 83–4

Pelling, Margaret, 'Appearance and Reality: Barber Surgeons, the Body and Venereal Disease in Early Modern London in A I Beieir and R Finlay (ed.), *The Making of the Modern Metropolis: London 1500–1700* (1986), pp. 82–112.

Pollitt, Ronald L, 'Bureaucracy and the Armada: the Administrator's Battle', *Mariner's Mirror*, 60 (1974), 119–32

Prestwich, Michael, *Plantagenet England 1225–1360*, Oxford, Oxford University Press, 2005

Prochaska, Frank, *Royal Bounty: The Making of a Welfare Monarchy*, New Haven, Yale University Press, 1995

Quétel, Claude, *History of Syphilis*, tr. Judith Braddock and Brian Pike, London, Polity Press, 1990

Rediker, Marcus, *The Slave Ship: A Human History*, New York, Viking, 2007

Reidna, Ravo, *Tallinna Mustpeade Vennaskonna Maarja Altar: The Altar of Holy Mary of the Tallinn Brotherhood of the Blackheads*, Tallinn, Art Museum of Estonia, 1995

Revell, A L, *Haslar the Royal Hospital*, Gosport, Gosport Historical Society, 2000

Richardson, Harriet (ed.), *English Hospitals 1660–1948: A Survey of their Architecture and Design*, Swindon, Royal Commission on the Historical Monuments of England, 1998

Roberts, Charlotte and Cox, Margaret, *Health and Disease in Britain from Prehistory to the Present Day*, Stroud, Sutton Publishing, 2003

Roddis, Louis H, *A Short History of Nautical Medicine*, New York, Paul B Hoeber, 1941

Rodger, N A M, *The Safeguard of the Sea: A Naval History of Britain 1660–1649*, London, Harper Collins, 1997

———, *The Command of the Ocean: A Naval History of Britain 1649–1815*, London, Allen Lane, 2004

Rotberg, R I, *Health and Disease in Human History: A Journal of Interdisciplinary History Reader*, Massachusetts, MIT Press, 2000

Savona-Ventura, Charles, *Knight Hospitaller Medicine in Malta*, San Gwann, Publishers Enterprises Group, 2004

————, *Contemporary Medicine in Malta 1789–1979*, San Gwann, Publishers Enterprises Group, 2005

Scott, H H, 'The Influence of the Slave Trade in the Spread of Tropical Diseases', *Transcripts of Royal Society of Tropical Medicine and Hygiene*, 38 (1943), 169

Shaw, J J Sutherland, 'The Hospital Ship 1608–1740', *Mariner's Mirror*, 22 (1939), 306–27

Shepherd, John, *The Crimean Doctors: A History of the British Medical Services in the Crimean War*, Liverpool, Liverpool University Press, 1991

Shepherd, John A, *Spencer Wells: The Life and Work of a Victorian Surgeon*, Edinburgh and London, E and S Livingstone, 1965

Sheridan, Richard B, *Doctors and Slaves: A Medical and Demographic History of Slavery in the British West Indies 1680–1834*, Cambridge, Cambridge University Press, 1985

Siraisi, Nancy G, *Medieval and Early Renaissance Medicine: An Introduction to Knowledge and Practice*, Chicago, Chicago University Press, 1990

Steckel, Richard H and Jensen, Richard A, 'New Evidence on the Causes of Slave and Crew Mortality in the Atlantic Slave Trade', *Journal of Economic History*, 46 (1986), 57–77

Stevenson, Christine, *Medicine and Magnificence: British Hospital and Asylum Architecture 1660–1815*, New Haven and London, Yale University Press, 2000

Stewart, L, 'The Edge of Utility: Slaves and Smallpox in the Early Eighteenth Century', *Medical History*, 29 (1985), 54–70

Thomas, Hugh, *Rivers of Gold: The Rise of the Spanish Empire*, London, Phoenix, 2004

————, *The Slave Trade: The History of the Atlantic Slave Trade 1440–1870*, London, Phoenix, 2006

Walton, John K, *The English Seaside Resort: A Social History*, Leicester, Leicester University Press, 1983

Watt, James, 'Surgeons of the *Mary Rose*', *Mariner's Mirror* 69/1 (1983), 3–19

Watts, Sheldon, *Epidemics and History*, New Haven and London, Yale University Press, 1997

Wilson, F P, *The Plague in Shakespeare's London*, Oxford, Oxford University Press, 1927

Woodman, Richard, *Neptune's Trident: Spices and Slaves 1500–1807*, Stroud, The History Press, 2008

————, *Masters under God: Makers of Empire, 1816–1884*, Stroud, The History Press, 2009

Ziegler, Philip, *The Black Death*, Stroud, Sutton Publishing, 2003

Zivanovic, Srboljub, *Ancient Disease: the Elements of Palaeopathology*, tr. L F Edwards, London, Methuen, 1982

# Index